the good
of politics

Engaging Culture

WILLIAM A. DYRNESS
AND ROBERT K. JOHNSTON,
SERIES EDITORS

The Engaging Culture series is designed to help Christians respond with theological discernment to our contemporary culture. Each volume explores particular cultural expressions, seeking to discover God's presence in the world and to involve readers in sympathetic dialogue and active discipleship. These books encourage neither an uninformed rejection nor an uncritical embrace of culture, but active engagement informed by theological reflection.

the good of politics

a biblical, historical, and contemporary introduction

james w. skillen

Baker Academic
a division of Baker Publishing Group
Grand Rapids, Michigan

© 2014 by James W. Skillen

Published by Baker Academic
a division of Baker Publishing Group
P.O. Box 6287, Grand Rapids, MI 49516-6287
www.bakeracademic.com

Printed in the United States of America

Library of Congress Cataloging-in-Publication Data is on file at the Library of Congress, Washington, DC.

ISBN 978-0-8010-4881-4 (pbk.)

Scripture quotations are from the Holy Bible, New International Version®. NIV®. Copyright © 1973, 1978, 1984, 2011 by Biblica, Inc.™ Used by permission of Zondervan. All rights reserved worldwide. www.zondervan.com

14   15   16   17   18   19   20   7   6   5   4   3   2   1

In keeping with biblical principles of creation stewardship, Baker Publishing Group advocates the responsible use of our natural resources. As a member of the Green Press Initiative, our company uses recycled paper when possible. The text paper of this book is composed in part of post-consumer waste.

green press INITIATIVE

contents

acknowledgments

It was a considerable privilege to receive an invitation from William Dyrness and Robert Johnston to contribute a volume to the Engaging Culture series. And it has been a pleasure working with Baker Academic editors Robert Hosack and Lisa Ann Cockrel and the great team at the Baker Publishing Group. Thank you all very much.

Behind the writing of this book stand so many teachers, colleagues, scholars, practitioners, and friends that I cannot begin to count or list them. But I want to thank at least a few from whom I've received much help and encouragement, particularly during the years I traveled throughout the United States and much of the world as the director of the Center for Public Justice.

First of all I want to thank my wife Doreen for her love and for guarding the time and space needed for concentrated research and writing. She also provided much-appreciated proofreading and other skills along the way. In a wider circle, thank you Bruce Wearne, Steve Snoey, Rockne McCarthy, Stanley Carlson-Thies, Harold Heie, Wendy Sereda, Charles Glenn, William Harper, Jonathan Chaplin, David Koyzis, Roy Clouser, Timothy Sherratt, Steve Meyer, Ronald Sider, Max Stackhouse, Dennis Hoover, Bob Goudzwaard, Albert Wolters, Calvin Seerveld, Raymond Van Leeuwen, Jean Porter, Michael Goheen, Craig Bartholomew, Adolfo Garcia de la Sienra, Nathan Berkeley, Sander Griffioen, Henk Gerrtsema, Danie Strauss, Albert Hengelaar, Alan Cameron, Tyler Johnson, Benyamin Intan, Yadi Lima, Lay Hendra Wijaya, David Kim, David Van Heemst, Adrianna Menasse, Kathryn Yarlett, Steve Bishop, and Chris Gousmett. None of them bears responsibility for the final product, but for what each has contributed I am very grateful.

James W. Skillen
January 2014

introduction

Natural disasters are not the only things shaking the earth. The world's political and economic institutions are quaking, and many are crumbling. The Arab Awakening that began in 2011 is changing the face of the Middle East and North Africa. Protests in China, Russia, and dozens of other countries continue on a low burn—low at least for now. Growing numbers of Europeans are skeptical about the future of the European Union and are protesting against their national governments. Many other countries are in turmoil—even civil war—where weak governments are unable to subdue opposing factions. And citizens in the United States are disgusted with Washington's paralysis, caused in part by divisions between those who want the federal government to do more and those who want to shrink it before it does any more harm.

Two decades ago, the end of the Cold War seemed to open the way to greater peace, prosperity, and democracy. Yet that is when degrading poverty in many parts of the world became more visible. That is when the work of radical Islamists broke out into the open, leading to 9/11 and to the long, divisive wars in Afghanistan and Iraq. That is when close observers noticed that religion had not gone into hiding as many had predicted it would because of so-called secular progress. Today, talk of religion and politics is all the rage, in part because real struggles of a political-religious nature are raging all around us.

What a time to reexamine Christian engagement in political life! What a time to try to gain a deeper understanding of political society, the responsibilities of citizenship, and the task of government. Regardless of the difficulties that will undoubtedly hamper such a quest, I feel compelled to undertake it and welcome your company on the journey.

Three Basic Questions

In 1789 the first vice president of the United States, John Adams, declared, "We have no government armed with power capable of contending with human passions unbridled by morality and religion. Our constitution was made only for a moral and a religious people."[1] In 2006 author Darryl Hart wrote, "[Christianity] in its classic formulations . . . has very little to say about politics or the ordering of society. . . . [It] has little to say explicitly about the sort of polity in which Americans have been living for the last 230 years."[2]

Those contrasting judgments raise three basic questions I want to address in this book. The first is this: What is the relation between politics and its cultural context (including religion and morality)? Second, what is government for and how should its responsibilities be properly exercised? And third, what, if anything, does Christianity have to say about political life and the ordering of society, and what, if any, political responsibility does the Christian faith urge upon those who profess to follow Jesus Christ?

When John Adams made the comment just quoted, he took for granted an Americanized version of Protestant Christianity that he believed was a necessary foundation of the new republic. The kind of government the Constitution established was, in his estimation, incapable of "contending with human passions" if the people did not maintain a strong sense of moral responsibility grounded in the fear of God. If Adams was correct, might we surmise that the instability and weaknesses of American government today are due to a weakening of the moral and religious character of the people?

When Darryl Hart made his comments, he was convinced that Christianity is something "spiritual and eternal . . . [a faith] occupied with a world to come rather than the passing and temporal affairs of this world."[3] If Hart was correct, might we surmise that America's problems (and perhaps the problems of many other nations in the world) exist because of mistaken attempts by Christians (and people of other faiths) to take political action in the name of their faith?[4] Which of these judgments is closer to the truth? Is some form of Christianity a necessary foundation of the American republic, such that without it the republic will fail, or is Christianity something spiritual that should be kept at a distance from "the passing and temporal affairs of this world," whether in the United States or in any other country?

At first hearing, the convictions of Adams and Hart seem at odds with each other. On further reflection, however, we can see that they share something. They both assume politics is separate from cultural life. If citizens do not bring good morality and religion to bear on political life, then, from Adams's point of view, there is no hope for the endurance of America's constitutional system. This represents a rather low view of politics. The political system apparently requires something from the outside to keep it honest because its internal operations cannot withstand contending human passions. Hart may hold a different view of politics, but he too believes that any Christian influence on government comes from something transcendent to, and separate from, the political system. Spiritual Christianity should certainly shape the moral behavior of Christians who might, thereby, have a positive influence in public life, but that does not mean Christianity should be expected to have something to say directly to the work of government.

Where do these views of politics, culture, and religion come from? Are they widely shared by Christians in the United States and elsewhere in the world? What are the grounds for such convictions? And how different are the views of Christians in other parts of the world from the views of American Christians? Insofar as politics, culture, and religion are dimensions of human experience everywhere, and insofar as Christianity is a global religion that makes universal claims, it would be a big mistake to imagine that American practices and controversies can be isolated from those in the rest of the world. Moreover, American life is now so tightly bound up with global developments, it would be foolish to imagine that we can get a clear understanding of Christianity and political responsibility by paying attention only to the American experience.

We know, for example, that Islam is a way of life that recognizes a direct connection between God and every aspect of life, including law and government. Many Christians share this conviction even if they hold a different view of God and God's relation to society and politics. We also know there are Christians and people of other faiths who believe religious faith should be kept at a distance from government and politics. In Egypt, for example, Coptic Christians have rarely challenged the discrimination they experience in their largely Muslim society. "Instead," writes commentator Heba Saleh, "they have retreated behind their church walls and shunned public life, leaving their Pope to negotiate with the state on their behalf. In practice this has meant church support for whoever is in power, against minimal and increasingly frayed guarantees of Christian rights." But young Egyptian Christians now reject some of that passivity, as was evident in Cairo's Tahrir Square in 2011 and 2012. Many young Christians, says Saleh, "are tired of the church's discourse which asks them to stay away from politics and let [the church] speak for them."[5]

We have just gotten started, but it appears that many additional questions follow quickly from the three basic ones I posed at the outset. For example, can politics really be distinguished as a realm separate from culture? Isn't political life simply one of many dimensions of culture? If there is reason to distinguish the two, is the same thing true of business and commerce, science and education? Are they also distinct from culture? If every expression of human life is considered distinct from culture, then what remains of culture? Regardless of how many distinctions and separations we make, the question remains: How are all of these arenas of responsibility related to one another? For they are all expressions of human life.

Perhaps even more problematic for the journey on which we have embarked is how to understand and assess the variety of expressions of Christianity in the United States and around the world today. If it is difficult to understand how culture and politics are related, it is perhaps even more difficult to get a grip on what Christianity is and how Christians ought to conduct their political lives. American Christians may be conservative or liberal, passive or active, pro-government or antigovernment. Does Christianity support any or all of these?

American religious sociologist Robert Bellah once asked, "Could there be a sense in which the American republic, which has neither an established church nor a classic civil religion, is, after all, a Christian republic, or should I say a biblical republic, in which biblical religion is indeed the civil religion?"[6] If one answers Bellah's question in the affirmative, then the distance between Adams and Hart grows even larger. If the answer to Bellah's question is no, we still need to decide how Christianity should be related to the United States, which is understood to be neither a Christian nor a biblical republic.

In addition to trying to answer those sorts of questions in a descriptive and evaluative way, I have an additional ambition for this book. I want to make judgments about how Christians *should* exercise civic responsibility and why it matters. Arguing for a path of action, however, makes it clear immediately that there is no neutral place to stand above the political fray; there is no way to start from scratch without presumptions and presuppositions. Consequently, I will have to tread carefully as we move along, trying to be as clear and as fair as possible in making arguments, sorting out diverse points of view, and offering recommendations. In the process, I hope the reader will find encouragement to do the same.

From Puritan Church Colony to American Civil Religion

Christianity has seen significant growth in Africa, Latin America, and parts of Asia during the last half century, even as it has lost adherents and influence in Europe. In the United States there is an expanding array of practices and beliefs within well-known church denominations as well as in newer independent churches. There has also been growth in the number of other religions and spiritualities in the United States. Although the public media typically treat evangelical, fundamentalist, and Pentecostal Christians as a single large bloc of right-wing conservatives in morals and politics, millions of people affiliated with those groups do not fit that stereotype. Moreover, while American social-gospel Protestants of a more liberal theological stripe have been declining in number and influence since World War II, there has been growth in the influence of African American Protestants and Roman Catholics during the same time period.[7]

Writing from a jail in Birmingham, Alabama, in 1963, Martin Luther King Jr. penned his now-famous letter in which he expressed anguish over a view of the church that many black (as well as white) pastors held. King was writing to defend his decision to come to Birmingham to help organize nonviolent acts of civil disobedience in protest against long-standing racial discrimination and government-condoned violence. "I have heard so many ministers say, 'Those are social issues with which the gospel has no real concern,' and I have watched so many churches commit themselves to a completely otherwordly religion which made a strange distinction between body and soul, the sacred and the secular."[8] That cannot be right, he argued. "There was a time when the church was very powerful. It was during that period when the early Christians rejoiced when they were deemed worthy to suffer for what they believed." Back then, Christians were not hesitant to enter a town with the good news and suffer the consequences of being mocked, attacked, or jailed. "But they went on with the conviction that they were 'a colony of heaven,' and had to obey God rather than man. . . . They brought an end to such ancient evils as infanticide and gladiatorial contests."[9] If that represented extremism, King wrote, then he would join in practicing it.

> Was not Jesus an extremist in love—"Love your enemies, bless them that curse you, pray for them that despitefully use you." Was not Amos an extremist for justice—"Let justice roll down like waters and righteousness like a mighty stream." Was not Paul an extremist for the gospel of Jesus Christ—"I bear in my body the marks of the Lord Jesus." Was not Martin Luther an extremist—"Here I stand, I can do none other so help me God." . . . So the question is not whether we will be extremist but what kind of extremist will we be. Will we be extremists for hate or will we be extremists for love? Will we be extremists for the preservation of injustice—or will we be extremists for the cause of justice?[10]

King's speeches and actions can be understood only against the backdrop of America's slave history and its post–Civil War systems of discrimination and violence against African Americans. That history alone raises serious questions about the degree to which America ever was (or is) a "Christian" nation.

King's questions about Christian "extremism" also reflect a significant peculiarity about our American use of the Bible, particularly the Old Testament, in political rhetoric. Many Americans have found such use of the Bible acceptable, while many have not. In the founding era of Puritan New England, almost 150 years before John Adams, and more than 300 years before Martin Luther King Jr., the conviction of early leaders such as John Cotton (1584–1652) was that their "errand into the wilderness" was a God-directed mission, following in the historical line of God's covenants with Israel through to the coming of Christ and eventually to the settlement of New England. "America, Cotton explained, was the new promised land, reserved by God for His new chosen people as the site for a new heaven and a new earth. . . . All of history is converging upon 'the cosmic climax of Boston's founding.'"[11] Alexis de Tocqueville, the nineteenth-century Frenchman famous for his outsider's assessment of the United States, concluded that "the foundation of New England was something new in the world. Puritanism was almost as much a political theory as a religious doctrine."[12] From the standpoint of Cotton and Tocqueville, Christianity was indeed intimately intertwined with American culture and politics by combining the biblical idea of a divine covenant with the American nation.

From this we might well conclude that Bellah's earlier question calls for an affirmative answer: America has been shaped so strongly by the faith and political thought of the Puritans that the nation must have been (and perhaps still is) a "biblical republic." But what are the grounds for Cotton's belief, and how would someone in our day who espouses that belief explain the relation of "Christian America" to Christian communities in other parts of the world? Would they say America is the *only* Christian nation or would they say it is the nation that stands at the *center* of God's action in history? Even here at home, how does one account for Christians who do not believe America is a Christian nation?[13]

Much of the inspiration for the Revolution in 1776 came from allusions to God's delivery of Israel from slavery in Egypt, leading them through the wilderness to a new land of promise. By the time of the Revolution, it was no longer only Puritan Calvinists who spoke of their church-led colony as God's new Israel. Americans, whether Christian or not, had begun to use that language to speak about the country as a whole.[14] Later in the nineteenth century, when the federal government could not prevent the outbreak of civil war and North and South became the killing fields of antagonistic Christian-republican crusades, we might imagine that the myth of America as God's new Israel would have fallen into disrepute and been discarded. To the contrary, use of civil-religious language about martyrdom and blood sacrifice intensified as the slaughter became an unjustifiable total war. Horace Bushnell (1802–1876), a leading Protestant pastor and journalist, wrote, "The shed blood of soldiers, North and South, white and black, would stand as the vicarious atonement for the newly realized, organic Christian nation-state." This was not simply a metaphorical atonement in Bushnell's mind, according to historian Harry Stout, "but quite literally a blood sacrifice required by God for sinners North and South if they were to inherit their providential destiny."[15] The Civil War, writes Stout, came to be interpreted as "the crimson baptism of our nationalism, and so it continues to enjoy a mythic transcendence not unlike the significance of the Eucharist for Christian believers. . . . The incarnation of a national American civil religion may have been the final great legacy of the Civil War."[16]

Two Different Exodus Stories

As it turned out, however, there was not just one version (or denomination) of the American civil religion that developed before and after the Civil War. Two versions emerged in dialectical tension with each other, but both stories retold Israel's Exodus story in a modern, Americanized way. The first version of the story, the white Anglo-Saxon Protestant (WASP) version, began with the courageous Pilgrims journeying to the new world under God's guidance. Theirs was an exodus from oppressive Britain (Egypt) through the Red Sea of the Atlantic into a new promised land where they were set free to build their city on a hill as a light to the nations. By the time America as a whole adopted this version of the new-Israel identity, the nation's ideal of freedom was conceived in direct opposition to the British monarchy (Pharaoh); thus, the Declaration of Independence. The 1789 Constitution was written to guard against the possibility of a future Pharaoh (too strong a central government) who might try to snuff out the flame of liberty. The president of the republic was to function as a modest executive, responsible to carry out the legislative decisions of Congress, which the founders tethered carefully to the states. By means of the Constitution, the people granted to the federal government very limited responsibility, namely, the regulation of interstate commerce and defense of the states and the people from foreign aggression. All other powers remained with the people and the states, which were understood to be the real centers of political life. The federal government was to be a servant of the states, not the dominating head of a national political community.

The second exodus story is very different. Slaves created it mostly in song, drawing on the same biblical inspiration that had empowered the WASP story. For the slaves, however, the original promise of America, articulated in the Declaration of Independence, was that all human beings should be free and equal because the creator had endowed them all with the same rights. In this version of the story the Pharaoh, who thwarted the fulfillment of the Declaration's promise, was not a foreign king but America's WASP slaveholders. Moreover, the federal Constitution failed to carry forward that promise because it supported slavery, so the Constitution itself was deficient and in need of revision. An exodus from the oppression of slavery would have to take place within the Egypt of America, opening the way to the liberation of the entire nation. Only then could America become what the Declaration promised: a land of freedom and equality for all. The exodus in this story, quite in contrast to the WASP version, required strong action by the federal government to abolish slavery and eventually to establish equal civil rights for everyone in the *national* polity. As a result of the Civil War and the eventual success of the civil rights movement, the federal government and the US Supreme Court gained a measure of supremacy over the states in education, employment, housing, and many other matters.

In these conflicting versions of America's exodus story, we find not only two different descriptions of the "new Israel" but also differing ideas of freedom. Freedom in the first story meant freedom from Britain, freedom from a strong central government, and freedom for property-owning whites. Freedom in the second story meant freedom from unjust laws and a defective Constitution, leading to equal treatment of all Americans—black, white, red, and any other color—within an all-inclusive national community.[17]

One of the greatest American speeches ever delivered was Martin Luther King Jr.'s "I Have a Dream."[18] Fifty years ago (on August 28, 1963), King spoke from the steps of the Lincoln Memorial on the Mall in Washington, DC, the centennial year of Lincoln's signing of the Emancipation Proclamation. King told the vast audience that his dream was "deeply rooted in the American dream that one day this nation will rise up and live out the true meaning of its creed—we hold these truths to be self-evident, that all men are created equal."

What is not often noted about King's speech is the degree to which he kept alive and pushed forward the civil-religious vision of America as God's chosen nation. Not only did he quote or allude to biblical passages, applying them to America, but the powerful rhetoric of his dream also envisioned America's nonracist future joined with the kingdom of God in one glorious fulfillment. "I have a dream that one day every valley shall be exalted, every hill and mountain shall be made low, the rough places shall be made plain, and the crooked places shall be made straight and the glory of the Lord will be revealed and all flesh shall see it together." With this faith, he said, "we will be able to transform the jangling discords of our nation into a beautiful symphony of brotherhood." The speech reached its rhythmic, inspirational, and prophetic climax in the ten pulsing repetitions of "let freedom ring" from every town and mountaintop across America. "And when we allow freedom to ring," he concluded, "we will be able to speed up that day when all of God's children—black men and white men, Jews and Gentiles, Catholics and Protestants—will be able to join hands and to sing in the words of the old Negro spiritual, 'Free at last, free at last; thank God Almighty, we are free at last.'"

The contrast between the WASP and the African American exodus stories exposes an additional weakness in America's civil-religious nationalism. While the two exodus stories present contrasting visions of God's "chosen nation" and of who should be included in its first-class membership, they do not tell us much about what the republic's government should be or what it should do to govern justly. The end of slavery, followed a hundred years later by the constitutional establishment of equal treatment for all citizens, certainly represented positive progress from the standpoint of public justice. Yet those constructive achievements brought change chiefly at the constitutional level by redefining membership (citizenship) in the republic to include people of all races. That change has not by itself, however, clarified the nature and responsibilities of government. We might say that the underlying expectation in both stories is that if membership in the nation is properly identified, then governing will take care of itself. Yet this tells us almost nothing about the specific purpose and limits of government or about the nature of a "political" community—a republic—in contrast to churches, business enterprises, families, and other nonpolitical organizations.

There is yet another matter to add to our agenda. A significant minority of American Christians believes that Christianity is radically incompatible with any version of the American civil religion. Stanley Hauerwas, at Duke University's divinity school, condemns the myth of Christian America for the reason that it is an enemy of the church and Christian faith. Hauerwas, following John Howard Yoder, believes not only that American nationalism is a danger to the church but also that liberal democracy itself stands at odds with the Christian way of life. Christians of all colors should be working to build the Christian community, not bending their efforts to sustain the false myth of American new-Israelism and secular liberalism.[19] Despite the critical stance of Christians like Hauerwas, however, a far greater number of Americans, including large numbers of Christians, still take for granted, even if unconsciously, America's civil-religious heritage as essential to America's well-being and as a legitimate companion of their Christian faith. There is little hope for the nation's future, they argue, if it does not recover its traditional (Judeo-Christian) moral and religious commitments. And many of those most worried about America's decline are the ones nurtured on the WASP exodus story and its assumptions about what makes America great.[20]

Double Separations

The introductory comments above are probably sufficient to suggest some of the difficulties facing us as we venture to think deeply and critically about the meaning of Christian engagement or nonengagement in the political arena. But another closely related matter will also require our attention in the chapters that follow. On one side are those who believe political life is an integral part of human culture, expressing an important dimension of our natural human sociability. That is a minority view in the United States, however. On the other side is the dominant view that politics is not natural; it does not belong to our original created nature; it is not part of culture. Politics and culture belong in different categories.

The idea that politics and culture are categorically different is typically defended by most Protestants on the grounds that government was instituted by God because of sin. Government may be necessary to protect us from dangers to life and property and to punish evildoers, but it is not an expression of what we are by nature. Consequently, many Christians treat the institutions of government with considerable suspicion. Since government has the power to compel by means of force, it can be used in morally indefensible ways. Culture, by contrast, is original to human nature. Culture is family and friendship, music and literature, science and education, industry and commerce, religion and leisure. The latter are expressions of our human nature. It would be best if humans didn't need government at all, but if God ordained it to restrain and punish evil, then it should be kept under tight constitutional control as it carries out its minimal responsibilities.

By curious contrast to this way of talking about government and politics, Americans sound a different note when speaking of their beloved *nation*. The major difference has its roots in the WASP version of the American civil religion. If government and its bureaucracies are held in suspicion and often referred to as "them" over against "us," the beloved American nation represents and symbolizes the freedom Americans cherish as central to their identity. Americans laud their nation as exceptional, a light to the world, just as they cherish their individual freedom. America is a city on a hill, the vanguard of democracy, the enemy only of tyrants, totalitarian regimes, and terrorists who threaten human freedom. America, the idealized nation—the beacon of freedom and hope, God's new Israel—seems to be something quite different from politics and government. Is this because Americans associate the *nation* with their culture of freedom while associating *government* with limits to their freedom? If so, this sounds very much like a theme winding through the WASP exodus story. The African American version of the story does not present such a contrast.

This tension between nation and government is visible to a greater or lesser degree in most American election campaigns. One candidate calls for less government, lower taxes, and more freedom, while another candidate calls for government to act in ways that will enhance the lives of all citizens through greater equality so everyone can enjoy the rights and benefits of freedom. Both sides argue for the greater good of the *nation*, but they disagree about whether *government's* actions enhance or endanger the nation. The starting point for both sides is free individuals who have inherent rights, but the arguments for government to act or not to act range across a spectrum from "little or no government" at one end to "as much government as necessary" at the other end.

It appears that we have already outlined a sufficiently large agenda for one book and may have raised more questions than we can answer. However, we have not yet said enough to introduce Christianity on its own terms. Biblically speaking, the Christian way of life cannot be reduced to either a supporting role or an opposing role for politics. Christianity must be understood in the context of God's covenants with Israel that reach their climax, according to the New Testament, in the revelation of Jesus Christ. That revelatory, covenantal drama depends in its entirety on God's creation of all things. God's history with Israel leading to Jesus Christ cannot, therefore, be read simply as the lead-up to God's election of America.

Christianity, we believe, entails a way of life that is not spiritually separate from earthly culture and politics, but neither is it compatible with the American civil-religious way of life. On one side, the element of truth to be found in distinguishing Christianity from political and cultural life is that Christian faith depends on the transcendent creator, judge, and redeemer of all things. On the other side, the element of truth in the view that Christianity and culture are intimately connected is that Christianity is a way of life constituted by following Jesus Christ. And in Christ, everything about us as image bearers of God is caught up into God's judgment and redemption of creation. Those committed to following Christ enter a way of life characterized by repentance, forgiveness, renewal, and wholehearted service to God and neighbors. Nothing that is part of our human identity can be left out of this way of life. Life in Christ through the power of the Holy Spirit is spiritual in the sense that every dimension of life in this world is being renewed by the Spirit of Christ, who is carrying the faithful forward through faith and hope to fulfillment in God's kingdom.

With regard to the relation of politics and culture, then, we will try to show why neither amalgamation nor separation is the answer. While it is proper and necessary to distinguish between different kinds of human responsibility, such as family life, education, industry, art, science, and so forth, it is a mistake to pit politics and government (as unnatural) against cultural responsibilities thought to be natural. The element of truth in distinguishing various social, cultural, and political activities is that God has created us with many capabilities and is calling us to exercise diverse kinds of responsibility in disclosing what it means to be created in the image of God. To try to explain everything about humanity from only a political or economic or sexual or logical point of view, therefore, fails to do justice to the full complexity of who we are. At the same time, the element of truth in the conviction that politics is a natural part of human culture is that political life has to do with much more than restraining and punishing evil deeds of public injustice. If humans had not sinned, there would be no need for police forces, criminal courts, and penal systems, but those responsibilities are not the only ones that belong to the government of a political community, and they do not define the original, underlying meaning of political life.

Creator, Creatures, and Christianity

Fundamental to the perspective of this book is the conviction that human beings and everything else that exists are the creation of God. Biblical revelation makes clear that everything begins with God and everything other than God is God's creation. Thus, when we talk about creation, we will be talking about more than the *beginning*. With the author of Hebrews we believe "that the universe was formed at God's command, so that what is seen was not made out of what was visible" (Heb. 11:3). Yet that is just the beginning of what the Bible tells us about creation. We stress this point at the outset because many Christians in churches throughout the world practice Christianity as a religion of sin and salvation: humans are sinners in need of salvation, and Jesus Christ is the savior whom God sent to redeem sinners so they can have eternal life. But who is the Christ that Christians call Savior? And who are the human beings identified as sinners?

Notice how John's Gospel, the letter to the Colossians, and the letter of Hebrews all begin. They start by stating that created reality exists in, through, and for the Son of God who became incarnate in Jesus Christ. The good news begins, in other words, by telling us about Christ's mediation of creation. "Through him all things were made; without him nothing was made that has been made" (John 1:3). "For in him all things were created: things in heaven and on earth, visible and invisible, whether thrones or powers or rulers or authorities; all things have been created through him and for him. He is before all things, and in him all things hold together" (Col. 1:16–17). The Son of God is the one "whom [God] appointed heir of all things, and through whom also he made the universe," the one who sustains "all things by his powerful word" (Heb. 1:2–3). The biblical story, the good news of Jesus Christ, *begins with creation*, not with sin and the need for salvation.

What, then, about the identity of human beings? Who are the men, women, and children we know to be sinners? According to the Bible, the first thing to be said about humans is not that we are sinners but that we are created in the image of God. We have been made to be like God, made to walk and talk and work with God (Gen. 1:26–27). The image bearer of God is God's royal steward, God's vicegerent, with immense responsibility throughout their generations to govern and develop God's creation. That is the creature who has become a sinner, who has broken trust with the creator, who has turned away from the path of life to follow pathways to destruction. Therefore, we cannot begin to grasp the meaning of sin or God's judgment or the saving work of Christ if we do not see that humans and all other creatures are created to exhibit God's glory.

The story of sin is the deep and enduring tragedy that has marked human history, the tragedy to which we are now making our contribution. Sin and degradation are not moral abstractions in a story that floats above earthly realities. If it were not for the mercy and grace of God, human disobedience would lead to the utter ruination of God's purposes for creation, bringing dishonor to God and destruction and death to everything created. The saving work of Jesus Christ is not a spiritual mystery that floats above the material world in which we live. Nor is it a story that focuses first on the saving of sinners. The incarnation, death, and resurrection of Jesus Christ are oriented ultimately to the reconciliation of the creation to God and thereby to the revelation of the glory of God. And it is because of Christ's reconciling work that sinful human creatures are hearing the good news of redemption, the good news of their restoration to the high calling of being God's stewards and viceroys of creation. The story of salvation is the story of the creation's reconciliation, of the forgiveness of sins and the renewal of life in this age in anticipation of the fulfillment of all things in the presence of God, when every knee bows and every tongue confesses that Christ is Lord (Phil. 2:10–11).

The biblical story is not about the salvation of souls for eternal life, which leaves a vacuum of meaning about life in this age. There is no "secular space" that may legitimately be filled with the worship of golden calves and the pursuit of other (false) gods. Christians must find themselves in the biblical story from start to finish, from top to bottom, if they are to understand and give themselves properly to their cultural and political responsibilities in this age. For Christ is the Alpha and the Omega of all things (Rev. 1:8). He is not a part-time God or a redeemer of the spirit only. Upon his resurrection, Jesus declared to his disciples that all authority in heaven and on earth had been given to him (Matt. 28:18). The biblical story is not some kind of ancient background noise that fades away when the American story begins. The biblical story catches up the whole of created reality, encompassing all that exists and all that humans will ever be and do. That is why if we are to look carefully at the meaning of *Christian* engagement in the political cultures of our day, we must first find ourselves in the biblical story.

part 1

the biblical drama

1

God's kingdom coming

The Messianic Promise

"Lord, are you at this time going to restore the kingdom to Israel?" (Acts 1:6). What a remarkable question! According to Luke, this was the last question ever put to Jesus. It came from the lips of his apostles just before he disappeared before their very eyes. Think of it: these disciples had been with Jesus for several years, including forty days after his death and resurrection, during which time he spoke with them "about the kingdom of God" (Acts 1:3). How could they have any more questions? Surely Jesus had explained everything they needed to know about his mission, the meaning of his death and resurrection, and their responsibilities from that time forward. But no, they were still unclear about Jesus's relation to Israel and God's promised kingdom. Jesus had taught them to pray, "Your kingdom come, your will be done, on earth as it is in heaven" (Matt. 6:10). But what exactly were they praying for, and when would God's kingdom come on earth as it is in heaven?

Some of my Christian friends believe that the disciples misunderstood Jesus up to the very end. Jesus had not come to restore a political kingdom to Israel but to establish the church (a spiritual "kingdom") and to save souls for eternity. The kingdom that was of concern to Jesus was something quite different from the one Israel had in mind. Apparently, the disciples would have to learn this after Jesus ascended to heaven and the Spirit had come to guide them in their evangelistic work.

Yet that is not the way Jesus responded to his disciples, according to Luke. Jesus did not reject their question as if it were beside the point and irrelevant to his mission. In fact, except for the question of timing, his response encouraged them to keep alive the question about Israel and God's kingdom. As for timing, he told them, "It is not for you to know the times or dates the Father has set by his own authority" (Acts 1:7). But beyond that, the kingdom of God—a real kingdom—was indeed at the heart of everything Jesus preached and did during his life. He was born a son of Israel, he lived as a rabbi and prophet, and his deeds of healing the sick and forgiving sins trumpeted the arrival of Israel's Messiah and God's rule on earth.[1]

This is what Jesus's mother prophesied even before he was born. "The Mighty One has done great things," she sang in celebration. "He has brought down rulers from their thrones / but has lifted up the humble. / He has filled the hungry with good things / but has sent the rich away empty. / He has helped his servant Israel, / remembering to be merciful / to Abraham and his descendants forever, / just as he promised our ancestors" (Luke 1:49, 52–55). And the father of John (the baptizer of Jesus) prophesied with the same joy of hope fulfilled: "Praise be to the Lord, the God of Israel, because he has come to his people and redeemed them. He has raised up a horn of salvation for us in the house of his servant David . . . to show mercy to our ancestors and to remember his holy covenant, the oath he swore to our father Abraham: to rescue us from the hand of our enemies, and to enable us to serve him without fear in holiness and righteousness before him all our days" (Luke 1:68–69, 72–75).

So, there stood the disciples, a long time after they had first recognized Jesus as the Messiah of Israel, weeks after they had witnessed his death and resurrection, and yet . . . where was the kingdom of God? Why hadn't Jesus rescued Israel from Rome and brought down Israel's enemies from their thrones? When would every knee bow before the Messiah of Israel, the king of the earth, to fulfill God's promises? How much longer would they have to wait?[2]

With the authority and assurance that always characterized him, Jesus answered by giving them their marching orders. Leave the timing in God's hands, he told them. Here is what you need to know about me, about Israel, and about the kingdom of God: "You will receive power when the Holy Spirit comes on you; and you will be my witnesses in Jerusalem, and in all Judea and Samaria, and to the ends of the earth" (Acts 1:8). And then, suddenly, he was no longer there. Shocked, the disciples froze, unable to digest his words or to ask a follow-up question. But the follow-up came with the appearance of two men dressed in white: "Men of Galilee . . . why do you stand here looking into the sky? This same Jesus, who has been taken from you into heaven, will come back in the same way you have seen him go into heaven" (Acts 1:11).

Jesus, with the confident authority of a king whose domain runs to "the ends of the earth," tells his disciples, who are thinking small (from within the confines of Roman-controlled Israel), that the Spirit of God will come upon them and send them out to Israel and far beyond Israel to proclaim Jesus the king and lord of all. As N. T. Wright says, "Luke stresses that the newly inaugurated kingdom claims as its sacred turf, not a single piece of territory, but the entire globe."[3] That is the message Jesus was asking his disciples to carry; that is what they were to bear witness to. And no sooner had he disappeared from their sight than messengers appeared in front of them to confirm, from on high, the authority of his message. The one who just ascended into heaven will return in God's good time to put his feet on the earth again, and everyone will then understand (as John saw in a vision on Patmos) how God is fulfilling his promises to Israel: "'Look, he is coming with the clouds,' / and 'every eye will see him, / even those who pierced him'; / and all peoples on earth 'will mourn / because of him.' / So shall it be! Amen. 'I am the Alpha and the Omega,' says the Lord God, 'who is, and who was, and who is to come, the Almighty'" (Rev. 1:7–8). In his vision on Patmos, John heard the seventh angel sound his trumpet, followed by loud voices from heaven: "The kingdom of the world has become the kingdom of our Lord and of his Messiah, and he will reign for ever and ever" (Rev. 11:15). After John saw God's final triumph over the beast, he heard the faithful singing the "song of God's servant Moses and of the Lamb: 'Great and marvelous are your deeds, / Lord God Almighty. / Just and true are your ways, / King of the nations. / Who will not fear you, Lord, / and bring glory to your name? / For you alone are holy. / All nations will come / and worship before you, / for your righteous acts have been revealed'" (Rev. 15:3–4).

Luke concludes the book of Acts with Paul living in Rome, where he "proclaimed the kingdom of God and taught about the Lord Jesus Christ" (28:31). The good news about Jesus that Paul and the other apostles were proclaiming, says Wright, "is the news of the kingdom of Israel's god, that is, the message that there is no king but this god. More specifically, it is this Jewish message now crystallized as the news about Jesus, the Messiah, whom Paul announced as *kyrios*, Lord."[4] In the end, in other words, everyone and every nation, not just Rome and the enemies of the Jews, will find themselves at (or under) the feet of Christ Jesus, proclaiming God's glory and the righteousness of his deeds.

But what did that mean for the disciples after Jesus ascended to heaven, and what does it mean for us today? If Jesus is the king of kings and not only the head of the church, then what does his ascension and invisible lordship have to do with the governing of modern states and nations? Did the early church answer these questions correctly? Did the Christian emperors of the late Roman Empire and the kings of medieval Europe get it right? What about the rulers of modern states, whether monocratic, aristocratic, democratic, or dictatorial?

Everything under His Feet

The picture that comes to mind most often when one hears the phrase "everything under his feet" is probably the picture of Jesus that John saw in his vision recorded in Revelation, a picture of triumph. The Lamb of God triumphs over sin and all the forces of evil arrayed against God. That is also what Paul described for the Corinthians. The end will come, wrote Paul, when the risen Christ "hands over the kingdom to God the Father after he has destroyed all dominion, authority and power. For he must reign until he has put all his enemies under his feet. The last enemy to be destroyed is death" (1 Cor. 15:24–26). These and several other passages in the New Testament quote or allude to Psalm 110: "The LORD says to my lord: 'Sit at my right hand until I make your enemies a footstool for your feet.'. . . / The Lord is at your right hand; / he will crush kings on the day of his wrath. / He will judge the nations, heaping up the dead / and crushing the rulers of the whole earth. / He will drink from a brook along the way, / and so he will lift up his head" (vv. 1, 5–7).

This picture of retributive judgment, of a crushing triumph over the enemies of God, is not, however, the first and most basic picture the Bible presents when using the words "under his feet." Recall Psalm 8, which refers to Genesis 1. The psalmist is reveling in the majesty of the Lord, whose glory reaches beyond the heavens. Overawed by that majesty and the wonder of all that God has created, the psalmist asks, "what is mankind that you are mindful of them, / human beings that you care for them?" He answers, "You made them rulers over the works of your hands; / you put everything under their feet" (Ps. 8:4, 6; see Gen. 1:26, 28). This is the psalm the author of Hebrews also quotes (2:6–8). In these passages we hear a positive celebration of the good order of creation, of God putting humans in charge of everything on earth, with no suggestion of divine retribution or of any destruction of enemies. God created humans, in their generations, to govern, develop, and care for the earth. The expression of putting everything under their feet tells us, in those contexts, of the responsibility men and women have been given to rule and develop the nonhuman creatures and, in the process, to cooperate with one another in nurturing and using their own talents. Men and women are royal stewards of the king of creation. This is a picture of the proper order of creation in which everything finds its place and is given its just due. The good order of creation situates humans under God—under God's feet, on God's earthly footstool, as Isaiah pictures it (66:1)—with a responsibility to do justice to the nonhuman creatures of the earth placed under their feet. This is not a picture of punishment or the destruction of enemies who have dishonored God and misdirected humans into pathways of death.

For this reason God's acts of judgment in pulling down evil rulers and putting them under Christ's feet do not aim to eliminate governments and every other kind of authority in creation but rather to restore and fulfill the good order of creation. Paul makes this clear in the verses that follow the ones quoted above from 1 Corinthians: "Now when it says that 'everything' has been put under him [Christ], it is clear that this does not include God himself, who put everything under Christ. When he has done this, then the Son himself will be made subject to him who put everything under him, so that God may be all in all" (15:27–28). Humans, forgiven of sin and restored to life in Christ, will find their proper place and responsibility once again under God. In other words, the Son's act of submission to the Father is not the act of a defeated enemy, cast down by God. Rather, Christ's submission reveals the humility of a servant, and the Father's elevation of the Son to the position of supreme human ruler follows because of that faithful service through which the whole creation is reconciled to God. Explaining 1 Corinthians 15:20–29, Wright says, "This passage, the earliest Christian writing about the kingdom that we possess, retains the essential Jewish framework. Not only in the explicit biblical quotations, but in the entire sequence of thought, the point is that the creator god is completing, through the Messiah, the purpose for which the covenant was instituted, namely, dealing with sin and death, and is thereby restoring creation under the wise rule of the renewed human being."[5]

Christ's faithfulness unto death and his resurrection to life thus bring together both meanings of "everything under his feet." God *created* humans to develop, fill, and govern the earth in his service until the work of their generations is completed, and God says, "Well done, good and faithful servants; enter into your reward." This reflects the good order of creation. However, as the author of Hebrews says, even though the creator put everything under human feet, "at present we do not see everything subject to them" (2:8). The "not yet" is, in part, a consequence of the fact that the generations of the first Adam are still unfolding and have not yet completed their work. But the "not yet" is also due to human sinfulness. In their sin, all the generations of humankind together can never fulfill their vocation because they have turned away from faithful service to God and to one another and have brought disorder to creation. Nevertheless, says the author of Hebrews, human failure to serve faithfully as God's vicegerents is not the last word in the story. For the author's very next words are these: "But we do see Jesus, who was made lower than the angels for a little while, now crowned with glory and honor because he suffered death, so that by the grace of God he might taste death for everyone" (2:9). In other words, the Son of God, in response to humankind's sinful defection, humbled himself to become one of us and to suffer death for our sake in order to redeem humans, thereby reconciling all things, properly reordered, to God.[6]

You can hear in this passage an echo of Paul in 1 Corinthians 15:27–28 and Philippians 2:5–11. The Son of God became human and "humbled himself by becoming obedient to death—even death on a cross! Therefore God exalted him to the highest place and gave him the name that is above every name, that at the name of Jesus every knee should bow, in heaven and on earth and under the earth" (Phil. 2:8–10). Jesus Christ is thus doubly honored in glorification. As the One who conquers sin and death, he puts every enemy of God under his feet, subjugating or destroying everything that stands against God's creation purposes. And through his faithful service, Jesus restores the image bearers of God, male and female, to their rightful place in God's good creation as royal stewards, under whose feet God originally placed everything.

But Jesus Said His Kingdom Is Not of This World

Even if we can find some basis in the Bible for arguing that earthly governance is part of what it means to be created in the image of God, didn't Jesus say, "My kingdom is not of this world" (John 18:36)? Doesn't that mean the kingdom Jesus is establishing is very different from any political order on earth? After all, the very next thing Jesus said was that if his kingdom were of this world, then "my servants would fight to prevent my arrest by the Jewish leaders. But now my kingdom is from another place" (v. 36). How, then, is it possible for human political life on earth to find its fulfillment in the kingdom Jesus is establishing "from another place"? Doesn't an earthly political community, by its very nature, include fighting to defend itself? It looks as if there can be no connection between human political systems and the kingdom Jesus is establishing.

Keep in mind that in this passage in John's Gospel, Jesus is standing before the Roman governor of Jewish territory (vv. 28–40). That governor, Pontius Pilate, finds himself in an uncomfortable position because the Jewish authorities have asked him to convict Jesus under Roman law as a criminal against Rome. They say Jesus is misleading people to believe that he is God's chosen Messiah and thus the king of the Jews, something that should worry Rome. Pilate conducts a preliminary hearing of Jesus and concludes, to the contrary, that there is no reason to convict him. But the Jewish authorities are not satisfied with Pilate's preliminary judgment. Under Roman jurisdiction, the Jewish leaders have no right to execute Jesus for a crime against Rome (v. 31). Of course, they are convinced that Jesus has broken laws of their own covenant by making claims about himself that only God can make, and thus they believe he should be put to death for blasphemy. Yet they hope Pilate will deliver the outcome they want by putting Jesus to death for treason against Rome. Pilate is not persuaded, but he goes back to have another conversation with Jesus because he would still like to satisfy the Jewish authorities.

Pilate then asks Jesus, "Are you the king of the Jews?" If Jesus answers yes, then of course Pilate will have the confession he needs to execute Jesus because a claim of kingship would challenge the rule of Caesar. If Jesus answers no, then he is no threat to Rome, and Pilate can turn him back to the Jews. But Jesus does not answer either yes or no. The answer he gives, that his kingdom is not of this world, is intended to show that his authority and his mission do not fit the categories of either Pilate or the Jewish leaders. Jesus did not come to challenge Rome on its own terms in order to try to take over the land of Israel or even the entire Roman Empire. His mission is not to try to gain control of a territory and hold onto it by force for as long as possible, the way ordinary rulers do. The kingdom that God sent him to establish is indeed different from the kinds of political systems with which we are familiar. But that does not mean the kingdom of God is unrelated to earthly politics. Jesus even says to Pilate, "You would have no power over me if it were not given to you from above" (John 19:11). In that way, Jesus acknowledges the legitimacy of Pilate's position but does so on God's terms, not on Rome's terms. The mission of Jesus is to show both the Roman and the Jewish authorities that it is God alone who holds ultimate authority over them and holds them accountable to the terms of God's kingdom.

With the Jewish leaders, Jesus has a different kind of disagreement. Their actions show they are willing to cooperate with Rome on Roman terms in order to try to get rid of a prophet who is challenging their authority and, in their eyes, committing blasphemy against God. However, they should not be cooperating with Rome in this way because their law calls them to acknowledge God alone as their supreme Lord. They shouldn't be asking Pilate to judge a Jew with regard to his faithfulness to God's covenant with Israel. Jesus has come to tell the Jewish people that God's kingdom—the kingdom of heaven—is near. From Jesus's point of view, the Jewish leaders should be listening to him as the authoritative prophet from God, not seeking Rome's help to keep their own house clean.

The claim of Jesus that offended both the Jewish leaders and Pilate was that his authority came from another place, from God on high, and thus it had something directly to do with both Rome and Jerusalem. Pilate acknowledged no authority higher than the Roman emperor, who claimed to represent God on earth. If Jesus was correct, then he was indeed challenging the foundation of Caesar's claim to authority. Of course, if Jesus was a fraud or was mistaken in his claim, then he was no threat to Rome. The Jewish authorities believed they represented God, in accord with the covenant. If Jesus was correct, he was trumping their authority by the direct authorization of God.

Here is the crucial point that got Jesus into a fix with both Pilate and the Jewish authorities and led to his crucifixion. If Jesus had been preaching the arrival of a kingdom that had nothing to do with this world, a kingdom removed from "real politics," then neither the Jewish nor the Roman authorities would have been so upset with him. To the contrary, however, the claims that Jesus was making had to do with God's lordship over all kingdoms *on earth*, over every human authority *in this world*. Jesus presented himself as God's directly authorized prophet of the kingdom. His actions and words said even more; he was acting as if he were the promised Messiah, the promised Son of Man who had come to inaugurate the divine kingdom. Jesus, therefore, was either deranged and a fraud or his kingdom did pose a threat to everything Rome represented and his kingdom did challenge the position taken by the Jewish authorities.

If we understand the claims of Jesus about the kingdom of heaven in this way, we can see how relevant those claims are to every kind of human responsibility on earth, including human government. Jesus did not teach that his shepherding was "spiritual" and unrelated to life in this world. He did not say that his authority to teach disciples touched only theological matters. He did not teach that the brotherly, sisterly love he was urging his disciples to practice was sacred in contrast to their "secular" family relationships. To the contrary, the mission of Jesus in announcing the fulfillment of God's purposes with creation was to reconcile and redeem all that is human—all shepherding, schooling, family relationships, economic institutions, and political practices. God's kingdom does not originate in this world, nor is it confined to the life we live as sons and daughters of the first Adam. But that kingdom does have everything to do with human life in this age because our lives here and now have their entire meaning within the order of God's good creation and Christ's fulfillment of it.

Another oft-quoted passage in the New Testament should be mentioned here. It comes in Matthew 22:15–22, where the Pharisees are trying "to trap [Jesus] in his words" (v. 15), so they ask him a question. Much like the passage in John, their question has to do with political authority. The Pharisees ask Jesus whether it is right for Jews to pay the imperial tax to Caesar.[7] They assume that if he answers yes, they will be able to accuse him of violating Jewish law by legitimating Roman authority. If he says no, then he will be challenging Rome's sovereignty, and they can expose him before the Roman authorities as treasonous. Jesus realizes what is going on and asks for a coin. Then he asks whose image and inscription are on the coin, and they respond that it is Caesar's. Jesus says, "Give back to Caesar what is Caesar's, and to God what is God's" (v. 21). Those who are trying to pin him down are left speechless and walk away.

Many Christian circles have understood this response from Jesus to teach the separation of political obligation and obligation to God. Some even say it authorizes the separation of church and state. Caesar gets one thing; God gets something else. What belongs to Caesar doesn't belong to God, and what belongs to God doesn't belong to Caesar. But that distinction does not fit this text. Jesus came to announce the arrival of the kingdom of God anticipated by Israel. For him to say that a political authority should be paid a tax did not conflict with his mission. The apostle Paul would later say much the same thing in his letter to the Roman Christians: "This is . . . why you pay taxes, for the authorities are God's servants, who give their full time to governing. Give to everyone what you owe: If you owe taxes, pay taxes; if revenue, then revenue; if respect, then respect; if honor, then honor" (13:6–7). Jesus and Paul were not saying that political authority is separate from the realm of God's authority but that governing authorities hold their positions as servants of God. So why did Jesus's comment about the coin leave his questioners speechless?

Look carefully at what Jesus did not say. He did not say that Caesar had a domain of his own separate from God's domain, and, if one paid the tax to Caesar, it had nothing to do with what one owes God. Jesus did not say that God's domain is unrelated to this world. Jesus could assume that those listening to him understood the commandments, and the first commandment is to love God with all of one's heart, with everything that one has, and to serve no other god. Human creatures owe God everything, including their responsibility to pay taxes to a political authority. Caesar, by comparison, is not owed everything. He is not God. He may legitimately lay claim to a tax payment insofar as he holds a position of public service, but only God is owed everything. Jews knew, for example, that a tithe paid to the priests was an act acknowledging that everything, not just the tithe, belongs to God. Jesus confounded the Pharisees because he was exposing their own confusion about the very law they acknowledged as binding upon them. Give to God what is God's, namely, everything. And under that overall obligation, give what is due to every servant of God—rulers, priests, parents, tax collectors, teachers, prophets, and others.[8]

There is one more thing. The fact that the Pharisees walked away speechless was probably because they realized they had trapped themselves rather than Jesus. In the exchange, his authority was enhanced and theirs diminished. If they had stayed to acknowledge that fact, they would have shown that they owed something to Jesus. If Caesar is owed a tax payment, and God is owed everything, then what did the Pharisees owe the prophetic rabbi standing before them who just spoke the truth with unchallengeable authority? They owed Jesus their ears; they should become his disciples. Better to walk away.

What seems clear from these two biblical passages about the position and claims of Jesus is that he came to inaugurate God's kingdom. He did not come as just another man with ordinary human political aspirations. The kingdom he came to announce by word and deed was the kingdom his Father sent him to inaugurate. He came to do his Father's will, to proclaim and also to embody God's judgment of every authority on earth. Many did not understand his words and actions, which led to his death; but that mystery, too, underlines the truth of Jesus's statement that his kingdom is not from this world but from another place. The kingdom he represents will have no end; it will stand as the last word in response to every human government on earth through all of time. His is the climactic kingship, and it has to do with everything on earth. As Hebrews puts it, God spoke throughout history by many prophets up until now, "but in these last days he has spoken to us by his Son, whom he appointed heir of all things" (1:2). This Omega who is also the Alpha is the one who came to provide purification for sin, after which "he sat down at the right hand of the Majesty in heaven" (1:3). According to Paul, he is the one appointed by God to "judge the world with justice," and God "has given proof of this to everyone by raising him from the dead" (Acts 17:31).

The kingdom of God in Christ is not one among many competing kingdoms fighting for control of territories on earth; it is, instead, the highest court of justice for all nations. And ever since the ascension of Jesus Christ to the right hand of the Majesty on high, the only proper response by any nation or person is to repent (Matt. 4:17; Acts 17:30). Repentance in this case means more than apologizing or expressing sorrow for past mistakes; it means turning away from unjust, unloving ways of life to habits of justice. The inauguration of God's kingdom in Christ neither dislodges nor disbands our human political vocation.

To the contrary, it calls us to the obedient exercise of political responsibility. For the political communities and governments of this age, it means turning from practices and institutions of injustice to practices and institutions of justice. That involves complex and sophisticated statecraft, which requires solid training in the discernment of the demands of justice in the realm of pubic law and administration.

With that said, it is clear that no government on earth may claim to stand in for the resurrected and ascended Christ during the time he is "absent" from the earth. At the time of his ascension, Jesus assured his followers that he would send the comforter, the Spirit of God, the Spirit of truth, to indwell them (John 14:15–21). That same Spirit—the advocate—would also move forward with acts and signs that anticipate the final judgment. The Spirit, Jesus explained, "will prove the world to be in the wrong about sin and righteousness and judgment: about sin, because people do not believe in me; about righteousness, because I am going to the Father, where you can see me no longer; and about judgment, because the prince of this world now stands condemned" (John 16:8–11). The comforter, the advocate, now indwells, moves, nurtures, comforts, assesses, convicts, and judges life on earth on behalf of Christ—as the vicar of Christ—until the Lord's return. Christ, acting through the Spirit, is head of the church, but his rule extends over all things through the Spirit, including all political authorities and powers (see Col. 1:15–20).

"All authority in heaven and on earth has been given to me," Jesus told his disciples after his resurrection from the dead (Matt. 28:18). Of course, not everyone sees or believes in the continuing, patient, merciful governing authority of Christ over the governments and political forces of this age, but that is what Christians profess, by faith, to be true. All of human life in this age, including political life, depends on faith, for we cannot yet see or understand fully what will be established in the end. Faith may be misdirected because of trust in false gods that keep people from grasping the truth about their identity as the image of God and about Christ's patient and long-suffering lordship. Nevertheless, the supreme authority and rule of Christ over all things is what the Spirit is now proving and what believers are to proclaim by word and deed as they carry out their responsibilities in every sphere of life, including politics and government, until Christ's kingdom is revealed in its fullness.

Why Was Israel Wrong to Ask for a King?

In 1 Samuel we read the story about Israel asking the prophet Samuel to give them a king. Samuel was displeased by their request, but God said to him, "Listen to all that the people are saying to you; it is not you they have rejected, but they have rejected me as their king. As they have done from the day I brought them up out of Egypt until this day, forsaking me and serving other gods, so they are doing to you. Now listen to them; but warn them solemnly and let them know what the king who will reign over them will claim as his rights" (8:7–9). Samuel did what God told him to do and warned the people of the wrongs that a king would commit, but that did not deter them. So God said to Samuel, "Listen to them and give them a king" (8:22).

Some have read this story to say that God opposes monarchy in principle and is probably more in favor of a theocracy or priestocracy, or perhaps a constitutional republic.[9] Monarchy, from this point of view, is assumed to be a bad form of government since it represents a rejection of God. Consequently, when God told Samuel to give the Israelites a king, God must have done it as a matter of grudging condescension, perhaps as a judgment because of the hardness of their hearts. But reading Samuel's words in the light of the full range of God's covenantal dealings with Israel opens up other interpretations. God's disappointment with Israel, as the text makes clear, was not because of their attraction to kingship compared to some other form (or all forms) of government but because of their failure to recognize and follow the Lord God who was ruling and shepherding them. God had led Israel out of Egypt and covenanted with them in a singular way. What human king could have done that for them? If the children of Israel had been dedicated to God as they should have been, they would have trusted him and accepted the authorities God had given them from the time of Moses and the judges up to Samuel. They would have seen that their unity as a people and their protection from enemies were because of God's care for them. The Lord was guiding them in a unique way to the Promised Land where they would be established and show what a true kingdom should look like.

Israel's falling away from full trust in God led God to give them a king. And, indeed, because of their failure of faith, God told Samuel to tell the people what they did not want to hear: they were already in trouble and headed for more. Yet God's allowance of a king and warning of the negative consequences did not mean that God was imposing an evil institution on them. Instead, it was an allowance that would open the way to a further, historically differentiated disclosure of the creation's meaning in relation to God. By means of human kingship, when conducted on God's terms, Israel might learn again to know the Lord as their supreme king and themselves as God's royal representatives. In other words, since God was their ultimate king, a just king could mirror God's rule in a way parallel to the way human parents are supposed to mirror God's parenting care, or the way spousal love reflects the love between the divine bridegroom and his wife, or the way the shepherding of sheep reflects God's shepherding of Israel.

In essence, that is what Deuteronomy's kingship law makes clear. It instructs Israel about the kind of king they *should* have. The passage is of such importance for all that follows that I quote it here in full.

When you enter the land the LORD your God is giving you and have taken possession of it and settled in it, and you say, "Let us set a king over us like all the nations around us," be sure to appoint over you the king the LORD your God chooses. He must be from among your own people. Do not place a foreigner over you, one who is not an Israelite. The king, moreover, must not acquire great numbers of horses for himself or make the people return to Egypt to get more of them, for the LORD has told you, "You are not to go back that way again." He must not take many wives, or his heart will be led astray. He must not accumulate large amounts of silver and gold.

When he takes the throne of his kingdom, he is to write for himself on a scroll a copy of this law, taken from that of the Levitical priests. It is to be with him, and he is to read it all the days of his life so that he may learn to revere the LORD his God and follow carefully all the words of this law and these decrees and not consider himself better than his fellow Israelites and turn from the law to the right or to the left. Then he and his descendants will reign a long time over his kingdom in Israel. (Deut. 17:14–20)

In close connection with this passage in Deuteronomy are the kingship psalms, which eloquently depict a righteous king as revelatory of the divine king. When the king governs in a way that shows him to be at one with a righteous people, then together they reveal something about God's rule among his people, who are made righteous by following the way of the covenant.[10] Both the kingship law in Deuteronomy and the kingship psalms show that the meaning of kingship is not found in the monarch's dominance over the people but in his service to them in ways appropriate to the office and authority of government. According to Old Testament scholar Patrick Miller, the word "servant" in many of the psalms "is to be associated with two figures, the ruler and the torah lover," who merge into one. Psalms 15–24 "may be seen as defining proper kingship at the beginning of the Psalter. Obedience to torah and trust in Yahweh's guidance and deliverance are the way of Israel and the way of kingship."[11] The king is one of the people called to be a servant of God. The king holds a high office of leadership, but his calling is to be exercised in accord with the covenant with God. Thus, there is no room for pretension or a claim of superiority on the part of the person who serves in that office.

King and people can function as one of the communities that reveal something about God because such a community arises from the identity of those created in the image of God. Of course, a king (or any form of government) and the people in political community can become distorted and darkened through faithlessness, injustice, and the practice of oppression, leading to all of the associated evils God warned Israel about through Samuel and the prophets (see 1 Kings 12:1–24). What the psalms make clear in relation to Deuteronomy is what kingship should be and how a royal people can be revelatory of God as a partial and anticipatory disclosure of God's kingship that will be revealed in its fullness through the coming Messiah.

Conclusion

It was right for the disciples of Jesus to be asking about the kingdom of God and God's promises to Israel. Jesus had revealed himself as the promised Messiah, but the restoration of Israel and the fulfillment of God's kingdom were not yet fully evident. How could Jesus explain that? How much longer would the disciples have to wait? What they were waiting for was not simply God's destruction of their enemies. They were longing for the fulfillment of God's promises to establish shalom—peace, satisfaction, justice, bounty, and dwelling with God in righteousness and joy. The kingdom that Jesus came preaching would mean more than a final day of judgment. Rather than obliterating everything associated with earthly kingship, governance, law, and order, the kingdom of God would establish true justice under the messianic king, who would rule forever. From Abraham to Moses to David, on to the mother of Jesus and Jesus's disciples, the desire of Israel was to see God deliver all the good things only God can deliver. The whole creation has now been placed under Christ's feet, and soon the glory of God will be revealed in its fullness.

Where and how does political life fit under the creating and redeeming authority of Jesus Christ? How does Christ connect earth and heaven, the human and the divine in all of this? These questions lead to the next chapter.

the revealing
image

Persons and Polities

Many if not most people in the media and in the field of political science today think of humans as individual behavior bundles, motivated largely by self-interest. This understanding of the person has its roots in the idea that each person is (or should become) autonomous and self-directed. The modern ideal of the free individual with inherent rights, including the right to seek one's own happiness, has been shaped and reshaped along the way under the impact of the study of animal behavior. Those studies, however, have created problems for the ideal of autonomous freedom. Behavior patterns, according to scientists, are strongly shaped by one's DNA and by environmental conditions, such as parental training, advertising, peer pressure, and much more. In fact, humans may not be free at all but merely the sum total of their physical, biotic, and psychic preprogramming and social conditioning. The tension between the ideal of autonomous individuals, on the one hand, and a deterministic view of nature and human behavior, on the other hand, appears to be irresolvable.[1]

This complex view of human nature is carried into the study of nations and states, which are imagined to be like individuals writ large. Modern states are self-determining sovereigns, acting to advance their own interests. At the same time, states are driven by forces, such as the desire for security, national pride, and economic necessity, which may make it possible for their behavior to be scientifically explained. So is it freedom or determinism that shapes relations among states?

The ancient Greek philosopher Plato held a very different view of the individual (microcosm) and its relation to the political community (macrocosm).[2] The human person for him (modified to a degree by Aristotle) is a composite of body and soul with several functions and virtues that could be categorized as animal appetites at the lowest level, emotions and spiritedness at the next level, and reason at the highest level. A mature human is one whose life is guided by true knowledge and wisdom, gained by the disciplined training of reason that directs spirited action, which in turn keeps the appetites under control. From this point of view, it was also assumed that no individual is free and autonomous in the modern sense, nor is anyone simply a bundle of biotic and instinctual behavior patterns. The mature, rational man (for it can only be a few men, not women, who are capable of rational maturity according to Plato) becomes the most free and self-directed of humans only by submitting to the authority and discipline of reason. Reason is the normative condition of maturity, not the tool of an individual's will or desires. Maturity is not something achieved by willful assertiveness but something earned by mastering the art of reasoning.

From this view of the microcosmic individual, it is relatively easy to guess what the macrocosmic parallel is. For Plato and Aristotle, the most complete realization of mature human community is to be found in the well-ordered *polis*, the political community, or what we usually refer to as the Greek city-state. Humans are by nature social and political animals, and thus the full realization of human nature is found only in the best polis. The structure of the best and most just political community will look like this: the few rationally trained men will govern as philosopher kings; well-trained spirited men—guardians—will serve as the defenders and administrators of the polis, under the direction of the philosopher kings; and lower classes of men engaged in production, commerce, and slave labor will pursue their work in keeping with the organized administration of the guardian class. Here we see the individual writ large: reason (philosopher kings) ruling the will (administrative enforcers and defenders), which controls the appetites and passions (the lower classes).

In this idea of the city-state, a certain standard or form beyond the will of any person or class of persons determines what a just polity should be. The good polis is a *just* polis because it is rightly ordered; it is rightly constituted and rightly governed. The idea that the people at large should be free to shape the political community as they wish, through democratic means, is not only a foolish idea but also one that will lead eventually to a radically disordered polis. It would be like a person whose passions and appetites take control of the will and the mind. Disordered persons create disordered polities, and disordered polities encourage the development of disordered persons.

Which of these two views of human nature and political order is best? Should Christians begin with the assumption that humans are naturally free and autonomous or with the assumption that humans are by nature social animals with an inherent rational orientation toward political life? Are humans first of all autonomous individuals with diverse appetites and desires, or is each one a combination of appetites, emotions, and reason, requiring disciplined rational training for the realization of maturity in both persons and political communities? Or is there another way to conceive of human persons and rightly ordered political communities?

The biblical view of humans is quite different from the modern and ancient Greek views and is largely incompatible with both. However, this is not a generally shared consensus among Christians. Many Christians believe that God has set us free in Christ and intends for each person to be free. Every person has dignity before God, and a just political system ought to have as its highest obligation the protection of the dignity and rights that go with individual freedom. Moreover, individuals are not naturally political and should be free to form the communities and relationships they choose. Since humans are sinners, it also makes sense to expect that in the political arena people will seek to protect and advance their own interests. That's just human nature in its fallen condition. So, these Christians believe, the modern idea of the individual and the political process is pretty accurate, and that's why Christians should support a constitution that maximizes individual freedom and puts strong restraints on government's use of power. What Christianity brings to all of this is the understanding that apart from God's grace in Christ there is no hope for life after death, no way to get through this world of sin and to enter into the full freedom Christians have in Christ.

Many other Christians, though smaller in number in the United States, lean more toward the Greek view of human nature. Some parents and teachers still train children to control their appetites by a disciplined will that is under rational control. That training may in turn give rise to expectations that wise and thoughtful statesmen and stateswomen will step forward, motivated by more than personal interests and the narrow interests of their financial backers. This view of persons and polities may seem at first glance to be more compatible with Christianity. It also may seem more relevant to the condition of the international arena in our day. States are so tightly intertwined that world peace, environmental sustainability, and economic well-being require the cooperative efforts of wise statesmen from all countries to seek the larger common good of all. To imagine that a world of self-interested, self-seeking states—the macrocosm of self-serving individuals—has any possibility of surviving in a healthy, peaceful condition is foolish. Humans are certainly sinful, but, by the grace of God, they can also act rationally for the good of all in many circumstances and in high public office.

It may well be the case that there are elements in these two points of view that are compatible with a biblical view of human nature. But the deeper question is whether one can cobble together from those diverse elements a Christian view of the human person and the political community. What we need to do first, then, is to look more closely at the biblical view of human creatures. Doing that will bring into view the remarkable picture of men and women created in the image of God, created to be revelatory of God.

The Image and Likeness of God

The identity of humans as portrayed in the Bible does not ignore behavioral functions of diverse kinds. Nor does it disallow the hypothetical grouping of some of those functions into categories such as appetites, will, and intellect. But humans also function socially, linguistically, aesthetically, economically, and ethically. It does not help very much to group several or all of those functions under a category of sociability or rationality, because each has a distinctive meaning. Human creatures are highly complex and multifunctional, and their full complexity is part of what it means to be created in the image of God. Let's look briefly, then, at some of the important characteristics of the biblical view of human creatures.

The first distinctive characteristic is that humans are not only male and female, and thus jointly and interdependently the image of God, but also multigenerational creatures. This comes through clearly in the language and structure of Genesis, the biblical book titled and organized in terms of the generations of successive family lines, each tied backward and forward in the generational unfolding process: "God blessed them and said to them, 'Be fruitful and increase in number; fill the earth and subdue it'" (1:28a). This statement alone speaks against an individualistic conception of autonomous individuals. Not only are we interdependent as male and female, but only through the unfolding of many generations are humans able to work out their commission from God to fill and subdue the earth. Only as a multigenerational creature can the image of God fulfill God's calling, "Rule over the fish in the sea and the birds in the sky and over every living creature that moves on the ground" (v. 28b). To think of humans first and foremost as separate individuals, each supposedly free to be oneself, is to abstract the importance of personal identity and responsibility from the full reality of human life. Each of us is the person we are only in relation to God, to one another, and to everything else God has created. We are a particular kind of creature made to exercise high-level responsibilities in relation to God in the framework of the entire seven-day order of creation.

To speak of the generations of humankind also brings into view our sexual nature. The human generations unfold only by way of reproduction through sexual intercourse and child rearing. Moreover, we are the kind of creature, like the animals God created, that is dependent on food and water for life. Part of God's blessing of humans is the gift of food: "I give you every seed-bearing plant on the face of the whole earth and every tree that has fruit with seed in it. They shall be yours for food" (v. 29). And God gives this same gift to the animals and birds (v. 30). In other words, we are thoroughly embodied creatures tied to and dependent on other creatures, and in some cases we share with others the same food, water, and other resources. It is not surprising, then, that some students of human behavior choose to focus on the appetites, on instinctual behavior, and on conduct that is similar to that of animals.

The Bible, however, distinguishes human creatures from animals, birds, and fish. Humans have been created to walk and talk and work with God as high officials in God's creation-kingdom. We bear the kind of responsibility that belongs to no other creature. We have been created to love, serve, and reveal God through our friendships, marriages, families, development of the earth, education of young people, and, yes, *governing* of creation. Another thing the Bible does *not* do is refer to a particular human characteristic or function as the one that gives us our distinct identity. It is not reason, or love, or spirit, or soul that gives us our identity. Our distinctive identity is found in bearing the *image of God*. That is why the tripartite anthropology of the Greek philosophers as well as various dualistic anthropologies of body and immaterial soul (or body and mind) can be so inaccurate and misleading.

The multigenerational character of our human identity is the basis of cultures and traditions. Every important expression of human life in society today has historical roots and consequences. Industry, music, science, the languages we speak, diverse means of communication, and the latest inventions—all of them show dependence on the work of past generations. No person starts out in life as an unencumbered, autonomous individual. Long before one reaches an age of accountability with decision-making capability, one has learned to speak, eat, think, learn, and behave as a participant in a multigenerational cultural setting over which one had no originating control. Not all social and cultural developments have been good, but whether good or bad, healthy or unhealthy, they reveal the multigenerational character of humans.

Human life not only manifests a communal bond over time; it also reveals God. To be created in the image of God is to be a revealing image, a revelatory creature. Think, for example, of ways in which the Bible speaks of God wooing Israel as a bride, nurturing the people as a parent, tending them as a flock of sheep, teaching them as students to follow in the way of life, and governing them the way a righteous lawmaker, judge, or king governs citizens. These are not casual analogies or incidental metaphors. They carry great weight in conveying different facets of truth about who we are and about who God is in relation to us. To be the image of God is to be very much like God and thus revelatory of God in every aspect of our lives. To understand the biblical view of humans and the political communities they form, therefore, we need to start where the Bible starts, with creation.

The Seven Days of Creation

The creation story at the beginning of Genesis is presented in the framework of a seven-day week, and the days are clearly *God's* days, not sun-timed (twenty-four-hour) days as we measure the time of our days.[3] The greater light (sun) and lesser light (moon), for example, are not created until the fourth day of

God's work. And the seventh day, the day of God's rest, has no evening or morning. Moreover, God's "rest" does not mean that he slipped off for a nap or to relax after strenuous exertion, but rather that he celebrates the greatness, the grandeur, and the revelatory glory of all that is created. Another way to say it is that the seven-day order of creation shows that everything culminates in God's never-ending, seventh-day celebration. Moreover, the seventh-day climax, as the Bible subsequently makes clear, is the intended fulfillment of the whole creation, including the fulfillment of the responsibilities of the human generations.

This is what Hebrews 3:7–4:11 tells us, and it connects Genesis 2:2–3 with Psalm 95:7–11.[4] In the course of shepherding Israel, God held out the promise that the Israelites would eventually find rest at home with God, the kind of rest represented by the Promised Land. But the Israelites hardened their hearts, so God declared that they would never enter that rest (Ps. 95). Yet now, says Hebrews, God has spoken through Jesus by the Holy Spirit to promise once again that there remains a rest for the people of God. What kind of rest is it? The author is explicit in saying that the rest promised to those who do not harden their hearts is the very sabbath rest of God, the seventh day of creation. When the faithful have finished their life's work as sixth-day creatures, they will enter God's seventh-day rest (Heb. 4:6–11). In other words, God's creation holds together as a seven-day order in which all of God's work, which includes the work assigned to the generations of the sixth-day image of God, culminates in God's sabbath celebration with the people of God. This means that the diverse biblical expressions we use when speaking about heaven, eternal life, the kingdom of God, the new heaven and new earth, the new Jerusalem, and dwelling with God face-to-face—all of those expressions refer to the same climactic fulfillment of creation, namely, the celebration of the glory of God in God's day of rest—the creation's seventh day.

But we've gotten ahead of ourselves. While it is certainly the case that the seven-day week of God's creation implies a forward-looking movement from beginning to end, it is also evident that the presentation of God's seven-day creation in Genesis 1:1–2:3 reveals an architectural order from foundation to pinnacle. When we speak of the days in our week, we emphasize the progression of time, not the content of different days. When we say today is Wednesday, we understand that Tuesday has passed and Thursday has not yet arrived. We live one day at a time. But God's creation days are not like that. Each of God's days is defined by what God makes, and the created things of that day serve as the basis for the next day of created things, as a kind of hospitality center for them. All of God's creations continue in existence together as an architectural, ecological whole. Light and darkness (day 1) provide the setting for the separation of the water above from the water beneath (day 2). The waters above and beneath become the hospitality center for the water and dry land that are separated under the sky, with the land becoming the host of vegetation of all kinds (day 3). The greater and lesser lights (sun, moon, stars) then become the light-bearing servants of everything on earth, marking off seasons and days and years (day 4). And all of that provides hospitality for winged creatures and sea creatures (day 5). Then the earth, sky, sea, plants, lights, birds, and fish become the hosts of animals and humans (day 6). But the sixth day is not the end of the story. God's six days of created things, including the human generations, serve as the hospitable hosts of God's seventh-day celebration of the whole creation.

To speak of an architectural order of creation is to notice that the seven creation days hold together simultaneously. They are interlinked in revelatory grandeur. Unlike our emphasis on the separate time of each day, Genesis 1 emphasizes the distinct identity of the creatures of each day in their interdependent unity as God's one creation. If you pause and look around, you will see dry land separated from oceans and lakes, the sun shining, plants bearing fruit, animals reproducing, and humans engaged in different kinds of work—*all of which is taking place at the same time.* In other words, on biblical terms, the first, second, third, fourth, fifth, and sixth days of creation all develop interdependently, oriented toward God's day of rest. The first six days of creation are arrayed together before God's seventh-day throne as a footstool for the creator's feet (Isa. 66:1). The created things of each of God's days have their own glory and distinct honor; all are special in their own ways. Yet all of them depend on and host one another simultaneously in the unity of God's one creation order.

Old Testament scholar Raymond Van Leeuwen argues that Genesis 1 portrays the created cosmos as a royal palace with many rooms that the monarch fills with beautiful things. This is a well-ordered, well-governed kingdom, which honors and delights the ruler. The first three days of creation show the rooms of the palace being made, and the next three days (four through six) show the ruler filling those rooms with mobile creatures.[5] The creature most like the sovereign monarch is given the authority of a vicegerent or viceroy to rule the earth, manifesting one of the ways men and women image God. What does the ruler direct the vicegerents to do? To *build up* the earth (its rooms) through productive development and wise governance and to *fill* it with human offspring and the fruits of their sociocultural creativity so that those who image God can achieve all that God has given them to do. God the supreme monarch thus places everything under the feet of those made to be viceroys under the Lord of all (Ps. 8:6).

This is where our thinking about human government and politics must begin. Although there is no mention in Genesis 1 of legislatures, courts, and governors of political communities, neither does the passage mention universities, farms, art galleries, publishing firms, and large-scale industries. All such organizations and institutions have come into existence as human generations have emerged and built creatively on the achievements of past generations. Inherent in God's command to govern and develop creation is the task of public governance that will differentiate from other kinds of human responsibility in the course of social and cultural development over many generations.

The opening passage of Scripture is about the creation as God made it, calling each group of created things good and finally offering the judgment that they are "very good" (Gen. 1:31). This seven-day, architectural wonder is the creation order. It was taken for granted, for example, by Paul in 1 Corinthians 15:35–49. Unlike the contrast Paul draws in 1 Corinthians 15:20–28 and Romans 5:12, 15–19 between Adam as the one through whom sin came into the world and Christ as the one who overcomes sin, the contrast he presents in 1 Corinthians 15:35–49 is between the first Adam as God's good, sixth-day image and Christ as the last Adam through whom the resurrected faithful of all generations will inherit eternal life (seventh-day rest with God). "'The first Adam became a living being'; the last Adam, a life-giving spirit. The spiritual did not come first, but the natural, and after that the spiritual. The first man was of the dust of the earth; the second man is of heaven. As was the earthly man, so are those who are of the earth; and as is the heavenly man, so also are those who are of heaven. And just as we have borne the image of the earthly man, so shall we bear the image of the heavenly man" (vv. 45–49).[6]

From the perspective of this Pauline argument, God's sixth-day human creatures have been made for a multigenerational life of service in this age. But that is not all God intended for those born in Adam's line. That is only the beginning, the first stage, the natural mode of life, which is lived by faith, not yet by sight. Humans have been created for something more, namely, a life generated by the last Adam, the life-giving Spirit. Sin has of course degraded and darkened the life of the first Adam's generations and, through them, the whole creation. Death without hope, rather than life in anticipation of resting with God, is the consequence of sin, and that is our inheritance from the first Adam, Paul explains. But death and degradation are the consequence of sin; they are not original to those created in God's image. Even apart from sin, Paul explains, the generations of the first Adam do not have imperishable life. Only the life-giving Spirit can give imperishable, spiritual (seventh-day) life to the generations of the first Adam. The sabbath rest of God into which God will welcome the resurrected faithful is not a retirement phase of life in this age. No, it is a new kind of life—resurrection life, seventh-day life—in the last Adam, Jesus Christ.

In this biblical light, it is apparent that human culture and political responsibility, understood as part of the meaning of life in the image of God, must have as their ultimate horizon the culminating revelation of God's glory in sabbath fulfillment. In other words, everything God created, particularly human beings, is important and revelatory, and all of it is oriented toward a completion that cannot be found in this age, which is the unfolding of the creation's first six days, including the human generations. Yet everything about this age is related to the age of fulfillment to come. Consequently, Christians who focus only or primarily on the "next life" fail to see how their lives and labors in this age are part and parcel of what God will bring to fulfillment in the age to come.

By contrast, those who focus only on life in this age miss the revelatory and anticipatory meaning of who they are and what they are doing. To understand ourselves properly, in Christ, as image bearers of God, we must come to know ourselves in the full context of God's seven creation days.

Christ's Service and Authority

What God reveals in Jesus Christ has a twofold meaning with regard to everything God places *under his feet*, as we discussed in the last chapter. On the one hand, the incarnation, sacrificial death, and resurrection of Christ are at the heart of God's judgment of unrighteousness and triumph over sin and death. In Christ, God is rectifying and reclaiming the sinfully disordered creation. On the other hand, what God has revealed through the Son, who stooped in humility to become one with us, is the true meaning of faithful human service. In Jesus, God found a son of Adam with whom he could be well pleased, the one who was and did what God created humans to be and to do and who thus became qualified to lead a whole company of the faithful to the completion of their sixth-day labors and into the celebration of rest with God. The placement of everything under Christ's feet, in this second sense, means the restoration of creation and the fulfillment of everything God had put under human feet in the first place. Thus, God's retributive judgment against the enemies that threaten the destruction of God's creation has as its goal the reconciling recovery and fulfillment of the good creation in the sabbath rest of God.

There is another important thing to notice about the two senses of the expression "everything under his (or their) feet." In the positive sense, humans exercise constructive responsibility under God in ruling other creatures. In the negative sense, enemies of God challenge divine authority and wrongly lord it over other humans. The latter is the enemy whom Christ defeats. The enemy includes the acts of those who try to seize an authority God has not given them. In acting as if they were God, they put other human creatures under their feet. Augustine, in *The City of God*, made a point about this kind of disorder: "Sinful man hates the equality of all men under God and, as though he were God, loves to impose his sovereignty on his fellow men. He hates the peace of God which is just and prefers his own peace which is unjust."[7] By contrast, says Augustine, God intended no man "to have dominion over man, but only man over beast. So it fell out that those who were holy in primitive times became shepherds over sheep rather than monarchs over men, because God wishes in this way to teach us that the normal hierarchy of creatures is different from that which punishment for sin has made imperative."[8] We'll return to Augustine's point later to ask whether monarchy (and perhaps every other kind of government) is inevitably unnatural and a dominion made necessary by sin. But was Augustine correct to think that, because of sin, government necessarily has the character of a hierarchical dominion in which some people lord it over others?

Return for a moment to the passage in Matthew's Gospel about Caesar's coin (Matt. 22:15–22), which we discussed in the last chapter. When Jesus asked those who gave him a Roman coin whose image and inscription were on it, they said it was Caesar's. In that case, Jesus said, give to Caesar what is Caesar's. When he then said give to God what is God's, we can sense the unstated allusion Jesus was making to the image of God. The question was this: What "coin" on earth bears the image and inscription of God who is "emperor" of the whole creation? Humans, of course! And what does that suggest about what humans should give to God? The Jews knew the answer: humans owe God everything, the whole of their lives. Everything comes from God and is owed to God; we are simply God's stewards. Love the Lord with all your heart, soul, strength, and mind. That is what it means to be fully alive as God's image bearer. And for that reason, it is impermissible to think of humans as the microcosm of any institution on earth or as subordinate to anyone other than God. Biblically speaking, the macrocosm of human life is the seven-day creation in which humans are to live as the viceroys of God. In fact, the dynamic unfolding of the good creation discloses many ways in which humans mirror God: friendship, marriage, family life, priestly life, shepherding, public governance, and more. Every one of these reveals something about the meaning of God's relation to us. Yet none of them can be the entire macrocosm. To come to know ourselves fully as human beings will take place only when we dwell with all of God's people in face-to-face fellowship with God, as citizens of the holy city, as Christ's bride, as his brothers and sisters, and as priests and disciples of Jesus Christ in God's seventh-day rest.

Among other things, this means that humans are subordinate only to God. No position of human authority can be legitimate that gives one or more humans a godlike status of superiority over other humans. Diverse human relationships and institutions are intended to manifest different types of service—servant leadership—in relation to fellow humans. Augustine's insight follows closely upon the response of Jesus to the Pharisees about Caesar's coin. That coin with Caesar's image on it was intended by the emperor to say that everything and everyone in the Roman Empire was subordinate to Caesar, meaning that all humans belong "under his feet." When Jesus explained that the coin could serve its legitimate purpose in making a tax payment, he was subtly demoting Caesar from his position of pretended divinity to the position of a mere servant, one who has authority to claim a tax payment but not to demand everything from the people. Only God may lay claim to human beings in their entirety. Caesar may legitimately collect taxes in order to exercise his responsibilities as a public servant under God, but he, too, owes everything, including his governing responsibility, to God. His office does not make him more like God or put him closer to God than other humans.

Government and the Use of Force

It has often been assumed that the love Christ taught his followers to practice is at odds with the responsibility of governments to enforce justice, at least if the enforcement requires the use of physical force. For example, a central chapter in Richard Hays's book on Christian ethics, *The Moral Vision of the New Testament*,[9] makes a strong argument along this line, drawing conclusions similar to those of well-known theological pacifists John Howard Yoder and Stanley Hauerwas. The teaching of Jesus and the apostles, according to Hays, stands opposed to all use of force, whether by a murderer or by government officials. Therefore, since Christians are called to a vocation of nonviolence, they should refuse to hold any position of government authority that entails the use of force. But Hays doesn't give adequate account of the biblical distinction between the illegitimate use of force by a thief or murderer and the response to such acts by a government authorized to exercise retributive justice. His view depends on the confession of the Reformation-era Anabaptists who stated in their Schleitheim Articles (1527) that the office and responsibilities of government exist "outside the perfection of Christ."[10]

In challenging this interpretation offered by Hays, let's begin with two texts in Luke's Gospel that seem to support Hays's argument. The first is Luke 9:21–27, where Jesus tells his disciples that he must die. He says, "Whoever wants to be my disciple must deny themselves and take up their cross daily and follow me. For whoever wants to save their life will lose it, but whoever loses their life for me will save it" (vv. 23–24). Indeed, the entire teaching of Jesus and his death on the cross testify to his giving up his life rather than trying to hold on to it. Yet this teaching that the disciples should give up their lives in the service of Jesus has deep roots in the very meaning of creation. Humans have been created to give themselves up in service to God. They have not created themselves, and they cannot hold on to their lives in this age even if they try to do so. Life for the generations of the first Adam is expendable; it is perishable. Jesus became one of us, taking on the human vocation of being an expendable servant of God. To be sure, the death of Jesus brought with it the forgiveness of sins because God laid on him, as a sacrificial lamb, the sins of us all (Isa. 53:6, 8, 10). In that respect, Jesus did what sinful humans cannot do for themselves. Yet telling his disciples to "take up their cross" and follow him did not imply (as Hays seems to believe) that they would violate their commitment to Jesus by assuming a governmental responsibility to protect the innocent and uphold justice, requiring in some cases the use of force to restrain or punish those who break the law.

Government, understood biblically, is an office of public service, of giving up one's life on behalf of civic neighbors. Unjust acts by a government may not be countenanced; they are a violation of the office, not an inevitable expression of what government has been established to do. Using an office of government, or a position in a business, a school, or a church, for the purpose of self-aggrandizement violates the responsibilities of all those offices. The calling to follow Jesus in the service of God, in any and every sphere of life, requires the willingness to relinquish one's hold on the most precious gifts from God. We are to give over all gifts, all callings to God in service, yet we may be sure that in seeking first the kingdom of God we will inherit all things in Christ.

The second text in Luke's Gospel that seems to support Hays's argument (that Christians should not hold a government office that entails the use of force) is Jesus's tough rebuke of his disciples when he heard them arguing among themselves about who would be the greatest in the kingdom of God. Jesus said,

> The kings of the Gentiles lord it over them; and those who exercise authority over them call themselves Benefactors. But you are not to be like that. Instead, the greatest among you should be like the youngest, and the one who rules like the one who serves. For who is greater, the one who is at the table or the one who serves? Is it not the one who is at the table? But I am among you as one who serves. You are those who have stood by me in my trials. And I confer on you a kingdom, just as my Father conferred one on me, so that you may eat and drink at my table in my kingdom and sit on thrones, judging the twelve tribes of Israel. (Luke 22:25–30)

What Jesus countered here was the practice—the system—of government in which those in high office (kings) "lord it over" humans under them. The lords even considered themselves benefactors, condescendingly believing they were giving good things to those under their feet. There is an implication in this statement that the gentiles practiced something different from what Israel was taught to practice. That is the case, as we've already suggested in our discussion of Deuteronomy 17 and the Psalms. Jesus does not here condemn the work of government as incompatible with the way of life he is urging on his disciples. Instead, he is showing them that if they truly want to be "at the table" of honor with him in his kingdom, they must live now as servants, just as Jesus is doing. Jesus does not deny that there is a table of honor at which he and his disciples will sit. He even says that the seats will be thrones (of governing authority) from which they will judge the twelve tribes of Israel. This is to say that those who give themselves up in service now, all the way to death and without lusting for positions of importance, will be qualified in Jesus's kingdom to serve as judges even of the tribes of Israel.

The teaching in this passage is exactly parallel to that of Luke 9:23–26. Give up your lives in service for my sake, because you can't hold on to them and you can't elevate yourselves above others to a position of importance in God's kingdom. That is why today is the day of repentance! Right now, everyone should turn from self-importance and self-service and learn to give themselves up in service to God and neighbors. That is the way of life for which God created us, and it has been opened to men and women once again by God's mercy expressed through his Son and humble servant, Jesus Christ. Repent and believe this good news, disciples! Come and follow me!

It is precisely in the spirit of this teaching that we need to locate government's vocation, which is to uphold public justice, protect the innocent, and withstand those who would harm or kill their neighbors.[11] In other words, the office of government and the meaning of political community must be reconceived in the light of Christ's coming. Holding such a position of public authority does not have to mean, and should not mean, "lording it over others." To the contrary, in keeping with the law of love, it should mean acting as a servant of all civic neighbors in recognition that everyone, Christians included, stand equally before God, the Lord and judge of all.

Governmental Authority and the Law of Love

There is probably no passage in the Bible about government that is more frequently quoted and disputed than Romans 13:1–7. In it Paul not only urges everyone to "be subject to the governing authorities"; he also says those authorities have been established by God and in fact are God's servants, God's ministers. This teaching sits somewhat uneasily with the arguments of Hays and others who put it in tension with Romans 12, where Paul's teaching echoes Jesus's Sermon on the Mount.[12] Christians, Paul tells the Romans (12:9–21), should not think of themselves as superior. They should bless and not curse their enemies. They should live in harmony with one another and not repay anyone evil for evil but try to live at peace with everyone. And they should certainly not take revenge on anyone "but leave room for God's wrath, for it is written: 'It is mine to avenge; I will repay,' says the Lord" (v. 19).

Now, since the behavior described in Romans 12 should characterize Christians, interpreters like Hays say Christians should not hold an office of government as described in Romans 13 because there Paul explains that the governing servants appointed by God are in fact "agents of wrath to bring punishment on the wrongdoer." Those public servants are positioned to encourage the good, to be sure, but they "do not bear the sword for no reason." The reason, in fact, is to restrain and punish those who do evil, using force if necessary. Such action, as Hays sees it, is incompatible with the ethic of Jesus and the teaching of the New Testament. One of the difficulties of this argument, however, is that it appears to put God at odds with Christ. In Christ, God calls the faithful to pacifism, while outside of Christ, God appoints authorities to act in ways that are supposedly at odds with the Christian ethic. This interpretation also seems to be at odds with some of Jesus's own claims, as when he declared upon his resurrection, "All authority in heaven and on earth has been given to me" (Matt. 28:18). How can the authority of human government exist "outside the perfection of Christ" if all authority is now in the hands of the risen Christ?

This way of dealing with Romans 12 and 13 is not only problematic but also unnecessary. Note first that the whole of Romans 12 and 13, running to the end (13:14), is a Pauline admonition to live in accord with love. It begins (12:1) by urging believers to present themselves as living sacrifices, giving themselves up in God's service, not trying to hold on to their lives. It continues by urging believers to act with humility and not to think of themselves more highly than they ought (a passage quite parallel to Phil. 2:1–8). Believers are to function as one body, respecting all members of the body. Then comes the section about self-giving, not returning evil for evil, and overcoming evil with good (Rom. 12:9–21). Following the first seven verses of Romans 13, to which we will turn in a moment, Paul continues, "Let no debt remain outstanding, except the continuing debt to love one another, for whoever loves others has fulfilled the law" (13:8). In conclusion, Paul urges them to "wake up from your slumber, because our salvation is nearer now than when we first believed." Therefore, we should "put aside deeds of darkness and put on the armor of light" (13:11–12).

Now, it would be very strange to find in Paul's extended exhortation to live by the law of love a parenthetical argument about God's ordination of government that contradicts the law of love. Instead, every sign suggests that 13:1–7 is part of Paul's explanation of how we are to live in accord with the great love commandments. Notice first that God's establishment (ordination) of government is direct; it does not come indirectly through the church. Those who have put their trust in Christ should indeed turn the other cheek and not take revenge. They should be an example to others of what every person should be, thus helping to break the cycle of vengeance. Yet as long as God sends rain and sunshine on the just and unjust alike and has not yet sent angels to separate the wheat from the weeds in this age, then it is also true that believers—and everyone—should accept with thankfulness God's ordination of government to exercise a measure of divine retribution necessary for the protection of the innocent and the punishment of evildoers. God does not in this way give some people the right to lord it over others but rather establishes an office in which the officeholder has a responsibility before God to exercise the kind of justice that will displace cycles of private revenge. There is nothing about such an office of public service that is incompatible with subservience to the authority (and humble service) of Jesus Christ, whom God has appointed judge of the world with justice (Acts 17:31).

The authorization of government to act as the unbiased administrator of justice is one of God's gifts of mercy and long-suffering in face of human sinfulness. It is an expression of God's love for the human creatures Christ has come to die for and redeem. God is extending time and space for all sinners to repent and turn to God. And during that time, governmental authorities bear the responsibility to not only encourage those who do good but also protect the innocent from those who would harm them and punish those who commit crimes. Political authorities, too, should perform their service in accord with the law of love.

The fact that the office of government in a political community exists by God's ordination outside the authority of the offices of church authority is parallel to the fact that parental authority in the family, a teacher's authority in school, and an engineer's authority in construction projects exist by God's direct ordination as creaturely callings. Church authorities do not establish parental, educational, engineering, or political institutions. The latter all come from God, who created male and female in the divine image. All humans are made for friendship and family life, buying and selling, education and civic life. They do not get the authority to exercise those responsibilities from the church or via the church. Rather, the church—the bride of Christ, the people of God in Christ—is a community of faith drawn together by the power of the Spirit to reorient their creaturely responsibilities to the service of God. Jesus Christ is the Lord of all—Lord of marriage and family, of learning and agriculture, of science and the arts, of political and economic life. Christians have no authority to lord it over others in any of those arenas of life. The challenge for the community of Christian faith is to learn, as disciples of Christ, how to be faithful servants of God and their neighbors in every sphere of responsibility, including government and politics, all of which now stand under Christ's authority.

The difficulty we have in understanding this is that for most of its history the church was involved in trying to gain and then hold on to a position of authority through which it could rule over all other authorities, including governments. We have a deeply ingrained idea that Christ's lordship begins within the church and from there extends outward to the rest of the world and to all of reality. But Christ's authority is over both the church (the community of faith in Christ) and all creation, including those who are not professing Christians. Those living by faith in Christ certainly should *not* act out of self-interest and with an aim of self-aggrandizement to gain power over non-Christians. But insofar as God has authorized government to encourage and protect the entire public—for the common public good—there is every reason for Christians to honor that office and, when qualified and called, to hold such an office as one way to love and serve their neighbors in obedience to Christ. From this point of view, we can affirm the point made by Augustine that God did not create humans to lord it over other humans but to rule over nonhuman creatures. But I take issue with Augustine's idea that, because of sin, God established a hierarchy that does in fact put some humans in a position to lord it over others in order to maintain a degree of peace and order on earth. It is certainly possible to see governments acting unjustly when they put some people under their feet for the benefit of others. But that is unjust and not what governments should do. That is not what God called governments to do. In arguing this point in the pages that follow, I will try to chart a course different from the one initiated by Augustine.

Conclusion

The image of God—the revealing image, male and female—discloses something true about God and God's relation to us in everything we do, including our responsibility to exercise just public governance on earth. In Jesus Christ, the revelatory image of God has come into full relief. In becoming fully one with us, Jesus not only reveals what it means to live as self-giving servants of God in this age but also reveals, by way of his death, resurrection, and ascension, what God has planned for the faithful in God's sabbath glory. Earthly governance is part of what humans have been created to do, and in Christ Jesus we see how that responsibility should be exercised in anticipation of the final revelation of the new Jerusalem. Human life in this age is not a useless way station where we wait for our extraction and emigration to another world. No, our cultural and political engagements in this age are dimensions of our revelatory identity as the creature who images God, and those engagements, rectified and cleansed in Christ, anticipate fulfillment in the final unveiling of God's sabbath rest. The lives we live and the fruits we bear now by the renewing power of Christ's Spirit will be carried into the kingdom in which Christ rules forever to the glory of God.

citizenship
in the kingdom

One or Two Kingdoms?

If Christians are both earthly citizens and participants, by faith, in Christ's kingdom, does that mean they live in two kingdoms and have two citizenships? The idea of two kingdoms has been part of Christian thinking for a long time.[1] The biblical basis for the idea, as some see it, is Jesus's statement to Pilate that his kingdom is not of this world but from another place (John 18:36). Believers in Christ have citizenship in his kingdom, which is not of this world, and also have citizenship in the political systems of this world. However, the two-kingdom idea can lead in different directions. In the thinking of many, the political systems of this world are destined for judgment because they all stand opposed to the kingdom of God. For others, political life in this world is an expression of God's providential care of all creatures and therefore is not necessarily evil, but it is only a temporary means of restraining sin and punishing evildoers until Christ's kingdom comes. For still others, the kingdoms of this world can positively serve Christ's kingdom if they give special assistance to the church.

At least two things are missing from these variations of the two-kingdom idea. The first is an adequate account of how Christ's kingdom extends over all things in heaven *and on earth* (Matt. 28:18). In other words, much that is in the Bible tells us that there is only one kingdom, not two.[2] Second, the reach of Christ's lordship extends beyond the church and is not mediated only through the church. Therefore, we need another way to think about the difference between life in this age and life in the age to come in order to get at the relation between Christ's kingship and the governing responsibilities we bear in this age.

I argued above that friendships, marriage, family life, shepherding, gardening, and governing all reveal something about God and our relation to God.

Humans, created in the image of God, are revelatory of God. In that regard, it is relatively easy to understand that any human marriage is not the same as, and does not exhaust the meaning of, Christ's marriage to his bride. The same can be said for any friendship, enterprise, school, or political community. But it is not quite right to argue from that insight that we live in two marriages, or in two enterprises, or in two schools, or in two political kingdoms. Instead, we can recognize that our lives in this age, with their marriages, enterprises, schools, and political systems, anticipate by the very nature of their revelatory character the fulfillment of all human relationships in the divine-human community that is not yet fully revealed. God's eschatological (ultimate, fulfilled, seventh-day) communion with the faithful will have the character of a divine-human marriage, family, school of disciples, banquet feast, fellowship of friends, and political community. And it will take all of those to make manifest the full meaning of our revelatory and anticipatory experiences in this age. We can say, therefore, that there is only one kingdom: the kingdom of God from the beginning to the fulfillment of the seven-day creation, which embraces all human governing experiences in this age and is leading, by means of both judgment and blessing, to the time of fulfillment, the great day of the Lord, when all will be revealed.

In the framework of the seven-day creation order, there are indeed two ages of human experience with God: the first, by faith, throughout the generations of the first Adam, and the second, by sight, in the age to come when all of God's people are gathered together through the resurrection of Christ, the last Adam, into the fulfillment of God's kingdom. In this age, humans owe everything to the one king who rules over the one and only creation-kingdom that has ever existed. Moreover, with the resurrection and ascension of Jesus Christ, the climax of that kingdom is now open to eyes of faith in anticipation of its fulfillment in the age to come. From the perspective of our present experience, there is both an "already" and a "not yet" to the coming of the kingdom and its king, Jesus Christ. Political responsibility in this age, consequently, does not belong to a kingdom separate from Christ's kingdom but is one of the modes of service that humans everywhere owe to God and their neighbors in the one and only kingdom of God that is not yet fully disclosed. The fact that our sinful, faithless hearts lead us to rebellion and treason in God's kingdom does not diminish the reality of God's rule over the whole earth through Jesus Christ. And those who turn to the service of Christ in repentance and faith by the power of the Holy Spirit will find that part of the meaning of that repentance and faith has to be worked out in the political arena.

This Age and the Coming Age

The biblical presentation of human creatures as God's image bearers is quite different from the gnostic idea that has influenced the church from early in its history. Gnosticism is one of the dualistic ways of life that arose in the Greco-Roman cultural context and had some influence on developments leading to the two-kingdom idea.[3] To summarize briefly, gnostics taught that the world we now experience is a cauldron of conflict; our souls are in tension with our bodies. The soul longs for liberation from its bodily entrapment. The material world is associated with darkness, evil, and the oppression of a harsh if not demonic god (or gods). If the soul can find a way to the light by way of true knowledge (*gnosis*), it can transcend its bodily prison. Influenced by this kind of dualism, some early Christians developed the heresy that Jesus Christ is the good and loving God who offers true gnosis by means of which souls can find their way out of this world to eternal life. Some of those influenced by the gnostics then pitted Jesus against the dark and retributive God of the Old Testament. Reality consisted of two worlds pitted against each other in a radical dualism.

Although the church condemned gnostic heresies, their influence continues to show up when Christians tell the gospel story as one of Christ saving souls from this world for eternal life in another world. Influences from the heresy show up in the view that Jesus represents love and peace, in contrast to the Old Testament's judgmental God who guided Israel into holy wars against their enemies. From that point of view, God's covenant with Israel was a worldly straightjacket that led to death, whereas God's covenant of grace in Christ offers true (and perhaps secret) gnosis that liberates souls for eternal life.

This dualistic view of life distorts biblical revelation, which begins by telling us that the whole of reality is God's *good* creation. There is not one world of bodily entrapment that stands in conflict with a second world of souls seeking God. The seven-day creation encompasses everything, including God's sabbath rest. Eternal life does not begin with the rational soul's escape from this world but with the resurrection of the dead to a new mode of bodily existence in the climactic seventh day of God's one and only creation. The only platform on which anti-God forces can stand to conduct their evil work is the good creation of God. The opponents of God do not come from a separate world but are creatures of the one and only God, against whom they are committing treason. Yet even in their revolt, they remain totally dependent on the creator. The antagonists are parasitical creatures fighting on God's turf, for they have no separate turf of their own. Furthermore, the one through whom all things were created is the same Son of God who took on human flesh to bear God's judgment against sin and redeem the good creation for fulfillment in the presence of God. That world-transfiguring climax will reveal resurrected *bodies* on a renewed *earth*, not bodiless souls in an "earthless" heaven.

The biblical view of goodness and sinfulness in God's creation is quite different from gnostic views. The biblical view cannot be synthesized with either ancient or modern dualisms. Jesus came preaching the kingdom of God (the "kingdom of heaven" in Matthew's Gospel) in which God's will for the creation is fulfilled. Our Father in heaven is the one whom Jesus came to earth to serve as faithful Son in order to establish God's will on earth as it is in heaven. Paul uses the language of this age and the coming age, of life as we know it now in the natural body (of Adam's generations) and life that is to come in the resurrection bodies inherited by the brothers and sisters of Jesus Christ (the last Adam). Life in the age to come will be without sin because of Christ's sacrificial death and triumph over sin and death—but he triumphs over sin, not over created reality.

Government Established Because of Sin?

All of this is crucially important for a Christian understanding of cultural and political responsibilities. Those created in the image of God exist to reveal, not to hide, God. God created, not to obscure, but rather to disclose the divine glory. If God instituted government only because of sin, then we would have to assume that after Christ completes his triumph over sin and death, there will no longer be any need for government. Consequently, when the Bible speaks of the new heavens and new earth, we would expect it to do so by speaking only of the bride's marriage to her husband, of the ingathering of Christ's brothers and sisters into God's family, of the great banquet feast, and so forth, but it would say nothing at all about anything political or governmental.

However, that is not what John saw on the island of Patmos in his vision of the climax of all things. John saw that Christ's triumph over sin and death was leading to the fulfillment of God's *kingdom*, a new Jerusalem (a city well governed), with nations walking by the city's light (the Lamb of God) and the kings of the earth carrying their splendor into it (Rev. 20:11–21:27). The text says explicitly that in that city there will no longer be any curse because there is no longer anything for God to curse, yet the "throne of God and of the Lamb will be in the city, and his servants will serve him" (22:3). John describes what he sees with a strange mixed metaphor: "I saw the Holy City, the new Jerusalem, coming down out of heaven from God, prepared as a bride beautifully dressed for her husband. And I heard a loud voice from the throne saying, 'Look! God's dwelling place is now among the people, and he will dwell with them. They will be his people, and God himself will be with them and be their God'" (21:2–3). The city—a political community of perfect justice—is like a bride, and all who dwell in the city are a people at home with God, standing in righteousness before the throne of their Lord and king. The most intimate human relationship, marriage, which we have no difficulty associating with our created nature as the image of God, is joined in this picture with the new Jerusalem, the embodiment of a just political community.

The concluding passages of Revelation draw together a wide variety of human relationships that reveal something of God. A king is different from a shepherd of sheep, and a shepherd is different from a brother, father, sister, mother, friend, teacher, citizen. Yet Christ, like David, is our great shepherd and also our brother, friend, bridegroom, and king. Citizenship in earthly political communities is thus as much a part of the revelation of God and of our identity as God's image bearer as are marriage, family, friendship, discipleship, and shepherding. Or to put it another way, as we develop all of the cultural potential of human life in this age, looking ahead to the fulfillment of all things in the age to come, we need to see, in the Bible's light, that the development of well-governed political communities is one of the important dimensions of our service to God and neighbors in God's kingdom. In the new heavens and new earth there will be no curse, because there will no longer be any sin or disobedience to condemn. That will mean God's throne of justice has been fully established in our midst; it will not mean the end of government and political community.

Faith Is the Evidence of Things Hoped For

One of the primary problems we must confront is the tendency of Christians to dissociate life in this age from life in the age to come. We are prone to think of life in this world as closed off to itself. Here and now, we meet material needs, make reasoned judgments about day-to-day "secular" responsibilities, and develop talents to try to succeed in life and to enjoy it as much as possible. By contrast, faith in God has to do with "spiritual" things, supernatural grace, worship, evangelism, and hope for life after death. Since Christians believe that life in this world doesn't provide any experience of what life will be like in the age to come, we need faith to gain access to eternal life. Christian faith in this sense means believing in Jesus, who died for our sins and will return to raise us from the dead, and the connection between now and then, between here and there, is simply a matter of trusting, believing, and hoping for another life after this one is over.

But that is not what the Bible conveys. The life of the generations of human creatures both reveals God and anticipates the fulfillment of this age in the age to come. That is to say, the things God is doing with and through creation now, particularly with the image of God, are building up to a climactic fulfillment. What we anticipate by faith, therefore, is not life in another world separated from this one but rather the full disclosure of the meaning of our present lives and of the whole creation in the resurrection glory of God's seventh-day rest.

One of my favorite biblical metaphors that captures this drama is the building of a house or palace in which we will dwell with God in face-to-face fulfillment. In diverse passages of the Bible, beginning in Genesis 1, the image of God's royal dwelling place is presented in ways that show God making the stones and panels and contents of that house from the "material" of living people. Think, for example, of Hebrews 11:8–10[4] in which the author draws from the long history of God's covenantal dealings with the children of Abraham. In that history is the building of a tabernacle and then the temple, both of which represented God dwelling in the midst of Israel. But the promised land and the places of worship all pointed ahead to something more. Hebrews says that when Abraham followed God toward the land God promised to give him, he lived in tents, as did Isaac and Jacob. Yet Abraham was looking ahead to more than owning and living in that Promised Land, "for he was looking forward to the city with foundations, whose architect and builder is God" (Heb. 11:10).

Earlier in Hebrews (3:1–6), the author speaks about Moses as one who was "faithful in all God's house" (v. 2). Yet Jesus "has been found worthy of greater honor than Moses, just as the builder of a house has greater honor than the house itself. For every house is built by someone, but God is the builder of everything" (vv. 3–4). As the comparison of Moses to Jesus develops, the author shows that in the end there really is only one house, the house God is building. God's building project, in other words, takes place in this age over many centuries and through many generations. Finally, the author reaches this startling conclusion: "*And we are his house*, if indeed we hold firmly to our confidence and the hope in which we glory" (v. 6, emphasis added). You see, the dwelling place of God, the house, the palace God is constructing, is being built with materials that happen to be the people of God, including Abraham, Moses, and us today. We, too, are part of God's house!

In one sense, the faith by which Christians live looks ahead to what is not yet visible and finished, but the dwelling place is under construction right now through the multigenerational human vocations of God's royal servants. Moses has done that work in his role as judge, adjudicator, and public administrator, as have the faithful of all generations. We might think of an architect building a skyscraper in one of our cities. The building will not be evident to the public or available for use until it is completed, but every day construction workers are pulling in the metal, wood, glass, pipes, and electric wires that are becoming part of what will eventually be the completed skyscraper. Right now, all we can see is the architect's blueprint and the construction materials used to add one story after another. But all of that evidence assures the witnesses of a reality they do not yet see.

Peter also speaks this way about the house God is building, composed of "living stones" who are and will be God's "holy priesthood" (1 Pet. 2:5). In the psalm of Moses (Ps. 90), Moses begins with the confession, "Lord, you have been our dwelling place throughout all generations" (v. 1). God is the dwelling place of his people and is making the people into his house. On Patmos, John heard the awesome declaration, "Look! God's dwelling place is now among the people, and he will dwell with them" (Rev. 21:3). That dwelling place continues to be constructed from the building blocks of the faithful in this age as they carry out the service to which God has called them. As Paul urges the Philippian Christians, "Continue to work out your salvation with fear and trembling, for it is God who works in you to will and to act in order to fulfill his good purpose" (Phil. 2:12–13). And this is why, as we hold on to our sure hope of creation's fulfillment, we are to "spur one another on toward love and good deeds . . . and all the more as you see the Day approaching" (Heb. 10:24–25).

In the light of that biblical testimony, the two-kingdom idea is misleading. God's one kingdom, the one house, the one people, is being built during and throughout this age. Good government in this age does not belong to a kingdom separate from God's kingdom but is part of the building material God is using to construct the kingdom of our Lord Jesus Christ. Among those who are celebrated in the letter of Hebrews for their faith are those who "administered justice" (Heb. 11:33). In other words, one of the responsibilities humans should exercise by faith in God is the administration of justice in this age. Jeremiah portrays this dramatically and biographically in condemning Shallum for his unjust governance. Shallum was king of Judah and the son of Josiah, who had been a righteous king. "Woe," says the Lord, "to him [Shallum] who builds his palace by unrighteousness, / his upper rooms by injustice, / making his subjects work for nothing, / not paying them for their labor" (Jer. 22:13). "Does it make you a king / to have more and more cedar?" the Lord asks (v. 15a). No, God will drive Shallum out of the land, and he will die where his captives put him; that is the Lord's judgment and curse.

What stands in contrast to Shallum's unjust government? The Lord, speaking to Shallum, asks, "Did not your father have food and drink? / He did what was right and just, / so all went well with him. / He defended the cause of the poor and needy, / and so all went well" (15b–16a). That is a refrain heard throughout the law and the prophets. When the Lord condemns the people of Israel through Isaiah for their faithlessness and tells them to stop coming to worship him with their prayers and burnt offerings, he says, "Your hands are full of blood! / Wash and make yourselves clean. / Take your evil deeds out of my sight; / stop doing wrong. / Learn to do right; seek justice. / Defend the oppressed. / Take up the cause of the fatherless; / plead the case of the widow" (Isa. 1:15–17).

Now, listen to the question God puts to Shallum about the righteous behavior of his father, Josiah when he was king: "'Is that not what it means to know me?' declares the Lord" (Jer. 22:16). What does it mean to *know* God? If one is a king, a public official, it means *to do justice*, to do what is right and just. The relation between the earthly responsibility of a public official and the kingdom of God is intimate and direct. There are not two kingdoms; there is either faithful service in God's kingdom that both reveals and leads to knowledge of the Lord of the kingdom, or there is faithless performance that manifests injustice and ignorance of God, leading to God's curse. As the Bible says again and again, to *know* God is to *do* what God has called one to do. *Knowing truly is to do rightly.*

What will be revealed in the new heaven and new earth is not another world and another kingdom but the fulfillment of the one creation God now governs. The sabbath fulfillment of God's works, which include the human generations and the practice of their vocations, is being achieved through the faithful service of God's Messiah, the son of Josiah, son of David, Son of God. When Christ comes again to judge the living and the dead and to take as his bride the new Jerusalem, he will not be casting off the world in which we now live; he will be reconciling and fulfilling the whole creation through judgment and recovery. When Paul tells the Corinthians, "if anyone is in Christ, the new creation has come," he explains that this is from the God "who reconciled us to himself through Christ and gave us the ministry of reconciliation: that God was reconciling the world to himself in Christ, not counting people's sins against them" (2 Cor. 5:17–19). In other words, the "new" is the creation that has been reconciled and fulfilled. The "new" is precisely what God is making of human creatures drawn from the generations of the first Adam into the righteousness of Christ.

Governing Righteously with Justice

While it is true that from our present vantage point the fulfillment of God's kingdom has not yet come, God's call to us in Christ, by the power of the Holy Spirit, is a call to be at work in the kingdom. There is certainly a strong measure of expectancy inherent in living as disciples of Christ, but living with expectancy carries with it the obligation *to live*, to exercise our God-given responsibilities, knowing that God is working in and through us right now.

What does this mean for government and politics? We have many examples in the Bible of both faithful and unfaithful efforts in this regard. We just took note of the contrast between Josiah, the righteous king, and his unrighteous son, Shallum. Another clear illustration of a faithful and diligent public servant is Job. In Job 29, the righteous man (whom God allowed to fall under the curse of a satanic adversary's persecutions) reflects longingly on his earlier days of glory and joy. "How I long for the months gone by, / for the days when God watched over me," says Job. "Oh, for the days when I was in my prime, / when God's intimate friendship blessed my house" (vv. 2, 4). Where do those nostalgic reflections lead Job? They lead him back to the days when he was an elder at the gate—a local judge and public defender.

> When I went to the gate of the city
>   and took my seat in the public square,
> the young men saw me and stepped aside
>   and the old men rose to their feet;
> the chief men refrained from speaking
>   and covered their mouths with their hands;
> the voices of the nobles were hushed,
>   and their tongues stuck to the roof of their mouths.
> Whoever heard me spoke well of me,
>   and those who saw me commended me,
> because I rescued the poor who cried for help,
>   and the fatherless who had none to assist them.

Those who were dying blessed me;
    I made the widow's heart sing.
I put on righteousness as my clothing;
    justice was my robe and my turban.
I was eyes to the blind
    and feet to the lame.
I was a father to the needy;
    I took up the case of the stranger.
I broke the fangs of the wicked
    and snatched the victims from their teeth.
(Job 29:7–17)

Even though Job was not a king, the way he acted as a local official was in tune with the "law of the king" in Deuteronomy 17:14–20. The kind of governing officials God wanted Israel to have were the kind who would meditate day after day on the precepts of the covenant and follow a straight and narrow path, turning neither to the right nor to the left (see also Pss. 1 and 2). This is the message that comes through in every verse of Psalm 119, where a variety of words are used to convey the breadth and depth of God's covenant: precepts, statutes, words, promises, commands, decrees, laws. The psalmist recognizes that God's directing precepts and promises serve as "a lamp for my feet, a light on my path" (v. 105). God's laws and statutes are not abstract rules but a bond of love and trust between the Lord and Israel. God's decrees show the faithful how to follow the path of life.

The Bible's description of knowing and keeping God's law, particularly in regard to what we would call public lawmaking and adjudication, shows humans called to respond to divine *norms*, to normative directives that call people to action. When God calls Israel to do justice, to do what is right for the widow and orphan, God does not provide an exhaustive list of predigested rules to cover every possible circumstance but rather calls the responsible party to do justice, to exercise love and good stewardship in ways that fit the circumstances of their covenantal responsibility before God. The people of Israel can trust God and the creation's integrity in seeking the wisdom they need to respond obediently to God's normative words for life.

God organized Israel not only in terms of their tribal order but also in terms of just patterns of land use, ownership/stewardship, and family obligations. These were the basis for God's repeated expression of concern for the widow, the orphan, and others without family support and protection. Land was the basic capital of economic life, and it was never to be rented or sold off forever or for an indefinite time. The sabbath patterns were to control the length of time the land (and labor) could be rented or sold before it had to be returned to the original family or clan. These patterns and many others gave structure to Israel's social, economic, and legal life in its families, tribes, and the nation as a whole. And the words of the prophets tell us a great deal about how Israel failed to do justice and what God expected of them if they were to return to the path of covenant life.

In the course of history, from the time of God's covenant with Israel at Sinai until today, many things have changed, for better and for worse: the responsibilities of governing officials, the structure of states, the patterns of economic life, the obligations of family members, and most other conditions and institutions of human society. Nevertheless, the *normative* precepts of God still stand: love your neighbor, do justice, be merciful, be good stewards, walk humbly with God. The questions for us today are essentially the same as those of ancient times, but we must try to answer them in circumstances of greater societal differentiation, a shrinking globe, and a rapidly expanding world population.

Heeding God's Patience and Mercy in Upholding the Good Creation

In concluding this chapter, I want to draw attention to two key implications of the biblical witness that have normative significance for the constitution of political communities today. The first implication concerns the treatment of the diverse creatures of God's creation and the diversity of human responsibilities. The second concerns God's patience and mercy in dealing with human disobedience. We touched on both of these earlier, and in later chapters we will explore some of their implications in greater detail.[5]

First, in referring to the diversity of God's creatures and the diverse range of human responsibilities, I have in mind the human responsibility to do right by—to do justice to—everything God has put under our feet for stewardly development and wise governance. An old Roman adage sums up the meaning of justice this way: "Give to each its due." In biblical terms, that insight would go something like this: "Do right by every creature so that each receives what God intends for it." According to Genesis 1, each new day of creation is followed by the statement, "God saw that it was good." And after God's creating is complete, the text says, "God saw all that he had made, and it was very good" (v. 31). One of the implications of this text is that men and women, as God's stewards and viceroys, must pay very close attention to every creature, both to distinguish each from the others and to learn the meaning of God's judgment that the creation is good.

There are also important implications here for how humans should treat one another as they develop their diverse capabilities. Husbands and wives are to learn what it means to love one another as marriage partners, part of parental love is learning how to do right by each child, and teachers must learn how to assist each student in learning. The more things humans accomplish—the more new products, tools, and organizations they create; the more schools, hospitals, engineering firms, banks, and manufacturing companies they establish—the more they must distinguish carefully what is required to do justice in each case. Careful discernment also means learning to distinguish between just and unjust practices, between wise and foolish habits, between loving and unloving patterns in each sphere of informal or highly organized human activities.

Many of the proverbs and other wisdom texts in the Bible deal with these matters. Paul and other apostles frequently draw on those texts. Do not treat prophecies with contempt, says Paul, "but test them all; hold on to what is good, reject whatever is harmful" (1 Thess. 5:21–22). Hebrews urges believers to grow out of their infancy and become mature, for an infant "is not acquainted with the teaching about righteousness. But solid food is for the mature, who by constant use have trained themselves to distinguish good from evil" (Heb. 5:13–14). Not every human responsibility is exercised through government; most do not belong to the political community. Thus, part of wise discernment is learning to understand who is responsible for what. What is the proper responsibility of government in a political community and what responsibilities belong to families, schools, business enterprises, hospitals, and churches? How should justice be done to each one? Questions such as these pertain to the first dimension of learning to do justice to God's diverse creatures, and I believe that public justice demands government give each creature its due and give each type of human community and organization its proper due.

The second implication to highlight is God's mercy and patience in dealing with human disobedience. Human offences that cause harm and injustice call for judgment. "How long, O Lord, before you will come to save me from my enemies?" "Why, O Lord, do the righteous suffer and the unrighteous prosper?" These cries went up again and again from many an ancient Israelite, and they continue to go up from people today who are dying from starvation, being molested or misused, and suffering every imaginable kind of oppression or persecution. The dilemma is real. God calls for righteous living, and yet not every injustice and act of hatred is overcome. To believe that God is exercising patience and mercy in order to fulfill creation may not provide much comfort to one who is starving or suffering abuse. Righteous judgment may be coming, but it has not yet come. In the meantime, those who take pride in their folly and act unjustly are storing up evil deeds for the day of judgment. And those who repent and seek God's forgiveness are urged to learn patience and to be merciful even to their enemies. That is the pattern of life Christ exhibited and urged upon his followers.

That was the burden of Jesus's Beatitudes: "Blessed are those who are persecuted because of righteousness, for theirs is the kingdom of heaven" (Matt. 5:10). That is what Jesus taught through a parable about field hands who wanted to go out immediately and pull up weeds in the field. No, answers the master, "because while you are pulling the weeds, you may uproot the wheat with them. Let both grow together until the harvest" (Matt. 13:29–30). Those authorized to harvest the fields and to separate the weeds from the wheat, Jesus explains, are the angels. That is not something the field hands are authorized to do. For now, Jesus explains, his followers are to be patient as God is patient, and gracious as God is gracious in sending rain and sunshine on the just and unjust alike. During this time of God's patience, says Paul, Christians are to be "joyful in hope, patient in affliction, faithful in prayer. . . . Bless those who persecute you; bless and do not curse" (Rom. 12:12, 14). Leave vengeance in God's hands. "Do not repay anyone evil for evil. Be careful to do what is right in the eyes of everyone. If it is possible, as far as it depends on you, live at peace with everyone" (Rom. 12:17–18).

There are big implications in this teaching for citizens and public officials today. Christ is now king, Christians confess, and all authority in heaven and on earth has been given to him. Yet he has not yet carried through with the final judgment, and his angels have not yet come to separate the wheat from the weeds. Christ is therefore governing with great patience and mercy, not willing that any should perish, and is giving time for all to come to repentance. If these are the terms of Christ's rule at present, then it appears to follow that governments should function on those terms. This is what Christians should be advocating and working to promote. Governments are authorized to encourage the good and to restrain and punish evildoers. But public officials do not have the responsibility to separate believers from unbelievers in the field of this world, which is the territory in which God's kingdom is being established. Equal treatment of all citizens in a political community, regardless of their faith, would seem to follow from God's gift of rain and sunshine to the just and unjust alike (Matt. 5:43–47). It also seems clear that equal treatment of citizens follows from Jesus's instruction to his disciples that both weeds and the good plants should be allowed to grow up together in the field until harvest time (Matt. 13:24–30, 36–43).

The two implications for just governance can be summarized as follows. First, the particular and limited responsibilities of government must include the proper treatment of each creature, including each human person and each distinct kind of human relationship, organization, and institution. This means giving each its due—a mode of attributive and distributive justice. Second, just governance will entail equal treatment of all citizens, regardless of their faith, in ways that are patient and merciful, in tune with Christ's own patient and merciful rule.

In the chapters that follow in part 2, we will look at historical perspectives on the ways Christians have understood and engaged in government and politics from the time of the early church to the present day. Then in part 3, we'll return to the questions of what Christian engagement might look like today.

part 2

key historical
developments

Constantine, Augustine, and the fraught future of "Christian" politics

Roman proconsul, Statius Quadratus: "Swear, and I release you; curse Christ."
Polycarp: "Eighty-six years have I served Him, and he has done me no wrong: how then can I blaspheme my King who saved me?"
Proconsul: "Swear by the genius of Caesar."
Polycarp: "If you vainly imagine that I would 'swear by the genius of Caesar', as you may say, pretending that you are ignorant who I am, hear plainly that I am a Christian."[1]

Put to death in AD 156 for refusing to swear that Caesar is lord, Polycarp was one of many early Christian martyrs. Polycarp would not renounce the Lord and king who was far greater than Caesar.

The martyrdom of Polycarp takes us straight to the heart of our quest to understand how Christians should be engaged in political culture. Polycarp was convinced that Christians had to demonstrate their commitment to Christ. Under the threat of death, he acted with the same integrity that guided his life. Caesar was asking too much. Only Christ is Lord. Caesar was in no position to demand that Polycarp curse Christ. To understand Polycarp's decision we need to place ourselves in his shoes at the time of Jesus and the emerging church, a time when Jewish communities were also suffering persecution. It was a different world than the one we know today, but a world from which some of the most enduring "Christian" ideas and public practices emerged.

Life in the young Roman Empire was similar in many ways to life in other ancient empires, such as Egypt, Assyria, Persia, and China.[2] Ordinary people were *subjects*, not active citizens as we know citizenship today, and many of the rulers were acknowledged to be semidivine, the highest mediators between heaven and earth. A few people of wealth or in the service of the government or with the status of citizen enjoyed some privileges, but the vast majority of people in the cities and regions subjugated by Rome did not. (The apostle Paul was born a Roman citizen and used that status to appeal for a public hearing and trial.[3]) In fact, the status of citizen, which some people held in earlier Greek city-states and in the Roman Republic, was lost for more than a thousand years.[4]

The expansion of Christianity in the first centuries after Christ came chiefly from the conversion of gentiles—non-Jewish peoples—whose political, intellectual, and social experiences were predominantly Roman and Greek rather than Jewish. Therefore, the biblical idea of God ruling over the nations and having special covenants with Noah, Abraham, Israel, and David, leading to the revelation of Jesus Christ, did not serve as the primary basis of gentile public consciousness.[5] It was also the case, as Walter Ullmann points out, that the "state" as we know it today did not yet exist in that era, and the word "political," which was derived from *polis* (the Greek city-state), dropped out of use in the early Christian period. It came back into use only after recovery of the work of Aristotle in the thirteenth century. The term used in the Roman world was "government" (*gubernatio* or *gubernator*), often in conjunction with the word "jurisdiction" (*jus dicere*), which means the right to lay down the law.[6]

In the Roman Empire, the emperor's jurisdiction was unlimited. That is what Christianity challenged. By the time of Pope Gelasius I (the end of the fifth century), the battle lines between pope and emperor were being drawn over the relative positions of authority that each should hold in the empire. Gelasius, who argued that papal authority was superior to that of the emperor, spoke of the pope's *auctoritas* (authority) and of the emperor's mere *regia potestas* (ruling power).[7] The emperor, of course, did not agree to such a demotion, though eventually that is what took place because the emperors lost control of Rome and much of what we now call Western Europe. Oliver O'Donovan and Joan Lockwood O'Donovan write that Pope Gelasius's assertion of papal supremacy "defined the relation of ecclesiastical and secular authority in a form which would prove decisive within the Western Church for subsequent centuries."[8]

In the light of our argument in part 2, built on interpretations of key biblical texts, how shall we evaluate early Christian engagement in what became a Christianized Roman Empire? Did Polycarp's refusal to acknowledge Caesar's lordship express a general principle of noncooperation with government that all Christians should have accepted? That was certainly Tertullian's judgment fifty years later.[9] Or did Polycarp object only to the proconsul's demand that he curse Christ? If the emperor had honored Christ (or at least had not demanded

Polycarp's public denunciation of Christ), could Polycarp and other Christians have lived contentedly under Roman imperial authority?

Constantine the Great (c. 272–337)

These are critically important questions because around 312 Constantine (who was soon to become the emperor of the entire Roman Empire) was converted under a sign (or signs) that convinced him he would conquer victoriously in the name of Christ. By means of the Edict of Milan in 313, he recognized Christianity as a legitimate religion in the empire, and by the end of the century Christianity had been established as the only true religion. Constantine, like Polycarp, had come to believe that he owed everything to Christ, his superior, his lord and master.[10] Was there any problem, then, with Constantine using the power of the imperial office to establish Christianity throughout his realm?

In subsequent centuries the empire divided into Eastern and Western branches, with the church in each branch (Eastern Orthodox and Roman Catholic) supporting a system of government that carried forward many if not most of the elements of the Roman imperial system. The Eastern branch, with its center in Constantinople (founded by Constantine in 330 as a second Rome), continued to uphold the principle of imperial supremacy of the Christian empire, with the church as its subordinate partner. That system came to be called *caesaropapism*. The Western branch was reshaped over many centuries to become church-led, with ecclesiastical authority supreme over earthly rulers, as articulated in the Gelasian doctrine of two swords.[11] The Gelasian argument was that Christ gave the church both a spiritual sword and an earthly sword; the pope retained the sword of spiritual authority and delegated the sword of earthly power to those who governed under the auspices of the church. Did those developments, Eastern and Western, represent something positive in the transformation of an old pagan system into models of what Christian governance and a Christian society should be? Or, as many Christians believed then and believe today, did those developments represent a misunderstanding and misuse of biblical teaching that led to centuries of confusion and corruption for both the church and civil governments?

The O'Donovans write that those two views of the church's relation to imperial authority "were foundational for the social synthesis we have come to call 'Christendom.'"[12] On the one hand, leaders such as Eusebius (c. 260–339), the first major chronicler of church history and bishop of Caesarea, believed that the years after Christ "had been an age of mission, in which the triumphantly expansive word of monotheistic truth had laid hold on the conscience of the world, to the point where the demons had to yield their ground." He believed that Constantine's achievement of Christianizing the empire was the proper goal of the church.[13] Listen to Eusebius's praising of Constantine.

The only begotten Word of God reigns from ages which had no beginning, to infinite and endless ages, the partner of his Father's kingdom. And our emperor ever beloved by him, who derives the source of imperial authority from above, and is strong in the power of his sacred title, has controlled the empire of the world for a long period of years. . . . Our emperor . . . acting as interpreter to the Word of God, aims at recalling the whole human race to the knowledge of God; proclaiming clearly in the ears of all, and declaring with powerful voice the laws of truth and godliness to all who dwell on earth. . . . [I]nvested as he is with a semblance of heavenly sovereignty, he directs his gaze above, and frames his earthly government according to the pattern of that Divine original, feeling strength in its conformity to the monarchy of God.[14]

On the other hand, for Christian leaders such as Ambrose (339–397), bishop of Milan, the first centuries after Christ "had been an age of martyrdom, in which the purity of the gospel had thrown itself into conflict with the world, a conflict now to be continued by a firm and independent church leadership not afraid to call emperors to account."[15] Here is Ambrose in one of his sermons criticizing the emperor, who believed it was his prerogative to determine the extent and location of the bishop's authority: "I fear the Lord of the world more than the emperor of this age. . . . I would gladly go to the emperor's palace, were it consistent with the duties of a bishop to fight his battles in the palace rather than in church. But in the council chamber Christ is properly the judge, not the defendant. Who can deny that a question of faith should be heard in church? Let anyone with faith come here!"[16]

Here we have two contrasting views of the relationship between church and government. One calls for the church to support the Christian emperor, cooperating closely with him to bring the whole earth to acknowledge Christ's lordship, mediated to the world through the emperor's authority. The other view calls for a strong church that stands on its own authority over against the governing powers and ready to challenge them. Are these, then, the only two views that the early church could have adopted? Were other views conceivable, and if so, why were they left undeveloped?

Augustine of Hippo (354–430)

We can find help in responding to these questions by looking more closely at the work of Augustine, bishop of Hippo. Augustine was not only the most influential of the early church fathers; he is, arguably, the most important figure in the entire history of the church, both East and West. We know him not only from his many treatises and commentaries on biblical, theological, philosophical, and ecclesiastical subjects, but also from his path-breaking *Confessions*, the first autobiographical writing of its kind, written between 397 and 401.[17] From *Confessions* we learn of Augustine's early slothfulness and immoral life; his youthful adherence to Manichaeism, a gnostic religious dualism that pits an evil world against a good world; the influence of Stoicism that stirred within him a desire for wisdom; his study of Neoplatonism in Milan after moving there to teach rhetoric; and finally his conversion to Christianity in 386 under the influence of Bishop Ambrose, a conversion for which his loving mother Monica had long prayed. The story of his personal journey, told in the first part of *The Confessions*, expands in the second part to an exploration of the longer journey of the church throughout history.[18] In Milan, Bishop Ambrose helped Augustine to understand the Bible and to distance himself from Manichaeism. For the rest of his life, Augustine worked to articulate the Christian faith in opposition to non-Christian religions and philosophies that had so influenced him and the culture in which he lived. In later years he even published a book of retractions, correcting or renouncing things he had written earlier.

After his conversion, Augustine dedicated himself to the church, which he served primarily in Hippo, a major port city on the Mediterranean coast of North Africa (in what is now Algeria). There he was appointed bishop in 396. Already a prolific writer, he wrote even more after his conversion. His sermons, letters, and books reveal both the heart of a pastor, trying to encourage and build up the church, and the mind of an apologist, working to defend Christianity against misunderstandings and false charges coming from both inside and outside the church. In addition to *The Confessions*, his most important book for our purposes is *The City of God*,[19] written in his maturity over a thirteen-year period from 413 to 426. The book aimed to defend the church against charges that Christians were responsible for the decline of the Roman Empire, charges that intensified after "barbarians" sacked and burned Rome in 410. The book did more than that, however. It unfurled a wide-ranging inquiry into the mystery of God's providence, the nature of the Christian faith, and the role of Christians in this world. In these two books and several others, including his biblical commentaries, we gain access to Augustine's thinking about earthly government.[20]

Explaining and interpreting Augustine's views is not a straightforward exercise, however, for his writings convey at least three lines of argument that influenced subsequent history.

Opposing Cities: Love of God vs. Self-Love

The line of argument we'll consider first was not fully articulated until Augustine wrote *The City of God* late in his life. It revolves around the relation of two cities—two contrasting ways of life—the *civitate Dei* (the city of God) and the *civitas terrena* (the earthly city). This is a much-debated distinction, partly because there is ambiguity in Augustine himself about what the cities represent. In many passages the cities represent two communities in the course of their historical development. They are not entirely separate now but are ordered by fundamentally opposing loves. In other passages, however, the two cities appear to be distinguished as heavenly and earthly, as the eternal city in which only the elect in Christ have a part and the temporal city in which both Christians and non-Christians live while on earth.

Augustine first distinguishes the two cities by reference to their opposing loves. The city of God is motivated by the love of God made manifest in Jesus Christ; the earthly city is driven by self-love, which is rooted in human sinfulness. Self-love is the underlying motive of every person born in the line of Adam, whose fall into sin has marked us all. But by God's electing grace in Jesus Christ, an unknown number of sinners are being redeemed, forgiven, and redirected away from self-love to the love of God. The final destination of those driven by self-love is eternal damnation; the final destination of those redirected by the love of God is eternal life. The final separation and manifestation of the two cities is still to come.

There is clearly a stark *antithesis* between the two loves as they struggle against each other throughout history. Self-love, writes Augustine, can lead all the way to contempt of God, while the love of God leads all the way to contempt of self.[21] In the end, the two cities will be separated at the final judgment, and those who are raised from death to new life in Christ will join him in the presence of God forever—the city of God fully revealed. At one point Augustine interprets the Scriptures to say that the fulfillment of the city of God will be the completion of God's sabbath rest.[22] In this age, Christians and non-Christians cohabit the earth, either continuing in self-love, which leads to eternal damnation, or, by God's grace, repenting and turning to serve God through the love of Christ on their way to fulfillment in the city of God. This contrast raises a question, however, about how Christians and non-Christians can and should live together in this age. If the two communities are being drawn apart by competing loves, do they have anything at all in common, and if not, shouldn't Christians shun the ungodly who remain unrepentant? Should Christians perhaps even seek to withdraw from this world, particularly its politics, in order to serve God faithfully? Or, to the contrary, do the two communities have a great deal in common, requiring serious Christian engagement in what is shared by all people in this age?

Cooperating Cities: Shared Earthly Life

Those questions lead us to a second line of argument found in Augustine's writings. Augustine says the following, for example, about the ways Christians and non-Christians can, and should, cooperate while comingled on earth.

> [T]he earthly city which does not live by faith [in Christ] seeks only an earthly peace, and limits the goal of its peace, of its harmony of authority and obedience among its citizens, to the voluntary and collective attainment of objectives necessary to mortal existence. The heavenly City, meanwhile—or, rather, that part that is on pilgrimage in mortal life and lives by faith—must use this earthly peace until such time as our mortality which needs such peace has passed away.

As a consequence, so long as her life in the earthly city is that of a captive and an alien (although she has the promise of ultimate delivery and the gift of the Spirit as a pledge), she has no hesitation about keeping in step with the civil law which governs matters pertaining to our existence here below. For, as mortal life is the same for all, there ought to be common cause between the two cities in what concerns our purely human living.[23]

Following this line of argument we discover that the antithesis that had been drawn between contrasting loves gives way to a different kind of contrast, namely, between mortal life on earth, which is the same for all and in which Christians are captive sojourners, and eternal life in the heavenly city where Christians will find their permanent home.[24] The phrase "earthly city" (*civitas terrena*) now takes on two meanings. In the first sentence of the paragraph just quoted, as in Augustine's first line of argument, he describes the "earthly city" as those who are motivated by self-love and live without faith in Christ. But then, in the sentences that follow, he speaks of that part of the heavenly city that dwells on earth, living like "a captive and an alien" *in the earthly city*. However, from the viewpoint of the antithesis between two loves, it would be contradictory to say that the city of God lives in the city of self-love and is a captive in it. That is a contradiction because the city of God lives in and through the love of God, not the love of self. So the question is whether Augustine inadvertently equivocated when speaking about the earthly city (sometimes speaking about a community driven by self-love and at other times simply about earthly life), or whether he intended to say that Christians who are part of the city of God are at present actually held captive by self-love and should not hesitate to make common cause with those who live out of self-love and even contempt for God.

In this second line of argument Augustine says that those who live by faith in Christ and those who do not live by that faith can "combine their wills" to attain what is useful in this life. If that is true, however, the only basis he seems to recognize for such cooperation is the desire for "an earthly peace" achieved through the "harmony of authority and obedience among its citizens" which is what those who do not live by faith are seeking.[25] Is Augustine suggesting, then, that Christians may, and should, cooperate with the earthly city's self-love as long as they do so only with regard to life in this world?

Regardless of how one answers that question, it seems clear that Augustine believes life in this world is either a confinement that Christians want to leave behind or a way of life that implicates Christians in self-love as long as they need to cooperate with others in attaining what is necessary for earthly life. On earth, Augustine says, Christians are on a pilgrimage until their mortal condition passes away. Life in this world thus comes into view as "the same for all." Yet to put it that way brackets or sets to one side the antithesis between the love of God and self-love because the second line of argument suggests that the two cities can make "common cause" in this world over what concerns "our purely human living." Is it perhaps the case, then, that the realm of "purely human living" is not touched by (or caught in) the antithetical opposition between the two loves? Did Augustine intend to confine the impact of the love of God in Christ to a dimension of life that is almost entirely separate from the dynamics and decisions of "purely human living"?

This seems to be what Augustine conveys in comments that focus on Christian responsibility in this world. In *The City of God* he writes,

> This heavenly city then, while it sojourns on earth, calls citizens out of all nations, and gathers together a society of pilgrims of all languages, not scrupling about diversities in the manners, laws, and institutions whereby earthly peace is secured and maintained, but recognizing that, however various these are, they all tend to one and the same end of earthly peace. It therefore is so far from rescinding and abolishing these diversities, that it even preserves and adapts them, so long only as no hindrance to the worship of the one supreme and true God is thus introduced. Even the heavenly city, therefore, while in its state of pilgrimage, avails itself of the peace of earth, and, so far as it can without injuring faith and godliness, desires and maintains a common agreement among men regarding the acquisition of the necessaries of life.[26] .

If the people of God in Christ need only insist on true worship and the maintenance of their personal faith and godliness, then a great deal of earthly life can be viewed as simply a temporary commons that is not implicated in the antithetical tension between two loves. In other words, the antithesis between the love of God and self-love can be confined to the terrain of worship, confession of faith, and personal godliness. Beyond that, life on earth, which is far removed from life in heaven, can be considered a temporary, soon-to-be discarded, mortal condition that all humans share in common while on earth.

Does Augustine in this way resolve the apparent inconsistency between the two lines of argument we've been considering? The following statement from *The City of God* may suggest such a resolution: "In the earthly city, then, temporal goods are to be used with a view to the enjoyment of earthly peace, whereas, in the heavenly City, they are used with a view to the enjoyment of eternal peace."[27] Look closely, however, at what sounds like a clear and simple contrast. If Augustine intends to include in "the heavenly City" that part of it that now lives on earth, then it would appear that Christians may use "temporal goods" only "with a view to the enjoyment of eternal peace," *not* earthly peace. If by "the heavenly City" he is referring to eternal life in contrast to temporal life, however, then he could be saying that during the time believers live on earth, they may use temporal goods in one way, namely, with a view to enjoying earthly peace, and when they enter the heavenly city, they will use temporal goods in a different way, in the enjoyment of eternal peace. But that is where the contrast seems to break down, for there will be no temporal goods in the heavenly city of eternal life. His parallelism does not hold up.

What is missing from Augustine's thought, it seems to me, is adequate grounding in the biblical teaching of creation. Biblically speaking, this world and human life are God's revelatory creation, not a temporary confinement or prison to be escaped.[28] And while it is true that there is an antithesis between the love of God and self-love, the antithesis comes to expression because of sin within the context and boundaries of God's creation. Consequently, from a biblical point of view, the basis for cooperation between members of the two cities is the good creation upheld by God's grace. Insofar as humans are driven by self-love, sin does indeed twist and darken life into a prison. But sinful self-love is not what constitutes the good creation God loves so much. Sinners may resist God's grace and fail to realize how much they owe to God as creatures made in the divine image, but they cannot escape their creaturely identity or the rain and sunshine that fall on the just and unjust alike. The last word about life in this temporal world is not human sin and degradation but God's restraint and judgment of sin and his redeeming work in Christ that is reconciling the creation to God. Augustine did not sufficiently take into account the meaning of creation as the theater of the revelation of God's glory. That is why Augustine has, at least in part, disconnected the love of God revealed in Christ from the meaning of earthly life. A duality of earth and heaven, of this world as a prison and the world to come as a release, has a strong emphasis in Augustine's work. That contrast seems to reflect a continuing influence of Manichaeism, which he had by that time rejected in principle.[29]

Instead of a rich idea of God's creation as the common ground of all human creatures, Augustine makes use of an idea of natural order from Neoplatonism and Stoicism, modified to some degree by his understanding of the Bible.[30] He appeals to the law of nature and a hierarchical order of being that is common to all humans,[31] and even if that natural law and order have been effaced to a significant degree from the minds of sinners, Augustine believes there are vestiges, semblances, or images of the law still at work. They are what provide the basis for achieving a limited measure of justice and concord among people on earth, though admittedly such concord can never embody the true justice of the city of God.[32]

There is another difficulty here as well. Elsewhere Augustine says that the institutions of government (and some other institutions) are unnatural. They have been instituted or permitted by God as a response to sin, to restrain and punish evildoers. As Herbert Deane explains it, drawing from several of Augustine's writings,

> Since most men . . . are unredeemed and will be so until the end of the world, new means must be provided to introduce a measure of order, stability, and peace in the midst of the strife and conflict that mark earthly life. . . . [God, then,] has established new institutions, adapted to the new condition of sinful existence in order to keep a check on human greed and violence and to prevent society from

collapsing into complete anarchy and chaos. These institutions, such as private property and the entire legal and political order, are divinely ordained as both punishments and remedies for the sinful condition of man. Although they provide an element of order, stability, and peace in social life that would be completely absent without them, the earthly peace and order that they make possible are no longer natural and spontaneous, but must be maintained by coercion and repression.[33]

Now, if this is true, how can the vestiges of the natural law provide a basis for unnatural institutions? How are the natural and the unnatural connected? And how can institutions that God ordained because of sin provide a remedy as well as punishment for sin? Since Augustine identifies government with punishment and restraint (its retributive functions, established because of sin), and since he associates Christ's redeeming work with the city of God in opposition to the earthly city, he has no way to connect Christ's redeeming love and mercy with government's exercise of remedial and restorative justice. Consequently, for earthly purposes he attributes a remedial effect to the *unnatural* institution of government, which has been established to restrain the effects of sin. But what can be renewed by means of an unnatural institution's coercion?

Given his understanding of earthly government, Augustine is unable to propose a mode of Christian engagement that can appeal to a standard of true justice. Even if Christians may, on the basis of vestiges of the natural law and unnatural institutions, cooperate with non-Christians in trying to attain things necessary for this life, their responsibility in this world appears disconnected, to a significant degree, from the redeeming work of Christ that will establish true justice in the city of God. The work of earthly government, therefore, cannot be redirected by the love of God toward the city of God.

This outcome of Augustine's thinking has been one of the most influential in the history of Christianity. The relation of this age to the coming age began to be interpreted ever more systematically as a contrast between earthly confinement and heavenly bliss. This world is the world of sin in contrast to the world of release from sin. This world is governed by unnatural institutions in contrast to the next world, which will be governed by Christ. This is the world of temporary, coercive government in contrast to the world to come, where there will be no need for government. Even though Augustine says in many places that God is the creator of everything and that the creation is good, and even though he criticizes Manichaeism for its radical dualism, he misses or leaves undeveloped the integral relation between this age of God's revelatory creation and the creation's fulfillment in God's sabbath rest.

What we have uncovered, therefore, appears to be two incompatible pictures in Augustine's mind that guided his development of the two lines of argument just outlined. On the one hand, there is the picture of an antithesis between the love of God and self-love, between the love that constitutes the life of the city of God and the love that constitutes the earthly city. On the other hand, there is the picture of this world as common ground for the members of the two contrasting cities. Those living out of self-love see nothing beyond this world, so they work as best they can to achieve enough earthly peace to make possible the continuation of their various pursuits of self-love. Those motivated by the love of God, however, do see something beyond this world and look ahead in hope and faith to life in the city of God. But while they are held captive in this earthly prison, Christians, too, must work to obtain the necessities of life even though earthly life is simply a time of sojourning, a time of endurance as strangers who long to find a permanent home. Christians cannot find release from this world until Christ returns. Consequently, for the sake of relative peace and justice now, they make no scruple to obey the laws of the earthly city, making use (only because they must) of the kind of peace that non-Christians are seeking. The basis for cooperation thus appears to be either (1) a temporary sharing in the self-love of the earthly city, restrained by unnatural institutions, or (2) a sharing in common efforts to acquire the "necessities of life," a sharing that is somehow neutral with respect to the antithetical drives of the two loves that otherwise motivate the two cities.

In the way he draws this contrast, according to Deane, Augustine actually anticipated the later "two swords" doctrine of Pope Gelasius. The duality begins with Augustine's conviction that humans "consist of body and soul," and therefore, as long as we live in this world, we must be "subject with respect to our bodies to the powers of this world to whom is granted 'the governance of temporal affairs [rerum temporalium gubernatio],' while as far as our souls and their eternal salvation are concerned we must be subject only to God and not to any man who contravenes God's law."[34] Thus, the body-soul duality is connected to the duality of earth and heaven and to the institutional duality of earthly government and the church.

From the fourth century onward, the Western church increasingly took on the identity of an *institution*, consisting of spiritual authorities whose leading representative was the bishop of Rome. Ordinary members of the church were increasingly identified as laypeople, connected to the institutional church by participation in its services and sacraments. The idea of the church as a community of all the faithful—as the body of Christ—gradually lost its grip on Christian consciousness. There were at least two reasons for this. The first was that a hierarchy of governance—spiritual and temporal—became the defining characteristic of society, the society called *Christendom*. The second was that by the time of the High Middle Ages almost everyone in the society of Christendom was baptized as an infant. Consequently, the church as a community of faith was no longer distinguishable from the society at large. Everyone was part of Christendom. Thus, the important distinctions were no longer between opposing communities of faith motivated by contrary loves but rather between the ranks of institutional "authorities" and "jurisdictions" (ecclesiastical and governmental) within the single social order of Christendom.

Government Coercion in Service of the Church

That brings us to Augustine's third line of argument. Early in his Christian life, Augustine expressed the conviction that Christians should try to persuade unbelievers and heretics of their errors by word and argument, not by the use of force as the Roman imperium had done against Christians such as Polycarp. After Christianity was established as the religion of the empire, however, a dissident group of Christians called Donatists became ever more troublesome, especially in the region of Augustine's bishopric. Their actions led him to change his mind.[35] He became convinced that government's use of force could be legitimate if it helped to preserve the unity of the church. In the spirit of Eusebius, he wrote, "I have therefore yielded to the evidence . . . which my colleagues have laid before me. For originally my opinion was, that no one should be coerced into the unity of Christ, that we must act only by words, fight only by arguments and prevail by force of reason, lest we should have those whom we knew as avowed heretics feigning themselves to be Catholics."[36] The evidence Augustine accepted showed that many who were forced to abandon their heresies responded positively. Moreover, the use of force in this way helped to bring about a greater degree of earthly peace.

Pursuing this line of thought, Augustine reached an even more expansive conclusion about the relation of Christian rulers to the church. He decided that kings who are Christian can serve the Lord "when they do in His service what they could not do were they not kings. . . . Nay, verily, let the kings of the earth serve Christ by making laws for Him and for His cause."[37] This goes far beyond the idea that Christians may cooperate with non-Christians in trying to meet earthly needs until they are released from their mortal condition. What Augustine offers now seems quite inconsistent with his other lines of argument. The kings of the earth are applauded for using compulsion to support the church and are even encouraged to make laws for Christ and his cause. But how has Augustine come to believe that the kings of the earthly city can become servants of Christ's cause? His reasoning is pragmatic: the use of force seems to work by helping the institutional church hold on to its unity and defeat heretics. Augustine admits, "It is indeed better (as no one ever could deny) that men should be led to worship God by teaching, than that they should be driven to it by fear of punishment or pain; but it does not follow that because the former course produces the better men, therefore those who do not yield to it should be neglected."[38]

According to P. R. L. Brown, Augustine "was the only bishop in the early Church whom we can actually see evolving, within ten years, towards an unambiguous belief that Christian emperors could protect the Church by suppressing its rivals. He is the only writer who wrote at length in defense of religious coercion."[39] But how can the kings of this earth, whose kingdoms are at best enforcers of an earthly peace among sinners and at worst enemies of Christ, become servants of Christ? Is this consistent with Ambrose's view of an independent church authority? Who decides what the ruling authority should and should not do to support the church? Can this standard and *modus operandi* (method of operation) be shown to be consistent with Christ's patient and merciful lordship over all who dwell on earth? What is required for a government official to be a servant of Christ?

The matter of using force to help bolster church unity leads to another issue of great importance to this discussion, namely, the just use of force. The issue has most often been framed in terms of "just war" doctrine, or "just war" criteria, but it is more broadly about any use of force by government, including domestic policing. This goes to the very foundation of political community under government. If God established government because of sin rather than as part of the original responsibility of humans, then the use of force to restrain and punish evil is the basis and aim of government's responsibility, and that is the way Augustine understood it. In one of his letters he wrote,

> Surely it is not without purpose that we have the institution of the power of kings, the death penalty of the judge, the barbed hooks of the executioner, the weapons of the soldier, the right of punishment of the overlord, even the severity of the good father. All those things have their methods, their causes, their reasons, their practical benefits. While these are feared, the wicked are kept within bounds and the good live more peacefully among the wicked. However, men are not to be called good because they refrain from wrong-doing through their fear of such things—no one is good through dread of punishment but through love of righteousness.[40]

From this point of view, it is hard to see why a government should have any qualms about its use of force as long as it is able to punish and restrain evildoers sufficiently to keep itself in power and to keep some degree of order in its domain. In terms of Augustine's statement above, governments can leave to others (the church?) the concern about the love of "righteousness." Limits on how a government uses force can be grounded in pragmatic arguments, somewhat like Augustine's justification for using force against heretics. None of this connects government to the work of Christ, though Augustine approves of government acting in this way to support Christ's cause insofar as that cause is embodied in the true church.

As we look more closely at what Augustine said about justifiable warfare, however, we find that he regularly made arguments based on biblical revelation and the experience of Israel. He did not draw only, or even primarily, on the evidence of vestiges and semblances of the natural law in the work of government and the philosophical thinking of his day. Even though perfect peace and justice can never be achieved on earth, he believed that Christian love could and should influence even something as awful as the conduct of war. According to Deane, Augustine was at pains to persuade his readers that a government's use of force against criminals and in prosecuting just wars did not contradict the gospel precepts of love and turning the other cheek. Punishment of evildoers "is justified not only because it protects the innocent but also because it prevents the offender from continuing to misuse his liberty and from adding further crimes to his previous offenses."[41] Despite his considerable accommodation to the Roman imperial system, Augustine was the first to attempt a broader Christian argument to define the conditions and limits of the just use of force.

Here is a brief summary of Augustine's arguments, which set the direction for a so-called just-war ethic for centuries to come.[42] Augustine understood the point made by some, for example, that "a good ruler will wage wars only if they are just," but he added, "if he will only remember that he is a man, he will begin by bewailing the necessity he is under of waging even just wars. A good man would be under compulsion to wage no wars at all, if there were not such things as just wars."[43] This way of thinking about the evil of warfare led to the criteria that a government's decision to go to war must come only after every other means of resolving a conflict has been tried first; engaging in war justly, in other words, must be a matter of last resort.

Furthermore, a just war is possible only in response to "the injustice of an aggressor."[44] This point is now part of the criterion typically referred to as "just cause," meaning that warfare can be justified only if undertaken in response to unjust aggression or to unjust actions by another government or by people manifesting a genuine threat to peace and stability. The act of initiating war for self-aggrandizing purposes can never be justified. Another of Augustine's criteria is that the aim of a just war must be peace. In a letter (in 418) to Boniface, who was defending nearby Carthage against a siege by the Vandals, Augustine wrote, "Peace is not sought in order to the kindling of war, but war is waged in order that peace may be attained. Therefore [Boniface], even in waging war, cherish the spirit of a peacemaker, that, by conquering those whom you attack you may lead them back to the advantages of peace." A just peace also requires mercy after victory: "As violence is used towards him who rebels and resists, so mercy is due to the vanquished or the captive."[45]

It is also essential, as Augustine saw it, that war be undertaken by the declaration of a proper authority and with a proper attitude and right conduct. "The real evils in war," Augustine argued, "are love of violence, revengeful cruelty, fierce and implacable enmity, wild resistance, and the lust for power, and such like; and it is generally to punish these things, when force is required to inflict the punishment, that, in obedience to God or some lawful authority, good men undertake wars."[46] And when they find themselves in that position, they must conduct themselves with an attitude that does not exhibit or foster those evils. If we recoil at Augustine's approval of the kinds and degrees of coercion often used by governments in his day, we need to keep in mind that Roman political history was marked by a high degree of violence and militarism. S. E. Finer says with regard to the earlier Roman Republic that there had been no other political order, with the possible exception of the Assyrians, that was more militaristic and cruel. Roman soldiers were treacherous plunderers, extortion-ists, and cruel killers who reduced hundreds of thousands of defeated people to slavery and crucified thousands more.[47] Not much changed with the rise of the Roman Empire.

While there were some periods of lesser violence and greater peace in the years of Rome's imperial expansion, consolidation, and decline, Augustine lived in an era when Roman armies and regional governors, as well as invading "bar-barians," used force in ways that would be considered war crimes and crimes against humanity in our day. All the more, then, can we understand why many Christians refused to accept a role in, or cooperate with, government. When emperors and subordinate rulers became Christians, perhaps Augustine became too hopeful about the possibility of taming and restraining their unjust use of force. Or perhaps he did not expect great change but felt nonetheless that as a Christian bishop he should do everything possible to encourage Christian rulers to work for relative peace and justice on earth so that more ears would be open to hearing the good news about the eternal city.

In the centuries to come, the so-called doctrine of just war was expanded and systematized. A number of criteria, including a lawful declaration of war, just cause, last resort, limited means, and the probability of success, were grouped under the rubric of *jus ad bellum* (just entrance into war), while other criteria, such as the immunity of noncombatants and using means proportionate to the end of peace, were grouped under the rubric of *jus in bello* (justice in the con-duct of war). Some of those criteria have been written into international treaties governing military combat and into manuals used in training and governing military forces today.

Future Directions

What developed in the West after Augustine, as we will see, reflected primarily the second and third lines of his argument, namely, a church-led imperium with a hierarchical distribution of two swords (à la Pope Gelasius). The pope of the Roman Catholic Church kept the spiritual sword of superior moral and spiritual authority and delegated the sword of coercion to governments. Church officials and pious monks made vows to follow a high moral road that required chastity, poverty, and nonviolence, while they called on government officials and other laypeople to abide by ethical standards that accommodated family life, the holding of private property, and government's work of policing and war fighting. Church leaders would try to represent the city of God while encourag-ing those occupied with life in the earthly city to be as peaceable and just as possible within the confines of unnatural institutions and the need to survive.

Disagreements about the proper responsibility of Christians in this world continued after Augustine, however, and they continue to this day. The question, for example, of whether it is legitimate for Christians to participate in government, particularly in its policing and military responsibilities, is very much alive today. If it is legitimate, on what terms may Christians participate? If it is illegitimate, how do Christians conduct themselves as outsiders? If Christians do share responsibility with everyone for the common life on earth, surely they can leave the responsibilities of government in the hands of others while they concentrate on promoting the love of righteousness. Surely the demonstration of the love of God in nonviolent ways will do more than government's use of force to promote relative peace and justice in this world. That is, in fact, the conclusion drawn by a minority of Christians—mostly pacifists—ever since Augustine's time, not on the basis of everything he argued but on the basis of his characterization of the kind of love that constitutes the city of God.

However, most Christians after Augustine adopted a different approach built on the hierarchical ideas of social order that he espoused in the second and third lines of argument. The love of God in Christ, which will be fulfilled in the city of God, is the highest way of life, and those who lead the institutional church should live by its standards, not only refusing to hold any office of government (renouncing the use of force) but also choosing poverty and celibacy for themselves. In that respect the priests, bishops, and brothers and sisters with a "religious" vocation (a call to serve Christ full-time) will, as far as possible, represent the city of God on earth. Lower on the hierarchical scale of Christendom is a way of life shaped by a different, though also legitimate, ethic. At that level, government officials who enforce relative justice, farmers and others who own property and conduct commerce, and those who marry and raise children will follow a way of life fitting for life in this sinful age. Since God establishes governments, in Augustine's view, to coerce and restrain sinners, their function is at odds with the natural order of creation and with the perfect justice of the city of God. For God did not commission humans to rule over other persons. Christians with "secular" (this-worldly) vocations should try, nevertheless, to live as lovingly as possible, finding their relation to God's perfect love through participation in the church's mediation of the sacraments and habits of repentance and service. And governments may show their loyalty to God by making and enforcing laws that serve the church and its cause. This religious-secular hierarchy with two ethical pathways came to mark the High Middle Ages of Western Christianity in which the Roman Catholic Church and its canon law served as the highest authority in the single social order of Christendom. Many aspects of that way of life continue to shape the institutions, behaviors, and thinking of Catholics and Protestants to this day.

5

from Augustine
to the splintering
of Christendom

"The people cannot get enough of the spectacle of magistrates, suspected of treason, undergoing repeated torture. The people delay executions, which the victims themselves request, for the enjoyment of seeing them subjected to even more suffering."[1]

The time is the late fourteenth and early fifteenth centuries in northern France and the Low Countries. The quotation is from Johan Huizinga's famous book, first published almost one hundred years ago, about the autumn (or waning) of the Middle Ages. The scene is important to keep before us because part of this chapter may sound like a story of progress. But what we might see as progress in some aspects of society's development never overcomes all the negative, regressive, and highly destructive developments that continue apace. Witness life in our day with its unjust wars, corrupt public officials, white-collar criminals, sex and narcotics trafficking, crimes against humanity, child soldiers—all existing in a world we believe to be more civilized than that of the late Middle Ages.

The question, of course, is how to distinguish progress from regress. By what criteria do we judge that the public prolongation and celebration of an execution in fourteenth-century Europe was worse than what goes on in America's prisons today, largely hidden from public view? By what criteria do we judge that a contemporary constitutional state represents progress beyond the kingdoms and cities of the late Middle Ages? We raise these questions not to cast doubt on the possibility of making judgments about progress and regress but to draw attention to the fundamental importance of *criteria*. If there is a constructive Christian contribution to be made in the political, legal, and economic arenas, how do we judge what that contribution should be, and according to what criteria?

Huizinga's exploration of the culture of one part of Western Europe toward the close of the Middle Ages shows how people expressed themselves publicly in overt and passionate ways. "The end of the Middle Ages was an intoxicating time," writes Huizinga, "when painful justice and judicial cruelty were in full bloom. People did not doubt for an instant that the criminal deserved his punishment." In feudal circumstances in particular, the sense of justice "was still three quarters heathen and dominated by a need for vengeance. Though the church sought to soften judicial usage, by pressing for meekness, peace and reconciliation, it failed to change the actual sense of justice." To the contrary, that sense of justice "was rendered sterner still by adding to the need for retribution the hatred of sin." And with a sense of certainty, the people believed sin to be "whatever their enemy did."[2]

Has the sense of justice changed in the last six hundred years? Do we now believe that punishment should be softer, less vengeful, and without hatred of sin? If so, do our police agencies and courts deliver more justice today than did the medieval versions of those institutions? Do we now have less of the "heathen" in us? If so, may we attribute that fact to Christianity's contribution to the progress of civilization?

One of the striking things in Huizinga's story is that on many occasions high officials themselves, and not only petty thieves, were caught and punished. In that time there were laws and not only oppressive overlords. There were legal systems under which the privileged and not only the poorest and weakest subjects could, on occasion, be brought to justice. In fact, a few centuries earlier—between 1050 and 1150—a revolution in law, legal processes, and legal institutions emerged that became one of the most powerful influences in the development of Western civilization. According to Harold Berman, the Papal Revolution of 1075–1122 initiated the development of a system of canon law in the Roman Catholic Church and spurred on the formation of concomitant systems of nonecclesiastical law and government.[3] That was the beginning of the Western legal tradition and was achieved by a creative synthesis of Roman, Greek, biblical, and Germanic elements.

Christian Politics before 1075

From its apostolic beginnings, Christianity spread north and west into Europe, south into Africa, and east into Asia.[4] In addition to Christianity, other religions were shaping the earth's political landscape in Asia, Africa, and the Americas. In the seventh century, Islam appeared and continued its rapid expansion after Mohammed's death (in 630) into territories that had once been under Roman rule and where Christianity had taken root. In the early centuries after Christ, Christians did much to change attitudes and social behaviors in positive ways, especially with regard to the treatment of families, women, and children.[5]

Nevertheless, Christian attitudes toward government generally reflected Augustine's dim view of what could be achieved on earth. To the extent that government could maintain some degree of order in a world marred by sin, it should be welcomed and obeyed. Where a Christian had the opportunity to serve as a public official, whether as emperor or as ruler of a small kingdom, he might try to enhance the church's influence and even make laws for Christ and his cause. But a vision for reforming this world was largely absent.

What did grow between the first and the eleventh centuries was a Christian community (*populus christianus*) gathered in congregations far and wide under the church's pastors and bishops and the rulers of diverse tribes, cities, regions, and feudal estates. And in the vacuum created by the decline of Roman imperial power in the West, the church was emerging as the leading moral and even legal authority. As for government, the rulers of smaller territories—Frankish, Visigothic, Vandal, Celtic, and Lombard—were taking over and were often at war with one another even after they were Christianized.[6] Some of those rulers saw themselves as Christian kings, responsible to uphold order and Christian unity within their realms.

The most important of the Christian kings was Charlemagne (742–814), a Frank who aspired to be "the new Constantine," a king-priest uniting governmental and spiritual authority in himself. According to Oliver O'Donovan and Joan Lockwood O'Donovan, Charlemagne's subjects believed he ruled not only "by God's grace" but also "in God's place."[7] There was, however, some mystery and ambiguity about Charlemagne's authority over the church because his coronation as "Emperor of the Romans" in 800 by Pope Leo III was interpreted by some as an act of submission to papal authority in Rome. And, in fact, the church tried to capitalize on that perception. However, bishops of the church in the Frankish territories were more closely aligned with Charlemagne than with the pope. Thus, the "church in which they and their kings were to minister as Christ's vicegerents was less the universal Roman imperial church than the West-Frankish *populus Dei*" (people of God).[8]

The Western church was not able very quickly to bring under its authority the peoples and governments of fractured Europe. But as it struggled to do so, it manifested one of the distinctive characteristics of Roman rule, namely, the penchant to write and codify law. When the Roman Republic had grown to become the mighty Roman Empire, it established a rather complex system of governance by law as well as by force. On the one hand, Rome ruled with an iron fist. The different tribes, nations, and cities that Roman emperors conquered were subjected to "the full military and civil power" of a Rome-appointed governor, and they had to pay imperial taxes. On the other hand, the local governors appointed by Rome were often local oligarchs,[9] and the imperial system at its height exhibited something of a federated character, though without representation of the subordinate units at the imperial center. This is where the importance of law enters the picture.

The complexity of the early Roman Empire's governance structure led to the development of an empire-wide system of law called the *jus gentium*, or law of peoples, an early version of universal law above diverse local law systems. The *jus gentium* did not displace local law; instead it established a layer of common law across all local boundaries—a law of rights, duties, and penalties for certain persons throughout the empire. Appeal to, and use of, the *jus gentium* occurred, for example, when the laws or judgments of local governments came into conflict with Roman statute law. Over time, these Roman practices produced a law-bound system of government that transcended the person and will of the emperor or ruler. The Romans, according to historian S. E. Finer, "were the first to conceive of a *res publica*, a nexus of goods, activities, and institutions which belonged *at large*."[10] In other words, emperors and rulers could come and go, but the system of law and political order would carry on.

For the most part, the laws and legal processes of Roman rule were created as a practical matter in the course of conquering, collecting taxes, keeping order, and settling disputes. No grand theory or philosophical system generated or guided them. The most important philosophical influence was probably Stoicism (think of Cicero), which emphasized the universality of natural law and the spark of divinity in every individual. Stoicism was also probably a factor in the development of another feature of Roman law, namely, a form of private civil law. It was the means by which individuals and corporate entities were enabled to engage one another by means of private contracts, in settling private disputes, and so forth. This was not a system of statute law drawn up and imposed by rulers but a body of rules and obligations holding for the conduct of business initiated among private parties.

All in all, Finer contends, the governing of society through law (and not only by autocratic will), which included the development of the *jus gentium* and private civil law, was "unmatched elsewhere in the world." The Roman system at its best entailed the recognition of law as something that could be invoked and appealed to by individuals and not merely imposed by rulers. It also meant that some individuals could, on occasion, take government agents and agencies to court and challenge them by "invoking the law as of right, not supplicating as a subject asking grace."[11]

In sum, we might say that if the distinctive contribution of Greece to Western culture came from its elevation, and even deification, of reason, the distinctive contribution of Rome came from its elevation, and even worship, of law in the familiar duplex of "law and order." Both the rational capacity and the legal/juridical capacity of humans are important dimensions of our identity and our ability to exercise diverse responsibilities. Yet the same can be said about our linguistic, history-shaping, economic, aesthetic, social, and ethical capacities. All of these were evident in Greek and Roman cultures, of course, but the elevation of rational and legal functions stands out. Insofar as we want to decide how Christians should engage in political and legal life in our day, we will have to come to grips with the deep influence of Greek and Roman cultures on Christianity (and vice versa), especially during the first fifteen centuries after Christ.

The Papal Revolution

Late in the fifth century, as we noted in the last chapter, Pope Gelasius I formulated a two-swords doctrine, contending that ecclesiastical authority was superior to imperial power. Yet partly because of the Roman bishop's lack of strength to enforce his claim, the Roman emperor (in Constantinople) maintained his own claim to preeminence, and rulers in the West (such as Charlemagne) eventually made their own declarations of superiority within their realms. Thus, the implications of Gelasius's doctrine could not be worked out to the extent he envisioned. When Justinian (483–565) became emperor of the Eastern Roman Empire a few decades after Pope Gelasius articulated his two-swords doctrine, he set out to reestablish the glory of the empire and the preeminence of its Caesar. He began by collecting and codifying the whole of Roman law—collections that became the famous and highly influential *Corpus Juris Civilis*, the *Digest*, and the *Institutes*, which Justinian believed would reveal the true greatness of imperial Rome. With these documents he was also making a detailed legal argument that as Roman Caesar he was the supreme sovereign of Christendom, the one "who directed and ruled the empire in accordance with Christian principles emanating from the fount of all Christianity, the divine majesty of the emperor himself."[12] For the next five centuries, the competition between emperor and pope continued as Roman imperial power declined and the Western branch of the church gained strength.

Then, in 1075, the great Papal Revolution began. The highly influential Archdeacon Hildebrand, not yet an ordained priest, let alone a bishop, was elected Pope Gregory VII.[13] The new pope wanted to settle the question of supreme authority once and for all. He believed this was not only a spiritual matter but also something "required by the justice (*justitia*) and the law (*ius*) of Christ."[14] Much like the emperor Justinian had done nearly five hundred years earlier, Gregory set out to establish the truth of his position on a comprehensive legal basis, appointing experts in theology and the law to develop what became the Roman Catholic Church's canon law. He and his successors composed what the O'Donovans describe as an elaborate legal brief in support of St. Peter's authority as the vicar of Christ, "of the structure and unity of the *corpus Christianum*," and of "Christ's earthly kingship."[15] Gregory declared that the bishop of Rome should henceforth be recognized as the supreme authority over the whole church, not excluding the Eastern branch and all lower ranks of clergy and laity, and over the entire empire and all governmental powers throughout Christendom. His pronouncement not only sealed the 1054 division between the Western and Eastern branches of the church but also heightened the conflict between pope and emperor until a settlement, reached in 1122, confirmed the supremacy of papal authority in the West. In that connection, Huizinga notes that a second metaphor became prominent in the medieval period alongside the two-swords imagery to symbolize the church's preeminent authority, namely, the image of two heavenly bodies, with the sun having primacy above the moon.[16]

In the first place, Gregory's actions added to the growing sense that the church should be busy with the ordering of this world and not only with nurturing faith in the world to come. The language of the day may have continued to distinguish between the earthly ("secular") responsibility of laypeople and the spiritual responsibility of the church, but the church was in fact becoming a fully engaged *earthly* institution concerned with governing and renovating earthly life and not only with mediating grace for eternal salvation. This represented a significant departure from Augustine.

Second, at the start of its second millennium, the church became, in full measure, a legally defined *institution* identified chiefly with its officials: pope, bishops, priests, and those who served them. The institutional church, in this sense, was marking out an earthly *jurisdiction* distinguishable from the lower-level jurisdictions of governments and other nonecclesiastical institutions. This institutionalization, codified in the new canon law, eclipsed the idea of the church as the body and bride of Christ inclusive of all believers. The church's legally defined institutionalization also included a new distinction between the pope's priestly *ordination* and his *jurisdictional* authority. According to Berman, the sharp distinction between these two elements became "one of the fundamental constitutional principles of the Church of Rome. Ordination was a sacrament, that is, a sacred symbol of divine grace. . . . Jurisdiction, on the contrary, was a power conferred by the church as a corporate legal entity. It was the power to govern by law—to 'speak law' (*jus dicere*) within the limits established by law."[17]

The meaning of "Christian politics" after Gregory thus became defined by the way the papal office governed the church through canon law and by the way it exercised its authority over earthly governments in recognizing, limiting, and giving moral direction to them. Of course, part of the history of the West, including the era inaugurated by Gregory, included protests, objections, and reform efforts by church and government officials, scholars, and mendicant movements, all of which laid the basis for new types of Christian political action in the future. But for a few centuries after Gregory, the latter efforts remained marginal.[18]

Third, the effort to elevate and cement papal authority above all other authorities necessarily forced nonecclesiastical institutions to clarify their jurisdictions. The church's canon law had much to do with this, as did the efforts of a growing cadre of "religious" and "secular" lawyers. However, since the primary concern in the eleventh and twelfth centuries was with jurisdictional questions of papal and governmental authority, the relation of social life in a broader sense to Christ's judging and redeeming work was not given significant attention. Some remarkable scientific and philosophical work was done in this period, but it manifested the greater influence of Greek rationality and Roman legality than of the biblical story of God's judgment and redemption of creation. Politically speaking, at least, the Roman imperial tradition proved more powerful than the biblical tradition in shaping the contours of the political order of Christendom.

Fourth and finally, altogether these developments solidified the relation between papal authority and life on earth, setting the direction of Christian political thought and practice for centuries to come. Whatever else the Roman Catholic Church was, the Gregorian initiatives made it the leading *earthly* authority in the hierarchically organized medieval society of Christendom. Diverse responsibilities in this world, including those of governments, were experienced as subordinate to the church's mediating authority. Thus, the *Christian* meaning and direction of life's nonecclesiastical responsibilities were understood to come from their relation to the church institution, not from within the creaturely identity of those responsibilities.

Reordering This World

During the first millennium after Christ, the more the church attempted to assert its independent authority in relation to the Roman imperium, the more it became involved in earthly affairs. There was no sudden reversal of the view that earthly life is a struggle of endurance in a fallen world. Nevertheless, as the church developed ethical guidelines for priests and laypeople, and, as it worked to moderate some of the harshest patterns of Roman rule, it was taking into its own identity many Roman imperial characteristics. While the church's leading bishops, and especially the pope in Rome, focused on organizing the church for the mediation of grace, their theological and organizational judgments increasingly came to bear on the reordering of governance of earthly life. With respect to the law, Berman explains that any effort by the church to "eliminate from the law those of its features which were repugnant to a Christian ethic suffered, in the East as in the West, from the absence of a vision of what kind of legal order a Christian ethic required."[19] The same can be said about government, economic life, commerce and trade, science, education, and more. This is not to say that the spirit of Christian renewal had no influence on the diverse activities of earthly life, but even when the church in the West turned its attention to the ordering of earthly society, its efforts in that regard were concerned chiefly with bringing the church's theology, sacraments, and administration to bear on human conduct.

Berman cites an example that shows how the church's attitude toward earthly life changed from the time of Augustine to the eleventh century. For about the first millennium of the church's history, the doctrine of the Last Judgment was about what would happen after Christ's return and the inauguration of the world to come. "Christian faith," Berman says, "was represented above all in the monastic life, where men and women who had 'died to this world' sought to live impeccable lives in the heavenly kingdom." Life in the decaying terrestrial city was a matter of waiting for Christ's return to judge the living and the dead.[20] Early in the eleventh century, however, the Roman Catholic Church (but not the Eastern church) developed a "parallel belief" in the "intermediate judgment" of each person at the moment of death. This was the doctrine of purgatory, "an intermediate time of 'purging'" between each person's death and the last judgment. Although baptism freed Christians from the debt of original sin, the new doctrine taught that justice required punishment for the sins committed by each person during his or her lifetime. This doctrine established a closer connection between the person's life on earth, which required an accounting of sins, and life after death.[21]

When the pope eventually assumed jurisdiction over purgatory itself, he gained not only a greater control over earthly behavior but also a degree of authoritative control over life after death. An elaborate system of penances and merits was developed through which a person's penitential acts and good deeds on earth could reduce the time of purging after death. All of this became part of the church's law and not merely part of its doctrine. Penance, which earlier had emphasized acts that would bring about reconciliation between the offended and offending parties, became a sacrament requiring the sinner to make confession to a priest. That in turn led to priestly absolution. In the church's exercise of its purported influence over judgment and redemption in order to try to affect earthly behavior (including the behavior of governments), it took hold of earthly life as the sacred taking hold of the secular. The Papal Revolution made the church's hierarchy the dispenser of sacral blessings and judgments on temporal life. We should not be surprised, then, to discover that what mattered most to many pious laypeople was discovering how to use sacraments and other supernatural signs to gain assurance of eternal life after death.

The belief that daily life has little lasting significance without a connection to the sacred led to a steady increase in the number of sacraments and "sacramentalia"—relics, charms, and superstitions that were intended to connect this life with the world beyond. By the fourteenth century, a number of bishops and theologians were expressing objections to the mounting clutter of saints, festivals, and days of rest. Pierre d'Ailly objected to the introduction of so many "new hymns and prayers or other arbitrary innovations and to the all too rigid intensification of vigils, prayers, fasts, and abstentions."[22] Jean de Gerson wrote a book against superstition, objecting to the "ongoing reduction of the infinite to the finite": the "miracle of the Eucharist is permeated with the most sober and material superstitions: that one cannot go blind or suffer a stroke on the day one hears a mass or that one does not age during the time one spends at the service."[23]

The church claimed to hold the keys to the kingdom, a power concentrated in the office of the pope, who, on earth, was designated the sole mediator of Christ's kingship. The development of the legal constitution of the church that began under Gregory VII continued under his successors, incorporating Roman doctrines of imperial sovereignty to define papal authority and jurisdiction. The pope became the supreme monarch on earth with *plenitudo potestatis* ("fullness of power"), which embraced both spiritual and temporal authorities. The pope was not only superior to the emperor but was also the emperor's judge. Pope Innocent III portrayed himself as the "mediator between God and man," an idea that led to the distinction between the pope's "ordinary power" and his "extraordinary power," which he exercised as Christ's vicar.[24]

The boundary between earth and heaven, between the earthly city and the city of God, became much less clear than it was for Augustine. Instead of an *antithesis* between two loves, there was now a *complementarity* between the secular and the sacred in the hierarchical ordering of Christendom. The church's laws and ordained clergy brought heaven to earth, while laypeople in a wide array of stations and ranks looked for ways to touch heaven from their position on earth.

The Church as a Law-State?

Berman contends that the Roman Catholic Church constituted itself as the first Western law-state, though he adds qualifications to that statement. "The church," he says, thus "had the paradoxical character of a church-state, a *Kirchenstaat*: it was a spiritual community which also exercised temporal functions and whose constitution was in the form of a modern state. The secular state, on the other hand, had the paradoxical character of a state without ecclesiastical functions, a secular polity, all of whose subjects also constituted a spiritual community living under a separate spiritual authority."[25]

Berman's argument here makes sense only from the perspective of the later collapse of Christendom. At the time, the church was simply solidifying its authority over governments by means of law. The church never became a law-state in the sense of establishing its own police and military forces throughout the territory of Christendom. The church's officials did not use the governmental sword directly but instead put governments on notice that the pope now had legal authority to exercise a degree of power (moral and spiritual) over a government's use of the sword delegated to it by the church. The church's achievement was essentially to reverse the order that had existed in the earlier Roman Empire, when the emperor claimed superior authority over the church but granted the church a measure of spiritual freedom and self-governance.

Part of what Berman means by describing the institutionalized church as a state is that it made use of the term and structure of a "corporation," synthesizing elements from the Roman law of Justinian, Germanic law, and Christian ideas of a corporate community. By means of its own law, the church distinguished sharply between the clergy and the laity, between the spiritual and the secular. Legal science in the twelfth century also "began to develop various branches of substantive law," including family law, inheritance, property, contract, and tort and criminal law.[26] As a legal, institutional entity, the church "formed itself into a complex bureaucracy with a professional court, a professional treasury, and a chancery."[27] All of these efforts to clarify the church's lawful, corporate jurisdiction meant, of course, that it was contributing indirectly to the specifying of the jurisdictions of nonecclesiastical parties, even if all of them in some respect were considered subject to the church's spiritual and moral authority.[28]

How did the church achieve all of this without having military and police power to enforce its laws and decrees? It happened for several reasons, says Berman: (1) because Christianity had become the widely accepted religion of Europe; (2) because rulers were dispersed and relatively weak as a consequence of the empire's collapse; and (3) because Rome had bequeathed to Christendom a "high level of legal consciousness and legal sophistication that came to prevail throughout the West in the twelfth and thirteenth centuries."[29]

The Jurisdiction of Governments

The jurisdictions held by governing powers were a subordinate part of the one community of Christendom in the High Middle Ages. That pattern continued for several centuries as long as Christendom maintained its unity. But the ground was being laid for what became the independence of temporal governments when the church's control of Christendom began to fail. In fact, the first resort of kings a few centuries later would be to claim *direct* (rather than indirect) ordination by God—the so-called divine right of kings. That, in turn, led to the recovery and modification of older imperial and Frankish ideas of monarchical superiority over the church. But that move did not come quickly. Even John of Salisbury (c. 1120–1180), who early in the twelfth century supported the idea that a ruler's title comes directly from God, argued that to become a prince one had to be chosen by God, and to be chosen by God "one must have the approval of the ecclesiastical authority. Since the prince is subject to God, he is subject also to the priesthood, 'who represent God on earth.'"[30]

At the heart of this jurisdictional dispute between church and temporal governments, however, lies a problem that a hierarchical answer fails to resolve. On the one hand, it may be relatively easy to recognize that institutions such as church and state are different in kind and exercise different types of responsibility. But on the other hand, the dispute between pope and emperor over supremacy could not by itself clarify the kinds of responsibilities and jurisdictions that should belong to each. Placing one or the other at the top of the social hierarchy does not address that question. Moreover, if the church in the biblical sense—the people of God, the bride of Christ, the body of Christ—is a community of faith that embraces all Christians in all aspects of their lives, then the diversity of responsibilities on earth cannot be adequately identified, distinguished, and related simply by an agreement that the pope or the emperor (or king) is Christ's vicar on earth.

Thomas Aquinas (1225–1274) and the Recovery of Aristotle

At the high point of the Middle Ages, in the thirteenth and fourteenth centuries, many social, economic, academic, political, and artistic changes in the West were unfolding simultaneously, and developments in the ecclesiastical and governmental legal systems were an important part of those changes. In that period, there were at least three ways to understand the church in relation to government and society. The first was the Augustinian idea of the church as the community of the faithful, being fashioned by the love of Christ into the city of God, a city that will be fully realized only in the world to come. Governments, by contrast, had a role in this world to restrain and punish sin and to uphold a sufficient degree of order and peace so that believers and unbelievers could cooperate in acquiring the necessities of life. In this view, not only did church and government share little in common, but they stood, to a certain degree, in antithetical relation to each other.

A second idea of the church, which became dominant after the Papal Revolution, was that of a legally incorporated institution identified chiefly with its clerical hierarchy and, in the West, preeminently with the pope. Laypeople, who were members of the church through baptism and other sacraments, were generally identified by their "secular" roles and responsibilities. The relation of the church to government in this frame of thought was one of complementarity rather than antithesis. The conflicts that did arise between them had to do primarily with boundary disputes over their respective jurisdictions within Christendom.

The third idea of the church was that of supreme authority in Christendom, which was conceived as an all-embracing Christian society with both sacred (spiritual) and secular (temporal) levels of responsibility. Christendom, in this picture, was more extensive than the church but was organized under the church.

By the time of Thomas Aquinas, this third idea supplied the framework for comprehending the whole of life, and it solidified the institutional distinctions of the second idea while almost entirely submerging the first idea. The church had become the leading institution of earthly (not just heavenly) society. Life in the earthly city was no longer placed in sharp contrast to the city of God. Government was now a junior partner with the church in the single society of Christendom, which joined earth to heaven in a grand hierarchy of being. One tendency, consequently, was for the institutional church to become more entangled in the affairs of earthly life. "Indeed," says Berman, "the very division between the ecclesiastical and the secular presupposed the mission of the church to reform the world, and consequently the mission of all Christians (but especially those in holy orders) to help make imperfect secular law conform to its ultimate purpose of justice and truth."[31] However, a second tendency became evident when social, economic, academic, and legal systems began to differentiate more rapidly. Those with responsibilities in other institutions began to think of the church institution more in terms of its spiritual authority than in terms of its earthly authority.

The most sophisticated intellectual attempt to comprehend these complexities in a rounded philosophical and theological system was made by Thomas Aquinas, the greatest theologian and philosopher of the church after Augustine. Aquinas drew on all strands of Christian thinking up to his day and also made use of the ancient Greek philosopher Aristotle, whose writings had only recently been recovered, translated, and reintroduced into the Western (Latin) mainstream by Muslim philosophers.[32] Among Aquinas's many achievements was his interpretation of political life as a *natural* community, part of human life by creation. In other words, unlike Augustine who believed that God established government because of sin to punish evildoers and maintain a modicum of order in a sinful world, Aquinas drew on Aristotle's idea of the polis as a perfect or complete natural community. Aquinas thought that political community is the most complete natural expression of human sociability.[33]

It is natural for humans to live in society, Aquinas reasons, and the ordering of society requires "that there exist among men some means by which the group may be governed."[34] In an early work, *On Kingship,* Aquinas argues by analogy as follows. Just as everything in the universe comes under divine government, "in like manner the members of the human body and all the powers of the soul are governed by reason. Thus, in a proportionate manner, reason is to man what God is to the world." Yet the rule of reason is manifest not only in individuals separately; "the analogy with the divine government is found in him [humankind] not only in this way that one man governs himself by reason, but also in that the multitude of men is governed by the reason of one man."[35] For Aquinas, as for Aristotle, that "one man" should be a monarch, but it is best for a monarch to head a government that has a mixed constitution in which the people have some share. "Hence," he writes in his later work, the *Summa Theologica,*

> the best system in any state or kingdom is one in which one man, as specially qualified, rules over all, and under him are others governing as having special endowments, yet all have a share inasmuch as those are elected from all, and also are elected by all. This is the best form of constitution, a mixture of monarchy, in that one man is at the head, of aristocracy, in that many rule as specially qualified, and democracy, in that the rulers can be chosen from the people and by them.[36]

Or, as Aquinas says elsewhere, the ordering of society for the common good "belongs either to the whole people, or to someone who is the vicegerent of the whole people. Hence the making of a law belongs either to the whole people or to a public personage who has care of the whole people."[37]

In thinking about government and the law in this way, Aquinas located governmental authority within the community itself (not outside it) as well as under the law of reason, the natural law. Law, he argued, is a "rule and measure" of human acts, and it therefore pertains to reason naturally. And justice in legal matters requires the ordering of all parts of society and of human nature toward the common good of "the body politic," which represents the fullest maturation of human society.[38] At the same time, as Jean Porter points out, Aquinas's idea of the common good does not reduce individual persons to political subjects alone. "While it is true that individual good is dependent in some way on the common good, we also see that the common good is dependent in some ways on the goods of individuals." Thus, "the boundaries of justice . . . include fundamental norms of respect for individual well-being," a well-being that is achieved through various relationships and responsibilities, not all of which are inherently political.[39]

Life in a political community, for example, cannot realize the highest good of the individual. That good is a supernatural gift of grace, the beatific vision of God that unites the believer with God in eternal life. The kind of government that pertains to eternal life, says Aquinas, can only be the government of God through "our Lord Jesus Christ." And the ministry on earth of "spiritual things" that pertain to Christ's rule has been entrusted to priests of the church, not to kings who govern "earthly things."[40] In other words, says Porter, "the political common good is not a particularly divinized form of temporal good, nor does it provide a special mode of access to union with God." In fact, there is nothing intrinsically common "about the individual's enjoyment of the beatific vision."[41] Moreover, as Aquinas says about the human virtues, "there is no virtue of which some activity cannot be enjoined by law. Nevertheless human law does not enjoin every act of every virtue, but those acts only which serve the common good."[42] "Human law cannot, therefore, prohibit whatever is contrary to virtue; it is enough for it to prohibit whatever destroys social intercourse, allowing everything else to be permissible, not in the sense of approving it, but of not attaching a penalty to it."[43]

We need to highlight several points here. First, the political philosophy of Aquinas was distinctively his own and not simply a repetition and endorsement of Aristotle's politics. Aristotle did not believe that human beings needed a trans-political, supernatural fulfillment beyond this world to achieve their ultimate purpose. For Aristotle, rational maturity is the ultimate end (or goal) of a rational individual, and life completed (perfected) in a mature political community is the true end (or goal) of human social life. That is as far as Aristotle could go. While Aquinas incorporated a great deal of Aristotle into his philosophy, he saw human nature and the political community in a larger context where the supernatural completes the natural. Politics can make no contribution to humanity's supernatural destiny. In saying that, Aquinas actually demoted Aristotle to the rank of a mere *natural* philosopher, contending that theological virtues, the church, and supernatural grace transcend any natural perfection that can be achieved rationally in a political community. Of course, Aristotle would not have appreciated or accepted his demotion by Aquinas, for it implied that Aristotle's philosophy was incomplete and imperfect. For Aquinas, however, Aristotle's work could be given pride of place at the natural level in the grand synthesis of Christendom. As F. C. Copleston puts it, "Aquinas was convinced that Aristotle's outlook on the world and on human life was incomplete and inadequate rather than simply wrong or untrue. Grace perfects nature but does not annul it: revelation sheds further light, but it does not cancel out the truths attainable by purely philosophic reflection."[44]

Aquinas's synthesis reflected the structure and spirit of Christendom in his day. On the one hand, Aquinas was trying to secure a firmer place for natural life, including politics, as something that expresses the rational nature of humans created by God. On the other hand, he was giving support to the conviction that what is natural, philosophical, and political is not sufficient to bring about the Christian fulfillment of life. He firmly located the ultimate end of life above and beyond the natural. The experience of God's supernatural grace by faith through the sacramental communion of the church opens believers to eternal life. That is what will bring about the highest level of human happiness, the true fulfillment of life. Grace perfects rather than annuls nature. Life in political community has its place, but it is not the highest place.

It is noteworthy in this regard that Aquinas's vision of eternal life was of the individual's union with God through a beatific vision rather than through the final revelation of the city of God as a political community and as a marriage, family, and community of friends of Christ Jesus. In his way of thinking, the supernatural end that transcends the natural is not so much a fulfillment of the natural as a superseding of the natural. Referring to a text from Aquinas, Porter says, "the happiness of the beatific vision is a complete good"; "it is not intrinsically increased by being shared with companions, even though this fellowship increases the well-being of happiness." Thus, there is no "simple parallel between the political common good and the supreme good of union with God."[45]

Second, the use that Aquinas made of Aristotle was enabled, in part, by the considerable diversification of society and governments in his day. Especially since the successes of Charlemagne in building an extensive Frankish kingdom beyond the reach of the Roman emperor (in Constantinople), conflicts and debates arose not only between pope and emperor but also between the church (at several levels) and many different governments. The larger and smaller kingdoms of continental Europe and England (as well as many cities and estates) were such that political life had to be understood in a greater variety of ways. Aristotle's political philosophy reflected life in a small polis, not life in the Roman Empire, and thus it proved more useful to Aquinas than it would have been to Augustine.

Nevertheless, the more Aquinas developed the idea of the naturalness and completeness of earthly political communities, the more he was sharpening the distinction between the institutional church of grace and the earthly political institutions of nature and reason. His distinction had more to do with the identities and purposes of the two institutions than with their rank in the hierarchy of Christendom. Seeking to understand the political community in this way led to a greater awareness that political life (as well as educational, scientific, and economic life) has its meaning within itself, even though Christians continued to recognize the superior, spiritual role of the church. While the church remained important for access to the forgiveness of sins and eternal life, it became less important for the discovery of life's meaning in this world. In sum, a comprehensive, hierarchical view of reality in which the supernatural completes the natural makes more room for the natural to be understood and enjoyed on its own terms, thus elevating the supernaturally oriented church further above natural life.

Third and finally, we should highlight several differences between Aquinas and Augustine. Augustine lived in an empire that was just beginning to establish Christianity and to be threatened from the outside; Aquinas lived after ecclesiastical primacy of the papal office had been securely established over much of Western Europe. Augustine was among the early Christian leaders struggling for the first time to articulate a Christian view of life in the face of non-Christian philosophies that dominated the Roman world. Aquinas could draw from a thousand years of social and intellectual contributions by Christian martyrs, monks, thinkers, priests, public officials, church councils, and papal decrees and admonitions. Augustine was a bishop with pastoral responsibilities, writing to address controversies that were shaping and rocking the world around him, a world that had not yet become Christendom. Aquinas was a scholar and teacher in the more settled and differentiated society of Christendom. His world was structured by the church's international canon law and different kinds of Christian organizations, including monasteries, universities, and more. And given the established hierarchy of church, government, and society, Aquinas felt free—even in the face of much criticism—to make use of "The Philosopher" (as he called Aristotle) in developing his own philosophy of the natural world as if there were no great tension between nature and grace, between this world and the next, between governments and the church.

Because the church had sanctioned the hierarchical organization of life, Aquinas did not struggle as Augustine had with the antithetical loves of the city of God and the earthly city. Augustine believed, for example, that private property as well as government was unnatural and had been established only because of sin. Aquinas, by contrast, viewed private property "as the concrete elaboration of man's natural dominion over material things in respect of his 'title to care for and distribute' them. . . . Ownership is a legal positivizing of the natural right of dominion that serves its primary purpose, the use of the earth's resources for the benefit of all, when its moral limits are observed."[46] Since Aquinas could take for granted that theology, scriptural revelation, and the spiritual life of the church serve to mediate God's grace for eternal salvation, and that the supernatural does not stand antithetically against the natural, he was able to approach the natural world on its own terms and in its own right as an expression of God-given goodness. The natural could be conceived rationally without appeal to supernatural revelation for correction or validation. And the philosophy of Aristotle could be taken up for that purpose without threat to ecclesiastical authority.

Within the framework of Christendom's hierarchy, Aquinas understood the natural law to be a reflection of the eternal law of God, yet he also believed that the natural law was accessible to reason without need of supernatural assistance. While one needs help from God to act as one should, one does not need "a new illumination added to his natural light in order to know the truth in all things, but only in those that surpass his natural knowledge."[47] "Now in human affairs a thing is said to be just from being right, according to the rule of reason. But the first rule of reason is the law of nature. . . . Consequently, every human law has just so much of the nature of law as it is derived from the law of nature. But if in any point it departs from the law of nature, it is no longer a law but a perversion of law."[48] The complementary dualities of reason and revelation, philosophy and theology, natural virtues and theological virtues, civil government and the church—all could find their place in a single social hierarchy from which the antithetical conflicts that Augustine struggled with had been almost entirely expunged.

Aquinas's argument for justifiable warfare shows, however, that he did not isolate philosophy from theology, or politics from the spiritual life, in separate, closed compartments. Just as Augustine developed his justification for a limited kind of warfare in the earthly city with detailed support from Scripture, so Aquinas made his case for justifiable warfare with constant appeal to Scripture and not primarily to Aristotle and other philosophers. Aristotle had offered no argument for just warfare. His view of what constituted a just polis took for granted that many if not most city-states would develop in less than mature ways. His criticism of the city-state of Sparta, for example, was that it made war and preparation for war its highest aim rather than seeing war as a means to the end of human maturity—the whole of excellence—in political society. Sparta had been relatively successful in conquering, but not in governing what it conquered, because it did not invest in preparation for good governance.[49] From Aristotle's point of view, Sparta was unbalanced and unwise, not sinful and unjust in a Christian sense.

While Aquinas incorporated into his philosophy and theology a great deal of Aristotle's understanding of human nature, his argument for what is just and unjust in warfare came almost entirely from Augustine with repeated quotations from the Bible.[50] Going to war for aggressive, self-serving purposes is sinful and wrong, he argued, not simply a mistake of elevating a means to an end. Justifiable warfare requires initiation by a proper authority for a just cause and with the right intention. A just cause is a wrong done by others that needs to be resisted, punished, or amended. And right intention means, as Augustine had argued, aiming for peace and not fighting with greedy and cruel motivations. A just war requires action that is proportionate rather than "inordinate and perilous," which leads to "slaying or plundering." There should be no destruction of women and children, or even of fruit trees (one of the means of life), in the enemy's territory. In the medieval synthesis all is supposedly harmonized, but listen to Aquinas's explanation of why the clergy should not engage in warfare. The first reason is that "warlike pursuits are full of unrest," so they would hinder the clerics "from contemplation of divine things." It would be unbecoming for ministers of the Mass, which entails the eucharistic sharing in the body and blood of the Lord, "to slay or shed blood." But if Aquinas is correct at this point, isn't there something fundamentally questionable about *any* Christian engaging in "unbecoming" actions that are "full of unrest" while trying to live in the love of Christ and taking part in the celebration of the Eucharist?

After the breakdown of the grand medieval synthesis in the centuries following Aquinas, the so-called secular or natural world would come to be understood in a different way under the influence of a new humanistic spirit aspiring to the freedom and autonomy of individuals. The "secular" would break free from, rather than remain a partner with, the "religious." The natural would no longer be willing to subject itself to ecclesiastical restraints or consider itself a lower level of existence in a grand hierarchy that culminates in supernatural grace. The secular world would insist on becoming independent and self-sufficient, no longer in need of the supernatural. That is not what Aquinas thought or would have anticipated, but looking back from our day we can see how the modern humanist could find such an opening in the philosophy of Aquinas (and in the medieval, hierarchical social order) that allowed for the detachment of the natural world from its place in the medieval hierarchy.

According to Copleston, "Aquinas thought of man as tending naturally and inevitably towards his perfection, towards the actualization of his potentialities as man, towards his final end or good. And he thought of the practical reason as discerning the acts necessary to the attainment of this end and as ordering them while forbidding their contraries."[51] To whatever extent Aquinas thought he had succeeded in incorporating Aristotle into a larger Christian view of the world that culminates in supernatural transcendence, the natural world in his view often appeared to be quite self-sufficient. When a large enough number of people became disenchanted with the church and with hope for life after death, the natural world could appear to them quite able to stand on its own. Medieval Christendom and Aquinas's philosophy were more fragile than he and others thought.

6

nations, states, and Protestant reformers

The aim of the Roman Catholic Church after the time of the Papal Revolution of the eleventh and twelfth centuries was to solidify the church's supreme leadership of Christendom. According to historian Christopher Dawson, "The emancipation of the church from imperial and feudal control and the assertion of the primacy of the spiritual power set free new spiritual forces and created the new international society of medieval Christendom."[1] The church sought its goal through the development of its canon law and corporate institutionalization, with authority concentrated in the papal office. The church's leadership envisioned a society in which every office and order of the church and every earthly practice, organization, and institution would find its place in the harmonious unity of Christendom. The comprehensive intellectual synthesis produced by Thomas Aquinas represented this vision and, in Dawson's words, served as the "crown and completion of centuries of continuous effort to achieve an integration of the religious doctrine of the Christian Church with the intellectual tradition of ancient culture."[2]

However, the church could not entirely control the dynamics of European life, and the unified society it envisioned was never fully secured. Even as the church's power and authority were strengthening, there were monks, such as St. Bernard, and civic leaders, such as Arnold of Brescia (in Lombardy, now in northern Italy), who criticized the church's earthly entanglements, seeing them as a cause of social conflicts rather than as the means of unifying Christendom. In Arnold's view, conflicts between the church and local officials in Brescia were the fault of "the temporal power of the bishop and the wealth of the Church." A solution would be found only by the return of the clergy and other church leaders "to the poverty of the primitive Church." Arnold even went so far as to argue that "priests who held property or exercised temporal authority could not be saved, that everything temporal must be resigned to the prince and the laity."[3]

By the end of the thirteenth century, in the decades following the death of Aquinas, the splintering of Christendom had already begun. Governments across Europe, particularly those in France, England, and Italy, were restive; urban dwellers grew antagonistic toward the church's interference in their affairs; monastic reformers struggled against the church's compromises with political power and other immoral practices; and university professors were writing treatises questioning many of the church's dogmas and practices. All of this, says Dawson, "proved fatal to the synthesis of religion and culture that seemed to have been achieved in the previous centuries." It was as though "the spiritual tide which had been steadily making for unity for three centuries had suddenly turned, so that everywhere in every aspect of life the forces that made for division and dissolution were predominant."[4]

Dawson, writing more than sixty years ago, may have had too romantic a notion of how much progress the church had actually made in unifying Christendom between the eleventh and the thirteenth centuries. The splintering of Christendom had multiple causes that included corruption, repression, jealousy, and overreaching ambition on the part of both ecclesiastical and governmental officials. Other causes of diversification, however, were ongoing developments in economic, political, academic, and artistic life that were outgrowing Greek and Roman categories of thought, as well as ecclesiastical dogma, canon law, and bureaucratic control. Marcia Colish, in her splendid book on the medieval foundations of the West, describes (along with much else) the amazing dynamism of the late medieval period evident in the creative development of vernacular languages and literature, science and technology, economic life, law and government, and ecclesiastical ethics, theology, and law.[5]

Consider just one example. Over the centuries, the church had articulated moral standards on matters such as usury—profit earned on a loan of money. Usury was forbidden by the church, as it had been for centuries, for reasons found in the Bible and other sources. Nevertheless, with the expansion of industry and commerce, usury had become a regular practice. Thus, while nearly every ecclesiastical and academic authority, including Aquinas, opposed usury, in actual practice the church's standard was simply ignored. In fact, says Colish, "usury was practiced with impunity by everyone active in the high medieval economy, from the popes and their bankers on down, despite the remarkably strong consensus of thinkers against its acceptability."[6]

To what extent, then, were the challenges to ecclesiastical authority arising because the church had mistakenly imagined it was jurisdictionally competent to provide moral and spiritual direction to those engaged in economic, political, scientific, and artistic life? And, by contrast, to what extent did the undermining of ecclesiastical authority arise because of a decline (or even rejection) of Christian faith and antagonism to the church's way of life? If it was the latter, then why was the faith declining or being rejected? And what was filling the vacuum created by the loss of Christian faith? If, however, the church's authority was shrinking because of a growing awareness that the church lacked competence to give guidance and make judgments in certain arenas of human responsibility, then what kind of authorities were filling the vacuum left by the church's shrinkage, and what standards of judgment were taking the place of ecclesiastical law and dogma in those areas? These are big questions that we cannot adequately address in this chapter. We ask them nonetheless because they are fundamental to any attempt to evaluate political and other changes taking place in the West between the fourteenth and the eighteenth centuries, changes that grew to influence the whole world.

Government and Politics

From the eleventh and twelfth centuries onward, people in many parts of Europe increasingly thought of themselves in national, local, and occupational terms. Vernacular languages were becoming more important. The seeds of nationalism were finding fertile soil across the continent. Occupational groups such as urban guilds and university professors were becoming more influential through their distinctive arts, crafts, and professions. In rural areas, such as those in England, the contractual relationship between feudal lords and their vassals, and eventually the relation between the lords and their suzerain king, grew into a regular process of "counsel and consent"—the king would consult with the lords on issues that would require their consent in order to secure their financial support. Those who had been mere *subjects* were becoming *active participants* in some of the economic, political, and military decisions that affected them. Eventually, knights of the shire and townsmen, as well as lords and church officials, gained a regular voice in the affairs of government. That process of representation led to the creation of the British Parliament. Moreover, the conviction was growing that the king himself should be subject to the law, although no enforcement mechanism was created to back up the idea. Nonetheless, what emerged in England by the fifteenth century was a peculiar form of mixed sovereignty, which political writer John Fortescue (c. 1394–1474) described as a combination of royal and political rule. The king was considered absolute in some areas and limited in others on which Parliament had a say.[7]

Cities and towns were also growing in both economic importance and political independence. Across Western Europe, particularly in the south, towns had the status of corporate bodies, a status dating back to Roman times. Citizens in towns had the status of free persons as compared with rural peasants or serfs who were bound to their lords. As Martin van Creveld explains, "In this way towns contradicted the very principles of feudal government which were based on the interlocking rights of superiors over inferiors. . . . Just as each nobleman was, to some extent, his own lord and exercised power inferior to, but not essentially different from that of the king, so towns had their own organs of government."[8]

The biggest challenge to the independence of town governments between the eleventh and sixteenth centuries was not the church or the disintegrating empire but the rising monarchies that were consolidating their control over national territories in England, France, Spain, and other regions. Those monarchies would eventually consolidate territorial power and create governing structures that would become the modern state. Two important exceptions to the pattern of monarchical subjugation of towns were the states that emerged in Switzerland and the Low Countries—the Netherlands. In those two locations, it was actually the towns and their surrounding provinces that took the lead through federated cooperation to unify their lands. With those two exceptions, says van Creveld, "the task of bringing the towns under royal control had been very largely achieved by 1660 or so."[9]

Monarchs were gaining territorial control at the expense of both the church and the empire. Moreover, lords and commoners in some countries, like England, were gaining access to, and a voice within, government at the expense of absolute monarchy. Towns and leagues of towns were gaining strength because of their economic, intellectual, and social importance, even as centralizing monarchies gained the upper hand in territory-wide governance. Developments on the ground as well as new thinking about political life were challenging the dominant idea that authority is simply a top-down delegation from God to the pope, an emperor, or a king. There was a renewal of what Ullmann calls the ascending (bottom-up) idea of political authority.[10] Oliver O'Donovan and Joan Lockwood O'Donovan explain that the people as a body or community began to be seen as the source of authority, and thus "the attributes of a legal corporation came to be applied to the people as a whole."[11] The growth of these ideas challenged the principle of papal authority especially in regard to temporal affairs. By the time of influential writers such as Dante Alighieri (1265–1321), Marsilio of Padua (1275/80–1342), and William of Ockham (c. 1285–1347), controversies and conflicts between ecclesiastical and political authorities were sharpening, and momentum was building for bottom-up reforms in government as well as for greater separation between ecclesiastical and political authorities.[12]

Dante, the great poet, wrote an influential treatise on government, arguing that the church's legitimate authority is spiritual, not earthly; on earth, rule should be in the hands of a single monarch or imperial authority. Even for the church to have the peace it needs for the conduct of its ministry, he wrote, it depends on government for such peace; therefore, in all temporal affairs the church should be subject to the earthly monarch. Marsilio went further. The clergy should have no exemption from civil law and its sanctions, he argued. In temporal affairs, those with religious vocations should be entirely subject to government, which is authorized by God through the political community, not through the church. Ockham countered the two-swords doctrine of papal supremacy by saying that governments existed long before the church was founded, so governing authorities could not have received their power by delegation from the church. Papal authority should have no role in the temporal affairs of government. In fact, Ockham rejected the view that the church has any real existence as a universal association. That is just an idea, much like the idea of a universal empire, and neither idea has any existence in reality. "What are fully real are local political and ecclesiastical communities, on a national, princely, or urban level, and the concrete positive laws they enact for themselves."[13]

At the turn from the fourteenth century to the fifteenth, the Roman Catholic Church experienced its Great Schism, when two and then three popes simultaneously contended for the position of highest authority. In 1414, a church council was held in Constance to try to end the schism and to deal with other disputes. The crisis and the council brought to the fore those associated with the conciliar movement. Conciliarists believed that ecclesiastical authority is lodged in the church as a whole body, represented in its councils, not in the pope. The chief spokesmen of the movement were Jean Gerson, chancellor of the University of Paris, Cardinal Pierre d'Ailly, and Cardinal Nicholas of Kues (or Cusa). They argued that the bishop of Rome was but one bishop among others even if he was the lead bishop. Moreover, from early in the church's history, decisions about orthodox doctrine and ecclesiastical governance had been made by church councils, most of which had been called and even presided over by Christian emperors. The church should not be conceived as a papal theocracy to which the rest of the church is merely subject.

For the conciliarists, writes Colish, "the whole church possesses sovereignty and delegates power to the ecclesiastical hierarchy." From this point of view, "the pope is the chief executive officer of a collective body made up of the faithful, who delegate power to popes through general councils. Councils and popes represent the faithful, who legally empower both to act on their behalf."[14] J. N. Figgis explains that the oft-quoted principle of the conciliarists was *salus populi suprema lex*—the well-being of the people is the supreme law, the natural law, which even a pope cannot abrogate. The pope is a member of the church "of which Christ is the head." The church, not the pope, "is the spotless bride of Christ."[15] Even though the conciliarists did not succeed in obtaining the changes they sought in the church's constitution and canon law, they helped to articulate the growing awareness that the church is not, first, a centralized institution of officials but a body with important local communities whose members need to be heard and represented by their bishops. This in turn fed the growth of popular identification with national churches. The movement also bolstered the conviction that the church as an institution should focus on spiritual matters and leave temporal affairs in the hands of those charged with them.

Figgis considers the work of the conciliarists as the last great expression of medieval constitutionalism, and Nicholas of Kues (1401–1464) gave clear expression of this. Kues, a Neoplatonist influenced by Aquinas and others, wanted to see the recovery of Christendom's harmony. That harmony could be achieved, he thought, by clarifying the relation between papal and imperial offices as joint representatives of the people. His argument was no longer the old Roman imperial one but one that appealed to the decisions of past church councils. Power and authority come from God to the church, he wrote in his main work, *The Catholic Concordance*. "The consent and agreement of the Christian community is the origin of Papal authority, which is a delegation from the people, and may be removed at their will." Likewise, the civil power is a delegation from the people and should be "free from ecclesiastical interference, and unhampered by clericalism."[16]

In all of the writings and arguments just mentioned, there was relatively little attention given to the actual practice of government and what is required to govern justly. The chief concern was with the ranking of authority between church and earthly governments, and the later medieval disputes continued as power struggles over which authority should exercise what kind of rule under what kind of constraints.

Martin Luther (1483–1546) and the Anabaptists

The Reformation of the sixteenth century was, in many ways, just a highly visible and historically powerful climax to developments that had been unfolding for several centuries. Thus, when Martin Luther nailed his Ninety-Five Theses to a church door in Wittenberg early in the sixteenth century, his charges and appeal for reform did not come from out of the blue.

Luther had both a positive and a negative aim: positively, to liberate Christians from the bondage of works righteousness and into the refuge of the unmediated grace of God and, negatively, to overcome every obstacle to that freedom of faith and life that the Catholic Church had erected. His positive aim had its roots in a reading of the Scriptures that convinced him salvation comes through faith in Christ by God's grace alone, not by any works or acts of penance a person does. Luther became an evangelist for the gospel of grace, which comes by the working of the Holy Spirit. This produced in him the conviction that every believer in Christ is a priest, thus his doctrine of the priesthood of all believers. And with that conviction came the judgment that every person in every station in society has a religious vocation. The church, in Luther's view, is, first, a spiritual community of the faithful, not a hierarchical institution in which priests from a higher position mediate God's grace to laypeople.

Luther's negative aim was expressed through his attack on the church's hierarchical organization, its burdensome practices imposed on laypeople (such as the buying of indulgences), and many of its theological dogmas. Yet his attack could not have been sustained without the backing of Frederick of Saxony, the German prince who became Luther's patron. Figgis says of Luther that "the whole bent of his mind was in favour of the sanctity of the lay power as against the ecclesiastical. Nor had he any means to his hand but the ruling classes of Germany. He therefore appealed to them and by so doing gave an immense increase to their power."[17]

Luther's positive and negative aims led to a more spiritualized understanding of the church and to a strengthened position for the earthly ruler. Harold J. Berman says that Luther's efforts contributed to the "delegalizing" of the church. "Where Lutheranism succeeded, the church came to be conceived as invisible, apolitical, alegal; and the only sovereignty, the only law (in the political sense), was that of the secular kingdom or principality."[18] Luther, however, did not follow Aquinas and others toward a view of political life as natural. To the contrary, he remained closer to Augustine, believing that God had established government because of sin and that Christians should submit willingly to their rulers as a sign of obedience to God. Luther's thinking led directly to the position adopted in the Peace of Augsburg (1555), namely, that the religion of the ruler should be the religion enforced within that realm (*cuius regio eius religio*). This was, in many respects, a recovery of the earlier Roman imperial position that had been adopted by the Eastern Orthodox Church and referred to as "caesaropapism": the ruler establishes true religion. In Luther's time, however, it was a local prince or national monarch who established the church in his or her domain, a position that came to be called Erastianism (after Thomas Erastus). But depending on who the ruler was, the approved church might be Lutheran, Reformed, or Catholic. Instead of the Roman Catholic pope ordaining rulers and delegating to them the earthly sword of power, the ruler now acted by direct ordination of God to support the one true church that he or she approved and supported.

In certain respects, Luther took the Augustinian antithesis between two cities and turned it into a dichotomy between Christians, who had no need of earthly government, and non-Christians, for whom the state was established. "If all the world were composed of real Christians, that is, true believers," he argued, "there would be no need for nor benefits from prince, king, lord, sword, or law."[19] Those who are not Christians, however, belong to the kingdom of this world, and it is for them that God has provided "a different government beyond the Christian estate and kingdom of God" (587). Earthly government exists "to bring external peace and prevent evil deeds"; the government of Christ aims "to produce righteousness." The two governments are quite distinct, and Luther appeals to Matthew 22:21, about rendering to Caesar what is Caesar's and to God what is God's, as support for his distinction (592). "Christ's government does not extend over all men; rather, Christians are always a minority in the midst of non-Christians" (587).

Luther combined his idea of the antithesis between Christians and non-Christians with Augustine's later argument that earthly kings can serve God by serving the church and aiding its cause. Luther personalized and internalized those Augustinian distinctions as he did the two ethical pathways approved by the church for two groups or classes of people—those with religious vocations, on the one hand, and those with lay vocations, on the other hand. The individual who lives by faith in Christ, Luther argued, lives as a member of a spiritual community that holds no position of power in this world, and lives only by love and without possessiveness or use of force. "Christians among themselves should have no temporal sword or law" (588). As citizens in this world, however, those same individuals act as earthly persons who obey the ruler and, if called to an office of governmental authority or a duty under government, may use force as God has ordained it. Though the sword is something the Christian does not need, it is beneficial and essential for governing non-Christians. "Therefore," Luther argued, "if you see that there is a lack of hangmen, constables, judges, lords, or princes, and you find that you are qualified, you should offer your services and seek the position, that the essential governmental authority may not be despised and become enfeebled or perish" (588).

No longer are there two groups or classes of people following different ethical pathways (the religious and the lay, the theological and the natural); there are now two different vocations within each person. "May a Christian be a secular official and administer the office and work of a ruler or a judge?" Luther asks. "This would mean that the two persons or the two types of office are combined in one man. In addition to being a Christian, he would be a prince or a judge or a lord or a servant or a maid—all of which are termed 'secular' persons because they are part of the secular realm. To this we say: Yes, God himself has ordained and established this secular realm and its distinctions, and by his word he has confirmed and commended them." If you want to know what your duty is as a judge or lord or lady, Luther wrote, you "do not need to ask Christ about your duty. Ask the imperial or the territorial law" (598–99). When a Christian goes to war, for example, "he is not doing this as a Christian, but as a soldier." In sum, according to Luther, the Christian "lives simultaneously as a Christian toward everyone, personally suffering all sorts of things in the world, and as a secular person, maintaining, using, and performing all the functions required by the law of his territory or city, by civil law, and by domestic law" (600–601).

Interestingly, when Luther turned to discuss just warfare and just economic relations (questions of usury and just price, for example), he did what Augustine and Aquinas did, building a great deal of his argument on scriptural revelation (602–8). In that respect, Luther's sharp distinction between the law of Christ and the law of the world, the Christian person and the secular person, is not so apparent. Yet it is clear from the language he uses that Luther associates the word "Christian" with church life, faith in Christ, salvation, and the spiritual life of the kingdom of Christ that embraces only the faithful. Political life, agriculture, and even the family are "secular" and therefore not Christian in the first sense. The antithesis, insofar as it functions, is between the world of salvation, faith, and the church, on the one hand, and the secular world of earthly responsibilities, on the other. Luther thus reflects, in his own more personalized way, the equivocations and paradoxes of Augustine's second view of the heavenly city and the earthly city.

When Luther reacted to the peasant rebellions by supporting the earthly prince's use of strong force to subdue them, he further elevated "secular" government to the chief expression of God's will for this world, including God's will for the earthly life of Christians. Although Luther stepped forth as a prophet of freedom in Christ, the meaning of that freedom was quite personal and spiritual. With regard to life in this world, his practical efforts came close to sanctioning an omnicompetent state, for he asserted "the right of the most religious and gracious King 'to visit, redress, reform, order, correct and amend all manner of heresies, errors, schisms, abuses, offenses, contempts, and enormities whatsoever, which by any manner of spiritual or ecclesiastical powers, authority or jurisdiction can or may lawfully be reformed, ordered [etc., etc.], to the pleasure of Almighty God, the increase of virtue, and the conservation of the peace and unity of this realm.'"[20] What was new with Luther, according to Figgis, was his idea of the "invisibility of the Church," which was "the condition and the counterpart of the visibility of the State."[21]

Sometimes called the Radical Reformers, the Anabaptist communities were diverse in origin and aims.[22] In fact, there is confusion about who the Anabaptists were because of the violent actions taken by Thomas Müntzer (1489–1525) and others in the Peasants' War of 1525. The peasant revolutionaries had been associated with Anabaptist separatists but turned violent in a way that caused pacifist Anabaptists to clarify their convictions and political stance in the articles they drew up in the German-Swiss border town of Schleitheim in 1527. Müntzer believed that history was about to end. Christ would soon bring final judgment to this world and establish the kingdom of heaven. The time had come, he proclaimed, for true believers to rise up and join in God's final acts of judgment and redemption.

Unlike the Müntzerites, however, most Anabaptists—diverse communities of German and Swiss Brethren (led by Conrad Grebel, Felix Manz, Balthasar Hubmaier, and others) and Mennonites (followers of Menno Simons in the Netherlands)—were pacifists who believed that the church, as described in the book of Acts, should be a community bound together in love, faith, and the sharing of all things in common. They were ready to disobey the civil authorities if necessary, but not by taking up arms. Yet Catholics and other Protestants did not always recognize the distinction between the violent and the pacifist opponents of civil authority. The appellation "Anabaptist" (to baptize again) took hold because of their refusal to accept the legitimacy of infant baptism, which had signified not only incorporation into the church but also incorporation into Christendom. The Anabaptists were convinced that only those who made a profession of faith should be baptized into the church community. They stood opposed to the idea of Christendom, a confusing amalgam that blurred the distinction between Christians and non-Christians, between church and world. Anabaptist opposition to Christendom went hand in hand with their refusal to take up arms either in self-defense or in government service. In that sense they were genuine social revolutionaries because they refused to support or participate in the government's use of force. They committed themselves to pacifism and to nonviolent resistance, believing that Christ taught his followers to live that way.

For the most part the Anabaptists accepted Luther's view that the church is a spiritual community, which has no need of the sword to maintain its existence. The Christian faithful should follow the law of love in Christ. In Augustinian terms, the Anabaptists wanted to live as faithful members of the city of God and not cooperate in earthly life with those motivated by self-love. "Concerning separation," they stated in the Schleitheim Articles, "we have agreed that a separation should take place from the evil which the devil has planted in the world. We simply will not have fellowship with evil people, nor associate with them, nor participate with them in their abominations."[23] The abominations the Anabaptists rejected included "all popish and neo-popish works and divine services, assemblies, ecclesiastical processions, wine shops, the ties and obligations of lack of faith, and other things of this kind, which the world indeed regards highly but which are done in direct opposition to the commandments of God."[24] In keeping with this commitment, they refused to accept Luther's idea that the God-ordained earthly prince should be recognized as a legitimate supporter of the church. They rejected Luther's notion that the Christian can also function as a "secular person," operating according to a different ethic for life in this world. They wanted their whole community of faith (a community of lay Christians without an ecclesiastical hierarchy) to live in accord with Jesus's Sermon on the Mount, as some of the religious orders sought to live, refusing to use force or to accept distinctions of wealth, and sharing all things in common.

What did they say about government and political life? The Anabaptists were close to Luther in their conviction that the power of the sword exists outside the government of Christ. But whereas Luther accepted princely government as God's approved strong arm to protect and support the true church and to punish heretics and other evildoers, the Anabaptists believed that God had ordained the government to restrain and punish evil apart from either establishing or persecuting the church. The state should have nothing to do with governing or giving privileges to the church, and Christians should not serve in political office. Thus, as the Schleitheim Articles declare, "the sword is ordained by God outside the perfection of Christ. It punishes and kills evil people and protects and defends the good." Secular authorities are indeed appointed by God to use the sword. "But in the perfection of Christ the ban alone will be used to admonish and expel him who has sinned, without putting the flesh to death, and only by using the admonition and the command to sin no more."[25] Christ "should have been made a king, but he rejected this (John 6:15) and did not view it as ordained by his father. We should do likewise and follow him. In this way we will not walk into the snares of darkness." It is not fitting for a Christian to serve as a magistrate, the Schleitheim confession argues, because "the authorities' governance is according to the flesh, but the Christian's is according to the spirit. Their houses and dwellings remain in the world, but the Christian's is in heaven. Their weapons of conflict and war are carnal with spikes and iron, but Christians are armed with the armor of God."[26]

Most Catholics and Protestants believed that the Anabaptists posed a great threat to society because their opposition to baptism and the use of force would lead to the dismantling of Christendom and of Christian states, cities, and princely domains. What else could hold society together if there were no common faith and morality? Up until the late fifteenth and early sixteenth centuries, the institutional church and its canon law were seen as the glue of Christendom. With the emergence of national and regional governments, the idea of a unified society became more national rather than universal in scope, but the conviction that a state needs a common faith to maintain its unity was not relinquished. Membership in one of the newly emerging states also meant membership in a common faith. The Anabaptists were the radicals who broke with that long tradition and thus threatened the social order. In doing so, they contributed little to Christian thinking about engagement in the art of government, but indirectly they had a major influence on the gradual recognition that communities of citizens and communities of faith are distinct in kind.

John Calvin (1509–1564) and Johannes Althusius (1557–1638)

John Calvin and Johannes Althusius were giants among the leaders of the Reformed (Presbyterian) wing of the Reformation with respect to political and legal life. Part of what distinguished them was their training in law and the practice of government. Neither began as a churchman or a monk, though both studied the Bible and theology. Their systematic approach to political and theological argument owed a great deal to their legal and classical education. That training also helps to explain the centrality of reason and law in their thinking about the Christian life and the church. The difference was the degree to which the Bible became their primary text for understanding all of life. For readers of the Bible, "knowing" is a matter of "hearing and doing"—hearing the Word of the Lord and responding in obedience. Reason would no longer serve as an *independent* guide to truth about the natural world. The Bible became central to Reformed worship and was placed on a pulpit in the front-center of the church, where it was to be read, heard, and expounded.

The Reformation's renewed attention to the Bible also helps to explain Calvin's emphasis on education and the training of leaders to carry forward the reform of church and society. To rethink everything from a biblical point of view demanded systematic and critical study, and that required mastery of the original biblical languages, not only Latin. The academy Calvin started in Geneva (a college and seminary) drew students from across Europe, some of whom went on to serve in or start similar academies elsewhere. Theodore Beza (1519–1605), who became Calvin's closest associate in Geneva and succeeded him in several of his posts, took over as the rector of the Genevan Academy in 1559. Althusius, who earned his doctorate in both civil and canon law in Basel, also studied with Reformed leaders in northern Europe and went on to teach at the Reformed Academy of Herborn in 1586, later becoming its rector. In 1604 he was invited to become the syndic (mayor, or head of the city council) of the town of Emden in East Frisia, a German town that bordered the Dutch provinces and served as a seedbed of Dutch Calvinism.

Calvin, a Frenchman, became a convert to the Protestant cause as a student after reading works by Luther, Philip Melanchthon, Martin Bucer, and other early reformers. He had to flee Paris in 1533 because of his Protestant associations and went to Basel, where he began to rewrite the Christian confession of faith. After 1536 he spent most of the rest of his life in Geneva as pastor, writer, civic adviser, and educational mentor of the Reformed cause. Calvin and others in the so-called Reformed tradition all showed the influence of Luther in their strong opposition to Rome and the Anabaptists as well as in their rethinking of the relation of church and government. They also joined the earlier reformers in confessing that salvation is a gift of God's grace alone, appropriated through faith alone, and that the chief end of life is to glorify God. They believed in the priesthood of all believers and that every Christian, not only those in priestly/pastoral offices, has a vocation from God.

Unlike Luther and the Anabaptists, the Reformed leaders sought a greater balance and cooperation between church and government. They wanted a strong church institution as well as greater accountability of the governing officials to the Bible, the church, and the people. Given their opposition to the Catholic Church, they, like Luther, contributed to the considerable shift of power from the church to civil governments, but they did so with greater insistence on the independence of the church as an institution equal in weight and authority to government. According to John Witte Jr., all wings of the Reformation contributed to the splintering of Christendom: "They broke the superiority of clerical authority and canon law and thereby vested new power in civil authorities and civil law."[27] As was the case with Luther, Calvin and the Calvinists had a great desire for order in society, and they stressed submission to the ruling authorities.

However, in the decades between Calvin and Althusius, there was significant movement beyond the stress on *submission* to government toward *active engagement* on the part of citizens and their representatives in the affairs of state. Reformed Protestants, much more than the Lutherans, worked to oppose government absolutism and tyranny. The basis for that opposition was laid by Calvin himself, who wrote that government officials who betray their office "are reduced to private persons" and "no longer hold an office of authority, but are mere 'brigands' and 'criminals.'" Commenting on Romans 13, Calvin wrote, "Dictatorships and unjust authorities are not governments ordained by God."[28]

Despite their opposition to Rome, however, the Reformed leaders of the sixteenth and early seventeenth centuries did not reject the idea of a unitary Christian society. Although they contributed to the fracturing of Christendom, they advocated what Witte calls a "miniature corpus Christianum" in separate states and cities.[29] From Calvin through to Althusius and beyond, they worked for the coordination of two kinds of authority—church and government—in a single organized society. In the last revised edition of his *Institutes of the Christian Religion* (1559), according to Witte, Calvin even "assigned the church a legal role in the governance of the earthly kingdom, and the state a moral role in the governance of the heavenly kingdom."[30] Calvin, like Ambrose and Augustine, wanted a strong church that is not subordinate to political authority, but also, like the later Augustine, he wanted governments to aid the church in its cause. Political compulsion, he believed, could promote religious liberty: "By teaching each person the rudiments of Christian morality, even if by force, the magistrate enables those who later accept Christ to be 'partially broken in . . . not utterly untutored and uninitiated in Christian discipline' and discipleship. By upholding minimal standards of Christian morality, the magistrate protects the 'public manifestation of religion' and provides a public and peaceful space for Christianity and the church to flourish."[31]

Althusius followed Calvin closely in this respect. He understood the political community to have both an ecclesiastical and a secular administration. That community, which he called the "universal association," is a single body with two major authorities, which are concerned, respectively, with "the welfare of the soul" and "the care of the body." The first is preoccupied with piety toward God, the second with justice toward neighbors. The first is administered by the ecclesiastical institution, the second by the secular institution.[32]

Calvin and his followers continued to work with the dualities of soul and body, sacred and secular, heavenly and earthly, and often associated those distinctions with the responsibilities of church and government. Yet they took as their primary starting point the sovereignty of God over all things and sought harmony between the complementary dualities under God's direct and unified authority. Although the Reformed leaders distinguished between ecclesiastical and governmental administrations, they did not accept the kind of tension or opposition between them that Luther and the Anabaptists did. Calvin writes in his *Institutes* that "whoever knows how to distinguish between body and soul, between this present fleeting life and that future eternal life, will without difficulty know that Christ's spiritual Kingdom and the civil jurisdiction are things completely distinct. . . . Yet this distinction does not lead us to consider the whole nature of government a thing polluted, which has nothing to do with Christian men."[33] Althusius writes, "Sacred and secular duties are distinct, and ought not to be confused. For each demands the whole man."[34] The unifying thread in this argument is more than simply a general reference to the sovereignty of God. Calvin's and Althusius's writings make constant reference to the Ten Commandments as the summary of God's will and of human obligations to God and neighbors.[35]

In the work of the Reformed leaders, "natural" or "secular" institutions were not subordinated to the church institution in a hierarchical fashion, nor did the leaders think of those institutions as being related to God only indirectly through the mediation of the ecclesiastical hierarchy. Those who followed in Calvin's line did not speak of the supernatural as the locus of church authority above and beyond the natural arena of government and other authorities. Rather, the whole of human life, both in this age and in the age to come, is directly dependent on and responsible to God.[36]

The Reformed perspective shows the influence of the conciliar movement as well as that of the Bible, all of which fed into the Calvinist emphasis on God's *covenantal* relation to his people. Calvin, more than Luther and the Anabaptists, goes back to the Old Testament, reading Israel as a model for the church in covenant with God. Luther pits gospel against law; Calvin teaches that the whole of covenant life, including the law, is renewed and fulfilled in Christ. While the covenant idea emphasizes God's sovereignty and the authority of God's appointed rulers, priests, and prophets, it also stresses the equality of all humans before God. Rulers are not gods but representatives of the people and also bound by covenant obligations. In this more integrated view of God's sovereignty over all things, the meaning of the Christian life (and the Christian person) expands beyond the activities of worship and the sacraments administered by the clergy of the institutional church. Although Calvin, like Augustine, still sees government as established because of sin, Althusius begins to treat political life as something given with creation or as an original and essential part of what it means to be human. Althusius, as we will see, developed an elaborate sociology of associations, which are organized as a natural expression of human sociability. Political associations are part of that natural sociability.

Nevertheless, in the work of Calvin and Althusius, the relation of Christ to earthly government remains a significant question. In part, this is because Calvin saw government primarily as an institution to restrain evil and to keep order in this world, and in part, it is because both men saw Christ as the Savior of sinners for eternal life, a work to which government can make no contribution. Moreover, Christ's saving grace is effective only for the elect, whereas the work of government touches everyone. Thus, as Calvin put it, "Christ's spiritual Kingdom and the civil jurisdiction are things completely distinct." The unity of life emphasized by the Calvinists is a unity of all things under God, but that does not necessarily mean that all things are subject to Christ, at least not in this age. In that respect, something of the older Augustinian, medieval, Lutheran, and even Anabaptist ways of thinking seems to be present in Reformed thought. One can draw from some of Calvin's statements the idea that government exists "outside the perfection of Christ." At the end of the *Institutes* he writes, "The Lord, therefore, is the King of Kings, who, when he has opened his sacred mouth, must alone be heard, before all and above all men; next to him we are subject to those men who are in authority over us, but only in him."[37] The reference to the "King of Kings" appears to be a reference to Christ, for the New Testament gives him that title. Yet Calvin does not refer to Christ by name but to "the Lord." Moreover, the entire paragraph from which that sentence is excerpted quotes only Old Testament passages with the one exception of Acts 5:29, where Peter says, "We must obey God rather than men." This suggests that Calvin was probably referring to Yahweh as "the Lord" who is "King of Kings," and in that sense the passage may be seen as anticipating the fulfillment of Christ's spiritual kingdom that is still to come. But Calvin's argument does not clarify how Christ's kingship is related at present to the civil jurisdiction that is "completely distinct" from Christ's kingdom. Many questions remain unanswered. If Christ's kingship is not directly related to human governments in this age, what is the meaning of references to a *Christian* society with both ecclesiastical and civil authorities? More important and fundamental, how is Christ the redeemer related to the Son of God through whom all things were created and in whom all things hold together?

Like Luther, Aquinas, and Augustine before them, Calvin and Calvinists continued to reflect on the just and unjust use of force. Calvin commented on this in his *Institutes*. Christians should not use force against their neighbors, he explains, but the Bible also makes clear that "murderers may not go unpunished," so God the lawgiver "puts into the hand of his ministers a sword to be drawn against all murderers."[38] The same line of reasoning holds for defense against foreign aggression, though Calvin admits that an argument for justifiable warfare "is not to be sought in the writings of the apostles; for their purpose is not to fashion a civil government, but to establish the spiritual Kingdom of Christ."[39] Yet, following Augustine's line of argument, Calvin insists that warfare can be justified if there is a just cause, a response free of a vengeful attitude, an official declaration made only as a last resort, and the goal of peace.[40] Althusius distinguishes justifiable entrance to war (*jus ad bellum*) from the just prosecution of war (*jus in bello*). He writes that engaging in war requires a just cause, an authoritative declaration made only as a last resort, a properly prepared military force, and the goal of restoring justice, order, and peace.[41] While there is nothing particularly new in these affirmations and qualifications, the arguments indicate one of the several lines of continuity from early Christianity through the Middle Ages and on through the Reformation.

Closely related to just-war reasoning was the argument developed by later Reformed leaders who defended resistance to tyrannical rulers. Soon after the infamous St. Bartholomew's Day massacre of 1572 in France, in which hundreds of Protestants were killed by the dominant Catholics, Theodore Beza published a lengthy tract titled "On the Rights of Rulers Over Their Subjects and the Duty of Subjects Toward Their Rulers" (1574).[42] He built on, and reaffirmed, Calvin's teaching that opposition to a tyrant is the responsibility of lower magistrates, not the people. But he went on to argue that a ruler exists for the people, not vice versa, and that God holds everyone, including rulers, accountable to the same natural and divine law of equity and justice. In addition to laying a basis for opposition to tyranny, Beza made a distinction between the kingdom and the ruler who holds a governing office in that kingdom.[43] With many qualifications and cautions, Beza finally throws his weight behind popular, forceful resistance to tyrants on three conditions: (1) only after "the tyranny has become thoroughly obvious," (2) only after "all other remedies have been tried," and (3) only after careful consideration has been given not only to what is permitted but also to what is expedient, lest the cure be worse than the disease.[44]

Five years after Beza's tract was published, an even more forceful defense of tyrannicide was published in Basel, titled *Vindiciae contra tyrannos* (1579).[45] It, too, distinguished the person of the ruler from the office held by the ruler. Is royal status "a possession or an office," the tract asks. "If it is an office, what does it have in common with a property? If it is a possession, then is it not at least a form of possession whereby the people, who conferred it, retain the propriety right?" A king, the document concludes, holds an office of the kingdom and does not possess the kingdom as his own property.[46] In part, what the anti-tyranny arguments do is to rearticulate the idea of a "public thing"—a *res publica*—which is a public-legal political community that cannot belong to the person of the ruler.

Althusius's contribution to political thought and practice that I want to emphasize here is his comprehensive social theory built around what he called *symbiosis* (living together, or social life). Althusius begins his book this way: "Politics is the art of associating (*consociandi*) men for the purpose of establishing, cultivating and conserving social life among them. Whence it is called 'symbiotics.' The subject matter of politics is therefore association . . . in which the symbiotes pledge themselves each to the other, by explicit or tacit agreement, to mutual communication of whatever is useful and necessary for the harmonious exercise of social life."[47] One difficulty with Althusius's use of the words "politics" and "political" is that every human relationship and association, by his definition, would appear to be *political*. The word "political" functions in this context as a synonym (or almost a synonym) for "symbiotic," "associational," and "social." However, in the way he explains human symbiosis, he sometimes narrows the reference of "political" to certain public associations, which he distinguishes from private associations like the family.

Despite his equivocation with the word "politics/political," Althusius approaches questions about social diversity in a distinctive and eclectic way that sometimes sounds like an attempt to synthesize Calvin and Aquinas. Althusius's aim is to categorize different types of association (or symbiosis) according to their distinctive purposes. While it is true that all types of association serve human needs, and that human life in all its dimensions has as its final purpose the worship of God, humans are associated in a wide variety of ways, including familial, ecclesiastical, and governmental ways. The needs of "body and soul, and the seeds of virtue implanted in our souls," says Althusius, have drawn humans together into communication. "These causes have built villages, established cities, founded academic institutions, and united by civil unity and society a diversity of farmers, craftsmen, labourers, builders, soldiers, merchants, learned and unlearned men as so many members of the same body" (18). Humans do all of these things as God's creatures, by their very nature. And Althusius believes it is important to understand each kind of association for what it is (or should be) and also to understand how all of them should relate to one another.

In developing this "science of politics," Althusius is closer to Aquinas than to Augustine, though he is guided generally by an Augustinian, Calvinistic confession of faith. Augustine believed that God created humans to rule over other creatures, not over one another. He saw ruling and subjection to rulers as a consequence of sin. Althusius, by contrast, says that "in every association and type of symbiosis some persons are rulers (heads, overseers, prefects) or superiors, others are subjects or inferiors. For all government is held together by imperium and subjection; in fact, the human race started straightway from the beginning with imperium and subjection. God made Adam master and monarch of his wife, and of all creatures born or descendant from her" (14–15). Not only does Althusius accept "imperium and subjection" as natural, he also reverses the analogy of government to marriage by saying that marriage is like a monarchical form of government.

Despite that authoritarian affirmation, the primary argument Althusius presents is much more communal. The efficient cause of association, he says, "is consent and agreement among the communicating citizens." The forms of symbiosis, which he goes on to distinguish, are of different kinds because, for example, a family is different from a private civil association. The family is a natural association "in which married persons, blood relatives, and in-laws, in response to a natural affection and necessity, agree to a definite communication among themselves." Moreover, marriage as a conjugal bond is distinguished from the family, which is a kinship bond (23–24).

Private civil associations, by contrast, have neither conjugal nor kinship bonds but are organized for purposes such as agriculture, industry, and commerce. In these cases tradesmen, craftsmen, farmers, and so on organize themselves not as family members but in their capacities as "bakers, tailors, builders, merchants, or coiners of money." And the associations they organize are collegiums (or collegia). Those who unite in a collegium are called colleagues or associates. The leader of a collegium is "elected by common consent of the colleagues, and is provided with administrative power over property and functions pertaining to the collegium" (29). The president of a collegium "is superior to the individual colleague but inferior to the united colleagues, or to the collegium over which he presides and whose pleasure he must serve" (29). The head of a collegium, in other words, is but an officeholder in an organization that has an identity of its own; the organization does not belong to its chief officer (or officers).

Althusius continues in this manner to describe an expanding and ascending progression of ever larger types of complex association. The city is the first *public* association he deals with, considering it something less than a universal public association. The city is an association formed not by individuals but by many private associations that come together to create it. In this case, once again, the nature of the symbiosis is communal, an association of associations, not the fruit of a contract among individuals. People who gather in a "crowd, gathering, multitude, assemblage, throng, or people," says Althusius, have no "symbiotic right" (no *jus symbioticum*) (34). The city's members are not the individual members of private associations. The private associations of families and collegiums join together not as spouses, kinsmen, and colleagues but in a way that now makes them citizens of the city in addition to the identity they have in other associations. "Thus passing from the private symbiotic relationship, they unite in the one body of a community" (35).

Highly important here is Althusius's insight that the jurisdiction of the city does not eliminate or absorb into itself the families and private civil associations that establish it. The nonpublic associations do not lose their identities and become nothing more than subordinate parts of the city. To the contrary, people will continue to be spouses, kinfolk, and colleagues in their families and private associations. But now in the city they will enter into an additional role and purpose. In fact, one of the requirements of a just city is that it should preserve and enhance the quality of private and family associations that form it.

Althusius next goes on to detail the nature and governance of the *province* and after that the *universal association*, which we would call a state, or republic, or political community. The province and the universal association require "holy" as well as "civil" administrations. A province "contains within its territory many villages, towns, outposts, and cities united under the communion and administration of one right (*jus*). It is also called a region, district, diocese, or community" (46). The "right" of those who belong to the provincial community is to share in its privileges and benefits. The "holy function" of a province is expressed in the cultivation of a "pious life," which requires "a correct understanding of God and sincere worship of him." The civil function of a province is to maintain "a just life," which includes "everything that pertains to the exercise of social life" (46–47). Thus, the province is to exhibit both piety and justice in its complex diversity.

Just as the city and province are composed of organizations and institutions on which the former depend, so the universal or major public association is composed of "many cities and provinces," which "obligate themselves to hold, organize, use, and defend, through their common energies and expenditures, the right of the realm (*jus regni*) in mutual communication of things and services" (61). The universal association, like other associations, has its identity from within itself, constituting a type of community for which its offices of government are fit. "For ownership of the realm belongs to the people, and administration of it to the king," says Althusius. "This right of the realm, or right of sovereignty, does not belong to individual members, but to all members joined together and to the entire associated body of the realm" (65).

Given all the elements of constitutionalism and federalism in Althusius's writings, we might wonder why he was not more influential across Europe, England, Scotland, and North America in the seventeenth and eighteenth centuries. The simple answer is that while he was quite influential in his time, his line of argument and example of engagement did not win the day. The reason is at least twofold. First, the consolidation of political power in national governments contributed to the religious wars that were not amenable to the kind of argument Althusius was offering. The Peace of Augsburg that allowed the religion of the ruler to become the religion of the realm meant that battles such as those in France and England between Catholics and Protestants were largely all-or-nothing battles for monarchical control. Questions about the relative autonomy of lower levels of political organization, families, and collegial organizations were not of primary concern. In the second place, many of those who were making arguments about the rights of individuals, freedom of association, republicanism, and even democracy were looking beyond the church, religion, and the Ten Commandments to find a more common and "secular" basis for resolving political conflicts and organizing societies. Althusius was among those still thinking of national societies as mini-Christendoms, communities of faith under ecclesiastical administration as well as communities of civic membership in the right of the realm.

In sum, the Reformed Protestants worked to articulate a more integrated view of society under the sovereignty of God, showing greater appreciation for the diversity of human callings and institutional responsibilities. They did this by giving renewed attention to the Hebrew Bible—the Old Testament—and to a critical assessment of both the church's canon law and civil legal systems. This is especially evident in Althusius's attempt to articulate a comprehensive view of the variety of types of human symbiosis. However, the Calvinists, from Calvin on through to the New England Puritans, remained constricted by the idea that the exercise of government's responsibility before God requires partnership with an established church that ministers to the whole society. Despite their many contributions to society and the reforms they promoted, the Calvinists offered no political answer to the religious wars.

Religious wars were not new with the Reformation, of course. They had been conducted in the Roman imperial world after Christianity took hold. They occurred for centuries between Christian and Muslim forces. They were mounted by Christian kings and authorized by the church's popes in the form of crusades to regain control of the Holy Land. And before the Reformation, there had been wars between competing Christian kings and other forces for control of the papacy. The difference now was that the Catholic Church was losing its religious monopoly in Western Europe, and the old order of Christendom was giving way to a new "order" of sovereign states, each with its own approved church.

7

from the Reformation to contemporary engagement

With this chapter we complete our historical overview and set the stage for contemporary engagement. In the preceding chapters we saw how significant Augustine's work has been in shaping almost all streams of Christian thought and behavior down to the present day. We noted the great influence of the Roman imperial system on the hierarchical governing patterns supported by both the Eastern and the Western branches of the church as they worked to build Christian societies on earth. We emphasized the importance for the West of the codification of Roman law by Emperor Justinian (527–565) and the development of the Catholic Church's canon law beginning in the eleventh century. We highlighted the remarkable turn by Thomas Aquinas, under Aristotle's influence, to an understanding of political life as a natural expression of human sociability rather than as something unnatural and established only because of sin. And we've tracked the emergence and persistence of a number of dualities that have shaped the ways Christians continue to understand and live out their lives: earthly city/city of God; body/soul; temporal/eternal; earthly sword/spiritual sword; natural/supernatural; nature/grace; secular government/sacred church; natural virtues/theological virtues; one ethical path for laypeople/another ethical path for the religious; law/faith; outside the perfection of Christ/inside the perfection of Christ.

In the preceding chapters we noted some of the causes and consequences of the splintering of Western Christendom, including political, economic, and scientific developments in late medieval society, the Protestant Reformation, and the formation of the modern state. While acknowledging the Reformation's considerable historical impact, we saw that it did not explode suddenly from out of the blue but was a powerful culmination of many trends that had been unfolding for several centuries. The most important changes arising from the Reformation included (1) further development of the conciliar idea of the church as a communal body, leading to the ideas of the priesthood of all believers and Christian vocations of laypeople; (2) the Anabaptist rejection of Christendom as the model of a Christian society; (3) the Calvinist use of God's covenant with Israel as a partial model for a Christian society; and (4) Johannes Althusius's construction of a symbiotic theory of a differentiated society and of federally organized political communities in which the offices of government are made dependent on the associations (communal bodies) they serve, thus helping to guard against arbitrary and tyrannical government.

The World beyond the West

Of course, there was more going on in the world than the developments in Europe, which have occupied our attention. (1) The eastern part of Europe on across to western Asia is where the Eastern Orthodox Church had its great influence. We cannot understand the political impact of Christianity without taking note of developments there. (2) Islam's most powerful and enduring empire—that of the Ottoman Turks—supplanted the Abbasid Caliphate early in the thirteenth century, captured Constantinople (the seat of the Roman Empire) in 1453, and reached its height around the time Calvin was preaching and writing in Geneva. (3) Imperial China, almost unknown in the West apart from its traded goods, was governed by the Ming dynasty from 1368 to 1644, when the foreign Manchus (Ch'ing) supplanted the Ming. The Manchu takeover came at the cost of as many as eighty million lives, yet the period that followed is considered one of China's most peaceful and prosperous. A brief word is in order about each of these.[1]

1. After Rome was sacked in the fourth and early fifth centuries, the empire's headquarters were moved to Constantinople—Constantine's city. Following the rule of Emperor Justinian, whose monumental achievement was to initiate the codification of Roman law, not much changed in the structure of imperial government for seven centuries, according to historian S. E. Finer. However, during those centuries the Eastern Roman Empire—which came to be called the Byzantine Empire—was engaged in constant warfare with Muslim forces and with "successive waves of barbarous Bulgars, Magyars, Serbs, Russians, Petchenegs, and the like in the north."[2] In 1071 the Turks defeated the Byzantine emperor's forces at Manzikert, which is "the decisive date in the decline of the empire." In 1204 Western crusading forces on their way to liberate the Holy Land took a detour to Constantinople, descending on their Eastern Christian brothers "in one of the worst orgies of destruction, rape, and looting in history."[3] That marked the end of an era in the East with respect to both church and empire,

though the Orthodox Church has remained influential to this day particularly in Greece, Russia, other parts of Eastern Europe, and the Middle East.

The greatest mission outreach of the Orthodox Church was to Kievan Rus in the tenth century. From the eleventh century until 1448, the metropolitan of the Russian Orthodox Church resided in Kiev. The church was protected, and even won relief from taxation, under the Mongols who invaded and took control of Kievan Rus in the early thirteenth century. In 1299 the church moved its patriarchal center from Kiev to Moscow. The rulers of the Grand Duchy of Muscovy (Moscow) led allies in defeating the Mongols in 1380, and the Muscovite kingdom grew to become the major power in what is now Russia. The foundations of the Russian national state were laid by Tsar Ivan III (1462–1505). In 1448 the Russian bishops elected their own patriarch without reference to Constantinople, and from that time forward the Russian Orthodox Church has chosen its own patriarch and is the largest of all Orthodox Churches. It was in the fifteenth century that the tsar and the church began to identify Moscow as the "third Rome," following the demise of Rome and Constantinople as the first two centers of the Christian Roman Empire.

The Byzantine Empire eventually collapsed, says Finer, not because of economic and military overextension but because of its political inflexibility and internal battles over control of the imperial throne.[4] The Orthodox Church bore some responsibility for that because it was the leading nongovernmental institution with enough independence, respect, and wealth to shape the culture and to give guidance to (or challenge) the emperor and lower officials. Yet, in Finer's view, the church acted mostly to maintain tradition, thereby suppressing dissent and critical thought. Church leaders believed that what had been handed down to them should be maintained with little if any change. That helps to explain the relative "barrenness of Byzantine intellectual achievement at the very time when the Roman Church was engendering Scholasticism" and Islam was fostering poetry, science, and mathematics.[5] As noted earlier, the Roman Catholic and Orthodox Churches separated entirely in 1054, and that schism marked the end of any significant influence between them until the twentieth century.

To some degree the caesaropapist Roman imperium did continue in Muscovite Russia after Constantinople fell to Islam in 1453. Although Russia was more Asian than Western after the Mongols conquered it, the tsars who subsequently ruled it were much influenced by Byzantine caesaropapist theology. Finer contends that "the Mongol legacy to the Russian princes consisted of techniques for carrying on political activities," but "Byzantium provided the grand ideology and model of a sacred absolutism over a single, united, and vast territory."[6] In the Christian-political confluence that began in Rus a thousand years ago and has continued to the present day, nothing new has come to the fore in regard to Christian political thought and practice. There have been a number of outstanding novelists, anti-imperial revolutionaries, and political critics, such as Leo Tolstoy and Alexander Solzhenitsyn, but little of a Christian-inspired, reforming approach to government and citizenship has emerged.

Beginning under Ivan IV (the Terrible), who declared himself tsar of all the Russians in 1547, and continuing through to Peter the Great (1682–1725), and to the importation of Western Enlightenment philosophy under Catherine the Great (1762–1796), changes in economic, educational, cultural, and diplomatic life did little to change the authoritarian political culture. Finer says that in all of his study of the history of governments, Russia under Ivan the Terrible was "the extremist example of arbitrary and capricious despotism to be found anywhere," and the absolutism of Peter the Great brought together "into a coherent and far more efficacious system all the strands of unfreedom which existed in the sixteenth century. . . . It was a system of universal bondage, unrestrained by any inherent limitations based on sacred or natural law."[7]

2. The Ottoman Empire, the second great Islamic empire, emerged about a century after the end of the Arab Abbasid Caliphate, which was extinguished by Mongols who razed Baghdad and massacred its inhabitants in 1258. Serving under the Turkish ruler (the sultan), a hierarchy of *ulema* (authorities in Islamic law and worship) functioned as local governors who administered both the *sheriat* (Turkish for *sharia*, Islamic law) as well as the rulings of the sultan who exercised his own prerogative power. Sharia "confined itself in practice to its traditional concerns with family, religious, and civil matters," whereas the sultan's law codes, known as the *kanunname*, "applied throughout the empire. Codification on this scale was without precedent in Muslim states, and indeed was unknown in the Europe of that time."[8]

It is important to point out, however, that the Ottoman Empire "lived by war and off war," as Finer puts it. In the period between 1400 and 1789, the Ottoman Empire was "in every case one of the four most warlike states." It was at war 70 percent of that time.[9] On the one hand, the imperial government "was conspicuously shallow in its penetration of everyday life. . . . Its role was to make war, acquire plunder, slaves, and revenues, raise taxes, and keep order. It was, in short, predator, revenue-pump, and policeman." On the other hand, the caretakers of Muslim ritual and sharia oversaw what we would call family and social services, taking "meticulous care of the domestic life of two-thirds of the empire's populations" while recognizing a degree of independence for artisans and merchants and various corporations of teachers, domestic servants, water-carriers, and more. According to Finer, "This was the subjects' field of 'citizenship,' little-interfered-with by governors."[10] And within the Ottoman Empire, "Orthodox Christians, the Jews, and the Armenians respectively composed three autonomous, self-governing communities called millets, headed by their own religious leader who [was] responsible for fiscal and public-order matters."[11]

Challenged by Western imperial ventures into Africa, the Middle East, and southern Asia from the sixteenth through the nineteenth centuries, and decaying from within due to financial crises and corruption that advanced from the sixteenth to the seventeenth centuries, the Ottomans barely held on to remnants of their empire until its final undoing in World War I. Although the official end of the Ottoman Empire was of more symbolic than substantive significance, it did signal to many Muslims, particularly in the Middle East, the victory of Western imperialism that, from their point of view, should never have succeeded. The end of the Ottoman Empire is one of the oft-mentioned points of reference for today's radical Islamists and a spur to Muslim activists and writers from the Mediterranean and Africa on across to Central Asia, India, Pakistan, Indonesia, and the Philippines.

3. When the Manchus (Ch'ing dynasty) took control of China in the 1600s, they continued the governing system of the Ming dynasty (1368–1644) and ruled until their own demise in 1911. In effect, according to Finer, "the same form of government prevailed in China for the entire 1368–1911 period, 543 years." "If the criterion of an effective governmental system is the ability to maintain the state's sovereignty, territorial integrity, and domestic tranquility," says Finer, "then the Ming must be reckoned one of the most effective in history."[12] When the alien Manchus took control of China in the seventeenth century, they were feared and held in suspicion by those loyal to the Ming, including the Confucian scholars who were the backbone of the imperial court and administration. However, after the Ch'ing emperor K'ang-hsi, a strong Confucian, began to honor and reward the court intellectuals and to promote elite education and training, he was able to win Ming support for the projects he initiated to celebrate Chinese culture.[13]

Part of the reason the Ch'ing dynasty was successful, according to Finer, is that the central government was relatively marginal to the life of the common people; it provided peace and stability without overtaxing them. China was happier under the Ch'ing than "under any previous dynasty, and as happy, if not happier, than any other state in the entire world."[14] The population expanded and enjoyed considerable prosperity in part because of the planting of New World crops and the use of new agricultural techniques. While the imperial government looked after dikes and drainage of the great rivers, local gentry "funded and organized the irrigation of the farmlands. It was they, too, who supplied funds for temples, poor-houses, hospitals, and schools." The entire social order was built on a strong Confucian social and ethical base. By means of schooling and the strong influence of the Confucian-educated gentry, "the peasantry internalized the Confucian patterns."[15] Confucianism was the moral glue of the society. Families and educators trained children for balance and harmony in life based on respect between father and son, older and younger brothers, husband and wife, and ruler and people. In fact, the government's authority depended on the people's regard for the ruler's moral example.

At the root of China's imperial system was the conviction that the emperor ruled as the Son of Heaven, endowed with the Mandate of Heaven, and his rule was supposed to reflect the harmony of heaven itself. When instability and signs of crisis arose, as they did with greater frequency in the nineteenth century, the ruler's authority grew weak and was undermined. "As the nineteenth century wore on," says Finer, Ch'ing governance "became more and more obsolete and the population pauperized by the pressure of limited land resources," which led to a growing number of local rebellions and attempts to overthrow the regime.[16] During the nineteenth and early twentieth centuries, Western commercial and missionary interests pushed their way into the country. The Japanese invasion of China further humiliated the rulers and contributed to a deepening crisis of confidence in most parts of China. The period of warlord conflicts came to an end only with the near triumph of Chiang Kai-shek's nationalists in the 1920s, who were soon overtaken by Mao Zedong's communists in 1949.

The Russian, Ottoman, and Ch'ing empires all reached their end in the first decades of the twentieth century. The consequences of those collapses are still with us, as are the consequences of European imperialism and Western attempts between World War I and the end of World War II to reorder the world on the basis of the Western state system during the very decades when the European colonial empires were collapsing. The twentieth century was the bloodiest and most destabilizing century in history and the one that brought almost everyone to an awareness that we live in one world. It was the century of rising nationalisms, including German Nazism; the century of the communist revolutions in Russia and China that led to the construction and collapse of the Soviet Union and to a new kind of socialist-capitalist system in China; and the century of Islamist revolts against Western imperialism.

New Religious and Political Dynamics in the West

In our historical survey of the West, we began by noting the influence of Christianity in the Greco-Roman world, focusing primarily on the church's relation to earthly governments. At various junctures we pointed to ways in which Christianity accommodated itself to Greco-Roman ways of life, including the Roman imperial system and Greek and Roman ideas of human nature. We now need to look briefly at the new humanism that emerged with the Renaissance and came to mature expression in the period referred to as the Enlightenment in the eighteenth and early nineteenth centuries.

The dynamism of the new humanism in the West was more than just philosophical or political in character and can be understood only against the backdrop of collapsing Christendom. If the Protestant Reformers sought to recover biblical Christianity from its late medieval corruptions, Renaissance scholars and artists wanted to recover the best of Greece and Rome that Christendom had obscured or discarded. Yet just as the Reformation's leaders could not entirely escape the cultural context of medieval Christendom, neither could the Renaissance proponents return to the classical world as it was. The humanistic spirit that came to expression in Renaissance studies and art and that influenced the Reformation was not the humanism of Plato or Aristotle or the poets and sculptors of Greece and Rome. The new humanism was a creative amalgam, something we might describe as a secularized revision of the medieval Christian-classical synthesis, something that was neither classical, nor Christian, nor medieval.

The humanism of which we are speaking reached spiritual maturity with the Enlightenment and the Romantic reaction to it. What was emerging was more than a new approach to philosophical thought, more than a forceful rejection of authoritarian government and aristocratic privilege, more than an unprecedented push for scientific and technological control of nature, and more than creative ventures in the arts and literature. The Enlightenment gave expression to a culture-wide, religiously deep way of life oriented toward reshaping the world, liberating human beings from every kind of bondage, in order to achieve what no philosophy or religion of the past had done. In this book we can't begin to do justice to the Enlightenment's captivating vision and sociocultural power. The spirit of Enlightenment and Romantic-era humanism is still very much at work today and not only in the West; and it is as strong, if not stronger, a force in the world now as either Christianity or Islam.

Our primary concern is with political life, which calls for mention of influential figures such as Niccolo Machiavelli (1469–1527). Many consider Machiavelli to be the first modern humanist political thinker because his book *The Prince* (in the genre of mirrors for princes) focuses entirely on what a ruler needs to do to maintain his position and to keep his city, republic, or kingdom in existence. No longer relevant for Machiavelli were classical and Christians concerns about the obligations of a ruler to do justice or to meet the demands of God or the natural law. The goal was mastery of life in this world rather than satisfying God or the pope in order to avoid judgment after death.

Englishman Thomas Hobbes (1588–1679) is the first modern humanist to theorize about politics using the new science of physics as his guide, a science that seemed to promise the eventual mastery of nature. Assuming that everything can be explained in terms of matter in motion, he imagined that the independent particles of political life are individual human bodies that want to keep themselves in motion (that is, stay alive). To do that, individuals make a contractual agreement to create a government strong enough to protect them from death at the hands of others. Whereas Thomas Aquinas would have asked, "What is the supreme human good (the *summum bonum*) toward which political life should be oriented?" Hobbes asked, "What is the ultimate human evil (the *summum malum*) that individuals want to avoid?"[17] Hobbes's answer was that humans want to avoid anarchy and death—the war of all against all as expressed in the wars of religion. That is why supposedly autonomous individuals contract to form a government (the Leviathan) that can rule with an iron fist in order to protect each person from threats to his or her life, including threats from religious fanatics.

The significance of figures such as Machiavelli and Hobbes is that they ex-pressed a new counter-Christian spirit that grew from the crises of Christendom and helped to shape the modern world. Thinkers such as the Spanish Dominican Francisco de Vitoria (1483–1546), Machiavelli's contemporary, and Calvinist Johannes Althusius (1557–1638), a younger contemporary of Hobbes, were more insightful and sophisticated in dealing with political reality, but they were too much part of the Christendom that was perishing.

In a sense broader than can be captured in political discourse alone, the words "enlightenment" and "humanism," when joined, have carried a promise parallel to the promises of gnosticism and Christianity, promises to answer life's deepest questions and provide a way to redemption and fulfillment. But whereas gnosticism promised a kind of mystical-intellectual insight that would lift one's soul out of the prison of this material world, and whereas Christianity promises forgiveness of sin and the renewal of life through Jesus Christ in this age and the age to come, Enlightenment humanism promises freedom and happiness *within* this world by human effort alone. The spiritual and intellec-tual excitement engendered by the Enlightenment persuaded many that they no longer needed to wait for salvation beyond this world. All promises of the soul's escape from the body and of heavenly transport to the city of God were judged to be foolish illusions that could be, and must be, dispelled by true knowledge—solid, measurable, empirical, scientific knowledge—of this world. Humans should work to master nature and themselves by rational means. Those who want freedom and control over their own lives should forge ahead with the radical reform of this world rather than hold on to pious talk of a better world to come. True freedom, then, requires the overthrow of every institu-tion (political, economic, or ecclesiastical) that stands in the way of that goal of knowledge and freedom.

This is a different idea of freedom and progress than those held by Catholic and Protestant Christians, but the former cannot be explained without the latter. The new idea of freedom transforms the biblical understanding of *creation* (God is the creator of all things, including humans) into the idea of self-creation. It turns the Christian teaching about *sin* into a doctrine of ignorance. And it replaces the *Christ who saves sinners by divine grace* with human self-salvation through knowledge that overcomes ignorance and liberates humans from subservience to all priestly, political, and economic authorities. There is in the new human-ism a forward-driving quest for truth and mastery of the world. This driving ambition is foreign to classical cultures and arises as an attempt to displace the medieval Christian story.

One of the key elements of the new humanism, inexplicable apart from Christianity, is the quest to transform this world by bringing at least some of heaven down to earth. Eric Voegelin describes it as a reverse form of gnosti-cism: instead of seeking knowledge that will release the soul from the ma-terial body of this world, the modern gnostic seeks the kind of knowledge that can transform this material world into the kind of world autonomous individuals want it to be.[18] Voegelin argues that this desire to "immanentize the eschaton" began with a medieval monk, Joachim of Flora (d. 1202), who believed that a third and final age of history—the age of the Spirit (following the ages of the Father and the Son)—was about to begin in his time, in this world. In some Christian circles, in other words, new hopes of purifying this world replaced (or were added to) the older expectation of life after death in a heavenly kingdom of the resurrected. Later, when that change of focus from heaven to earth became sufficiently dissociated from the church and Christian faith, it began to fuel new hopes about what humans could achieve on their own in this world.

In many respects John Locke (1632–1704) was the perfect transition figure between state-established Christianity and the modern "secular" state. On the one hand, he wrote as a Christian with theological conviction, wanting to arrive at a broad, nonsectarian understanding of Christianity that could be justified rationally. Government would then be able to establish a religion that could unify religiously divided England. On the other hand, Locke's move toward evidential rationality as the authority by which even Christianity could be justified went hand in hand with his development of a theory of the state that grounded political authority in a social contract drawn up by free and rational individuals. With Hobbes, Locke believed that politics and government are not natural to humans, but for that reason Locke believed government should be contractually limited to the task of protecting life and property and not allowed to possess absolute power. For the reasonable Locke, in contrast to Hobbes, freedom was a greater motivator than fear of death.[19]

Part of the English common-law tradition that Hobbes and Locke took for granted was a body of civil rights and freedoms. Some of those rights and freedoms had roots in the long historical development of private civil law going back to the Romans. The freedom of individuals to conduct their lives and to contract with one another privately on a variety of social and economic matters was made possible, however, within the framework of a public-legal order that established the limited jurisdiction of government. In essence, what Hobbes and Locke did was to imagine that autonomous individuals with their inherent rights and freedoms preexist society and create both society and government by means of something like a private contract. To put it perhaps oversimply, the contract theorists turned things upside down. Instead of seeing that a political community is necessary for (and goes hand in hand with) the recognition and protection of civil rights and freedoms, they imagined that individuals with inherent rights created political society and sustained it by their continuing contractual commitment to the protection of their freedoms. This view of individual freedom lies at the heart of the Western liberal tradition (which encompasses both liberals and conservatives in the United States) and the idea of limited government.

The American Experiment

The Declaration of Independence, which articulated the rationale for the American Revolution, made a great deal of the British monarch's violation of the colonists' civil rights ("the rights of Englishmen"). The Bill of Rights appended to the federal Constitution of 1787 is one of the consequences of the new nation's ideal of individual liberty and its fear of tyrannical government. A constitutionally limited government that guarantees the protection of individual freedoms is essential to liberal idealism and is evidence of the considerable influence of John Locke on the American founding. Yet we must remember that the colonists who joined in revolt against England were motivated by more than a desire to construct a liberal, constitutional government. What united them across ecclesiastical, economic, and professional lines was also a sense of common historical purpose that had been building over many decades. When the Declaration of Independence was finally penned, it appealed to the nations of the world to recognize the United States of America as a rightful member of the club. And America's vision of itself in that club was that of the exceptional nation among all nations, God's new Israel, a "new order for the ages." That sense of identity and mission brought together the ideals of both individual and national freedom. Government was to be a means to the end of freedom, and this is where the political significance of "rights" comes in.

The starting point for the American founders was life, liberty, and property for free individuals (white men at that time) represented in a free nation. Their appeal to God was to the one who had implanted those rights in individuals. And it was on the basis of those rights that they had chosen to establish a government for the purpose of protecting their rights and freedoms. In that respect, government owed nothing directly to God and could claim no authority over the people that the people did not give it. Government was accountable to its sovereign creator—the people—not to God. What emerged as the great American experiment, therefore, was a new nation idealized as a newly liberated Israel, which would be a light of freedom to the world of nations. Government played a secondary role in all of this, a role grudgingly recognized as necessary because of evils that threaten freedom.

What is perhaps most significant about the founding of the United States of America is the number of lines of historical influence that fed into it.

1. One line of influence was the Christian-imperial drive of the European nations—Dutch, British, Spanish, Portuguese, and French—that colonized the continent. The American colonies (including those in Latin America) were extensions of the rising European nation-states that were extending their reach to (a) find gold and develop agriculture and trade to add to the wealth of the imperial center; (b) keep up with or gain advantage over other nations that were doing the same; (c) explore the world for scientific and technological reasons, inspired by new confidence in scientific rationality and technological

power; and (d) take Christianity (either Catholic or Protestant) to the uncivilized heathen. All of these motives reflected a Western European view of the world that was internally fraught with the competing ambitions of Catholics, Protestants, and Enlightenment humanists (the CPE world). Native Americans and slaves (primarily Africans) were not part of the CPE world and thus were variously treated as (a) objects of God's loving outreach through Western Christian missions to save the souls of uncivilized sinners, (b) the heathen whom God judged to deserve enslavement by the nations chosen to civilize the world, and (c) disposable enemies whenever they threatened the progress of Western civilization.[20]

Throughout the history of the West's imperialistic outreach, there existed a tension, as old as Augustine, between the *justification* and the *condemnation* of the use of force. For some of the missionaries and church authorities (as well as a few among the political and economic elite), persuasion alone could be justified in efforts to convert and civilize the heathen. For other missionaries and church officials, however, force could be justified when seeking to convert the heathen or to compel them (through enslavement and other means) to become part of the civilizing process. The tension between these two views expressed itself, for example, in the behavior of North American colonists who either objected to or approved of taking Native American lands and using aggressive tactics to deal with them. The tension came through in the different attitudes toward government expressed by Quaker and Anabaptist groups in Pennsylvania and Delaware, on the one hand, and by some of the more aggressive frontiersmen and Westward-Ho nation builders, on the other.

2. A second line of influence was that of Christendom and the mini-Christendom ideal of a unified Christian society. This was as much the practice in early America as it was in Europe. Most of the North American colonies were organized under privileged or established Protestant churches, while in Spanish and Portuguese colonies the Catholic Church's preeminence was evident. With the US Constitution's mandate that the federal Congress has no right to establish a religion, a significant step was taken in the direction of disconnecting membership in the political community from membership in an ecclesiastical institution. However, part of what encouraged and made possible the fairly rapid separation of churches from state and federal governments was the popular conviction that the nation as a whole was "under God"—a God-chosen, God-blessed nation (white Anglo-Saxon Protestant [WASP] in character). In other words, the *privatization* of churches (with their attention to worship, evangelism, and theology, oriented toward eternal life) went hand in hand with the growth of a *national civil-religious faith* grounded in God's covenant with America, as we saw in the introduction. The fact that this secularized public faith became even more "secular" as time went on reflected the growth of Enlightenment humanism's influence in the lives of most Americans, including those who continued to hold tightly to a Christian (or other) faith in private life.[21]

3. A third stream of influence was that of the monastic and other purifying movements that emerged during the development and collapse of Christendom. The Puritans represented that influence, which made a strong impression on the new nation. America would stand at a purified distance from Rome and papal governance and from corrupt and authoritarian monarchies. Justifications of the American Revolution also sounded themes from the Huguenot's defense of tyrannicide. The ideal of a purified mini-Christendom, renewed by the Reformation into the ideal of a new covenant community, became a vision of America as God's new Israel. The fact that this is an important spiritual source of the American experiment has come to expression throughout American history in the *jeremiad*, a particular type of Puritan sermon, and now more often a journalistic essay, that bewails the failure of America to live up to its calling with the likely consequence that God's judgment (or some economic or military catastrophe) will fall upon it.[22]

4. A fourth stream was the set of constitutional obligations binding rulers and the ruled—practices that had been developing since at least the time of Magna Carta (1215). These practices eventually produced constitutionally articulated rights and freedoms as well as the division between executive and legislative branches of government with representative assemblies of legislators. This influence came not only from England but also from the conciliar movement and from later Enlightenment thinking. This stream fed into the federalist practices developed by the Dutch and the Swiss as well as by the Americans, all of them influenced by the Calvinist wing of the Reformation.

These different streams of influence have all shaped the ideas and motives of American Christian political engagement. For example, there continues to be a strong American tradition of Christian antipathy to political life. Since government was given because of sin to keep order in this world, and since Christians have a higher calling of service in Christ's kingdom, Christians should not waste time (or not much time) with political life but should concentrate on evangelism and other means of drawing sinners to faith in Christ. Fed by one stream of Augustine's thinking, those who hold this conviction believe that if Christians must cooperate with non-Christians in this world to obtain the necessities of life, they should recognize that they are doing so with a different motivation than the one that calls them to live in the love of God oriented to the city of God.

This line of thought and practice may come through in a Lutheran way that accepts the legitimacy and even the importance of government's role in this world and does not discourage Christians from serving in government. But such service is secular, not Christian; it is worldly, not spiritual; it is of law, not of faith. The view comports well with the conviction that government is a temporary means for keeping order in this world, not an agency of Christ's kingdom. Most Anabaptists would insist on a different answer to the seeming paradox of God's ruling the world through government and ruling the church through Christ. Christians should seek to live entirely within "the perfection of

Christ" and not participate in the offices of government. Americans who stand in one of these two traditions are the least likely to identify enthusiastically with the American civil-religious cause.

American Christians most likely to be comfortable with the American political system and one of the two versions of its civil religion are those in the Reformed tradition, including both Presbyterians and Baptists with Calvinistic leanings in theology. They are inclined toward either the WASP version of the Puritan-rooted exodus story or the rights-and-equality version of the exodus story with roots in the antislavery, civil rights movement. Of course, many in the Reformed tradition are critical of Americanism to the degree that it exhibits pride, idolatry, and unjust practices. But they have not, for the most part, developed a distinctively Christian view of life in the political community that takes critical distance from the civil-religious nationalisms that have characterized many states influenced by the Reformed tradition. In addition, many who distinguish church and state in the Calvinist fashion continue to live with unanswered questions about the connection between Christ's kingship and earthly politics. There is a tendency, influenced by Reinhold Niebuhr in the middle of the twentieth century, to view political life and government's obligation to enforce justice as something at a lower level than the direct expression of Christian love toward neighbors. This may sound more Lutheran than Calvinist, but it is an attitude supported by many in the Reformed tradition who distinguish between God's common grace toward everyone in this world and God's particular, saving grace extended only to the elect in Christ. From that point of view, the story and trajectory of God's saving grace in Christ, which moves toward eternal life for the elect, goes hand in hand with the story of God's providential guidance of history, which has positioned America as the beacon of hope for freedom, equality, democracy, and prosperity. And with Protestant efforts in the nineteenth and twentieth centuries to overcome the divide between these two stories, the Social Gospel movement gained great influence in its efforts to "immanentize the eschaton."

Baptists typically hold a very local, congregational, and democratic view of the visible church. The visible church is manifest in congregations of professing and baptized Christians, each of whom has a saving relation to Christ independent of the mediation of ecclesiastical authorities. In the American context, the separation of church and state is easily connected to the ideal of the individual's religious freedom from the state. There is a high degree of political libertarianism among Baptists, who tend to be suspicious of both big government and hierarchies of ecclesiastical authority. At the same time, however, this attitude typically coheres with a strong adulation of the American nation as God's light of freedom to the world. The WASP version of the American civil religion comports quite well, then, with a more individualistic understanding of the Christian faith, oriented toward eternal salvation. The story of saving faith in Christ functions at the spiritual level; and the story of God's promotion of individual freedom, democracy, and prosperity through America's example and leadership functions at the earthly or secular level.

Those Americans who are strongly motivated by Roman Catholic social teaching or by the vision of the American republic as an all-inclusive community of equality and nondiscrimination are more likely to approach political life as something natural rather than a consequence of sin. Catholics who to some degree heed the moral teaching of their bishops and the pope tend to see the government as the bearer of significant responsibility for economic and social equity and the support of family life. It is true that, for Catholics, political life belongs only to this world, yet since it is a natural institution, it is one of the important arenas of moral obligation through which Christians are to express their love of neighbors and God. In the Catholic view today, particularly after Vatican II in the 1960s and the impact of Pope John Paul II, the church hierarchy is not to exercise any direct authority over government but should act to offer moral admonition to citizens and governments alike, and Catholic laypeople should participate energetically in political life to help shape public life for the common good. Given the Catholic emphasis on social solidarity and economic fairness as important ingredients of the common good, Catholics as citizens tend to fall left of center on the American political spectrum. At the same time, given their strong emphasis on family, human life, and the subsidiarity of other institutions, they often stand right of center on certain so-called moral issues.

For many, perhaps most, Christians in the United States today, the historical roots of their political attitudes and affections may lie well below the level of consciousness. They may not recognize the names of Locke, Calvin, Aquinas, or Augustine. They may be unfamiliar with the traditions and secularizing trajectories of the American civil religion. Many influences of American pragmatism and of modern humanist educators, such as John Dewey and academic theorists such as John Rawls, may be so strong that Americans may not know the classical, Christian, and even early modern roots of the American way of life. Today, single-issue voting or activism oriented toward short-term goals has become the standard mode of American engagement in political life. And whether or not Christians and other Americans vote or do any lobbying, they may have a feeling of apathy or even powerlessness toward government.

How and why has American political life developed in the way it has during the last four centuries? In what sense, if any, is the Christian way of life compatible with the American way of political life that we know today? How should Christians face up to the full reality of government and politics in today's rapidly changing world? These are some of the questions that carry us on to part 3.

part 3

engaging
politics today

viewpoint
as standpoint:
where do we begin?

No one begins from scratch to take up his or her responsibilities as a citizen. From birth we are already situated, contextualized, and in the process of being socialized into the affairs of the country or countries in which we live at a particular point in history. Those of us living today do not begin where Israel, Athens, or the Roman Republic began, or where Augustine, Aquinas, or Althusius began. Yet those cultures and influential figures helped shape the context in which we now find ourselves. Consequently, we cannot avoid the questions: From what point of view shall we approach our civic responsibilities? Where shall we take our stand? In particular, what should Christian political engagement look like now?

One of the convictions we have articulated is that God created humans for political life. God did not establish government and politics only in reaction to sin. Underlying that conviction is the Bible's portrayal of humans as created in the image of God, male and female in their generations, made to be God's vicegerents, viceroys, developers, and caretakers of creation. Moreover, since everything that exists is God's creation, then everything about earthly life, including political life, is meaningful, telling us something about God's purposes for creation and about the meaning of our relation to God. Nothing about life in this world is neutral with respect to its origin and identity. If God created everything, then everything is dependent on and revelatory of God. Sin itself has its degrading and destructive character only in the context of God's good creation and its relation to God.

From a biblical point of view, therefore, what all humans share in common is their identity as God's image bearers, living in God's creation in relation to the

117

one who created them. Not everyone agrees with this judgment, of course, and that is why everything about the life we share in this world is also frequently in dispute. There are other views of human nature, such as the classical Greek and the modern individualist views, and there are many views of political life. Yet while there are different views, they are views of what we all have in common—human identity, the political systems in which we live, and so forth. Many of the differences are relatively simple matters of perception and received opinion that can be settled by exposing mistakes in perception or reasoning. Yet many of the differences are more fundamental, arising from basic beliefs that shape our perceptions and convictions. If I believe that God created everything and that everything is related to God, then that belief orients my life in a very deep way, framing my perceptions of the world and guiding the way I live. Likewise, if you believe that there is no God and the world in which we live is not God's creation, then your basic belief will orient your perceptions and way of life in a fundamental way. Basic beliefs are thus religiously deep in the sense that they shape our ways of life. We can't even begin to think and make judgments apart from basic assumptions about the meaning of life, thought, and human responsibility. And yet, it is also the case that our differing points of view and basic beliefs must constantly confront reality in the widest sense. Our views and convictions do not float in a vacuum or depend solely on our will to believe what we want to believe.

Living by faith thus appears to be one of the things we all share in common, even if we live by different faiths. A person might not be religious in the sense of believing in a transcendent God or engaging in traditional practices of worship. But living by faith has to do with more than cultic practices and the activities associated with churches, synagogues, mosques, temples, or feelings of spirituality. As a consequence, political life, like every other arena of life, is shaped by our often-contending basic convictions, worldviews, and ways of life. That is why people can differ so fundamentally over the nature and purpose of government. Political life is not a neutral terrain, even among those who are citizens of the same country. Thus, in order to engage wisely and constructively in political life, we need to take very seriously the basic beliefs people have about the meaning of life and, in this case, particularly about civic life.

To argue, for example, as we have been doing, that humans have been created for political life is to challenge a long-standing basic belief of many Christians going all the way back to Augustine. That is the belief that government and several other institutions were established by God only because of sin. While I agree that government's responsibility to exercise retributive justice is necessitated by sin, I have tried to show that such responsibility depends on the prior and original responsibility of government to uphold just distribution and attribution in a public, political community.

To disagree with Augustine (and those who follow in his line) on this point does not necessarily lead to the adoption of Aquinas's point of view, however.

Aquinas did teach that political life is natural to humans, but his understanding of political life depended chiefly on the work of Aristotle. Aristotle's view of human nature and the polis (the city-state) is quite different from the biblical perspective, so while we find a number of constructive features in Aquinas's view of political community, we have been trying to build on the biblical, covenantal framework for an understanding of the *creational* character of politics and government. In doing so, we have emphasized the revelatory and anticipatory character of life on earth. Just governance reveals something about, and points ahead to the fulfillment of, God's creation in the new Jerusalem under Christ's kingship, just as the love of husband and wife reveals something about and anticipates the fulfillment of the marriage of Christ and his bride. For Aquinas, the natural world is not so clearly connected to what is supernatural. The natural will be surpassed rather than fulfilled in the beatific vision of God. Nor is it very clear in Aquinas how the earthly polis is presently related to the city of God.

Against the backdrop of biblical revelation about God's creation of humans in the divine image and the judgment and restoration of creation through Christ, the mode of political engagement we want to explore and encourage in these final chapters is one that takes political life seriously as a dimension of our creaturely responsibility to serve God and neighbors. This mode of engagement is incompatible with all forms of idolatrous nationalism, tribalism, civil religion, and self-aggrandizing habits of individuals, institutions, and nations. Christian political engagement is also incompatible with attitudes and practices that belittle or despise government as a threat to human freedom, and it is incompatible with both individualism and collectivism. To assume that the individual is sovereign or that a politically organized community is the ultimate sovereign is to start at the wrong place to grasp the true meaning of political community in the grand scheme of God's relation to human creatures throughout their generations. Nevertheless, we live in a world where nationalism, tribalism, individualism, and collectivism appear to predominate almost everywhere.

In agreement with Augustine, I contend that humans were not created to lord it over one another, but I disagree with Augustine that domineering rule was instituted by God as a way to restrain and punish sin. To the contrary, I believe that government's practice of retributive justice should exhibit the same humility and nondomineering character as its practices of attributive, distributive, and administrative justice that would exist even without sin. Some people need to serve as the chief stewards—the leading officials—of government, but that does not mean they hold an office granting them the right to lord it over those who are not in positions of government authority.

The belief that God created humans for life in political communities goes hand in hand with recognizing that those created in the image of God (male and female) are more than political creatures. We have been created with many abilities and vocational responsibilities. Marriage, family life, agriculture, industry, education, scientific exploration, artistic creativity, worship of God—these and many others belong to us as creaturely endowments. Each of them needs to be developed on its own terms. No human authority is qualified to stand above and direct all of them. The political community has its own purpose and responsibilities in distinction from the responsibilities of other communities and organizations. This means that justice of a public-legal kind must be provided not only to all citizens of the political community but also to all nongovernmental institutions by recognizing and protecting their independent identities.

Christ's Kingship and Human Politics

According to the New Testament, Jesus Christ, whom God raised from the dead, is now seated at the right hand of the Majesty on high (Heb. 1:3). All authority in heaven and on earth has been given to him (Matt. 28:18). He has been given the name above every name, and before him every knee will bow and every tongue confess that he is Lord (Phil. 2:9–11). This is what the apostles taught. Christ's kingship is front and center in the biblical texts of the Christian faith. Jesus announced the arrival of the kingdom of God and continued to teach about it until the last hours he shared with his disciples after his resurrection and before his ascension to heaven (Acts 1:1–9). Within the horizon of Christian faith, there can be no question of whether Christ is the king above all kings and the lord of all lords. Our question is about what Christ's kingship means for life on earth now, for he taught us to pray for God's kingdom to come and God's will to be done on earth as it is in heaven.

From at least the time of Augustine to the present day, however, there has been a tendency to disconnect Christ's kingship and the city of God from the responsibility of human government on earth. For Augustine, the perfection of Christ's love and justice in the city of God is only ambiguously related to the earthly city. Government on earth is temporary and at best can serve God by serving the cause of the church. The two-swords doctrine of the Western church taught that the pope receives authority from Christ to administer the spiritual sword and to delegate the sword of earthly power to governments considered subordinate to the church. At best, then, the church mediates Christ's lordship to earthly governments, but generally speaking, the church's rule over Christendom meant that the earthly city was separated from the kingdom of Christ.

The Eastern Orthodox Church followed the original Roman imperial order, recognizing the emperor as the chief mediator of Christ's authority to earth, with the church subordinate to the emperor. But the mediational role of the emperor often meant that he exercised priestly and other responsibilities in a claim to omnicompetent authority on earth. The church in that framework served Christ by supporting the rule of the emperor, tsar, or king. That framework is the opposite of the Western disconnection between earthly government and Christ. In the East, the ruler represented Christ's kingship directly. Both the

Eastern and Western Christian views remained heavily dependent on Roman imperial presuppositions, which in my view is quite incompatible with biblical presuppositions.

For Aquinas in the West, political life and kingship are natural, and Christ's kingship is clearly supernatural. In that sense it is unclear how Christ the king is related to earthly governments other than by the indirect and temporary means of ecclesiastical mediation. Much the same can be said of the Reformers. Luther saw little or no relation between the earthly sword, needed to control non-Christians, and the spiritual authority of Christ over Christians. The Anabaptists were even more convinced that earthly government exists outside the perfection of Christ. And Calvin, who stressed the sovereignty of God over all things, sometimes distinguished sharply between the kingdom of Christ and earthly government to the point of dissociating them. From the time of the Reformation to our day, a variety of approaches that separate Christ's kingship from earthly government have continued to guide Christian thought and practice, reflecting most of the streams of Christian practice we discussed in part 2.

Ever since the collapse of Christendom, consequently, a great deal of room has been made for new ideas about the meaning of earthly political life. Believing that Christ's kingdom is spiritual, or not of this world, or only ecclesiastical, or only future, Christians have turned to nationalism, civil religion, liberalism, Marxism, and various forms of quietism (religious mysticism) and passivity as guides to their engagement or nonengagement in earthly politics.

One of the deep convictions that will guide us in the pages that follow is that Christ *now* governs this world as king of kings and is not only the head of the church. In that respect, the first thing to emphasize about Christ's kingship is its incarnational character, which is to say that the incarnate, crucified, and risen Jesus is the one whom God ordained as Israel's messianic lord and ruler of all nations. Christ's kingship is not that of a nonhuman divinity but of a fully human servant of God (Heb. 2). And because of Christ's faithfulness all the way to death, God elevated him to the throne on high, the throne of creation's climax in God's sabbath rest—the creation's seventh day. Christ does not sit on a supernatural throne above the natural world but on the throne of creation's fulfillment, which includes the fulfillment of human governing responsibility on earth.

Although Christ is not now present before our eyes in the way that the president of the United States or the president of Mexico is present, the Spirit of God is at work as Christ's vicar, drawing disciples into his service, convicting the world of sin, and overseeing the history of the unfolding generations of humankind toward the day of the Lord when Christ's kingdom will be fulfilled (John 16:1–15). Yes, this is a view held by faith, not yet by sight, but that does not make it odd in comparison with other views of history and politics. Democratic liberals have not yet seen the world filled completely with democracies living at peace with one another, but that is the faith-based vision that inspires their work to promote democracy in the world. Marxists have not yet seen the world organized, as they believe it should be, as a peaceful and productive community without need of government, but that is the faith-based vision that guides their day-to-day work.

The question for Christians is this: How should we engage politically, guided by the vision of Christ's kingdom that has not yet been revealed in its fullness? The obvious starting point should be to heed the teaching and example of Jesus whom we confess to be the Christ. We should do what he taught his followers to do: serve your neighbors in love, do justice, seek to live at peace with everyone, do not lord it over others but act as servants (Luke 9:23–27, 46–48; 22:24–32). In the political arena, therefore, we should work for the kind of political communities in which those who fill offices of government act as public servants to uphold public justice for the common good, willingly accepting their equality with all citizens under the law.

Christians should *not* try to use government to give themselves an advantage over non-Christians (Matt. 13:24–30, 36–43), nor should they presume that Christ's governing authority on earth is mediated through them or through the church. Rather, they should work to support constitutional patterns of government that assure equal treatment of all citizens, including equal protection of the rights of every person without regard to their faith. Christians should operate with the conviction that final judgment is in the hands of God and that as long as the enthroned Christ is ruling by mercy, patience, and long-suffering, we, too, should exercise our citizenship in keeping with that merciful patience extended to all humankind, including sinners like us. God sends rain and sunshine on the just and unjust alike (Matt. 5:45). From a biblical point of view, God's governance of all nations through Christ is true regardless of whether a government recognizes it to be true.

From this point of view, the antithesis between good and evil, between sinful governments and the justice of Christ's rule, is not an antithesis between heaven and earth, or between soul and body, or between church and state, or between Christians and non-Christians. Rather, the antithesis is between the way of life directed by and toward the love of God in Christ and the way of death directed by and toward self-love. The antithesis is between serving God in all things and serving false gods in disregard of the true God. What is seldom noticed is that the foundation on which the antithesis operates is the underlying reality—the original thesis—of God's creation, the good creation order.

The antithesis arises from the fall into sin, with the antagonism of brother against brother and neighbor against neighbor. It intensifies as self-love challenges the love of God in every arena of life. The way of death appears to have a self-sustaining "life" of its own, but that is an illusion. The antithetical stance of sinful creatures has no platform of its own on which to stand. It operates entirely within the creation and is constantly confronted and exposed by the true meaning of reality that it denies and violates.

Augustine's equivocations about the earthly city can be resolved only with a proper understanding of creation. After presenting the antithesis between self-love and the love of God, Augustine confused it with the distinction between mortal life on earth and immortal life in the heavenly city. But the second distinction does not have the character of an antithesis. Earthly life is part of the good creation and precisely what the generations of the first Adam were created for. It is only human sinfulness that stands against God and darkens the good creation. Christians and non-Christians do indeed cohabit the earth, for they share everything about creaturely life. And as sinners, both Christians and non-Christians participate in the misdirected love of self that is antithetical to the love of God in Christ. But insofar as repentant sinners are being renewed by the love of God in Christ, they begin to turn away from sinful, destructive patterns of self-aggrandizement and begin to live the kind of lives for which God created them. Augustine confused earthly life with sinful life at too many points and did so with government, failing to see political community as part of the good creation that is being redeemed by Christ for fulfillment in the city of God.

It is the combination of the belief that government was given because of sin and the belief that life on earth exists in negative tension with heaven that has led to the development of almost every approach Christians have taken to government and politics. What we need, therefore, is a better and more integrated view of the relation of earthly life to the fulfillment of creation in the age to come. We find some help in this respect from Aquinas and Althusius, who recognized that political life is natural for humans. Yet the work of both was fraught with other difficulties we are trying to overcome. Neither made an adequate connection between Christ's rule and human politics in this age and the fulfillment of Christ's kingdom in the age to come. God's judgment and redemption of creation in Christ has everything to do with the "natural" politics of this age in a way that Aquinas and Althusius did not develop.

Our sinfulness greatly hinders and degrades life in political communities, to be sure, but sin is just as much the cause of our degradation of family life, education, business, science, and the arts. Injustice, hatred, and discord that drive us away from our neighbors and lead us to ungodly acts of evil against one another cannot stand if there is to be any hope for life in any area of responsibility. At the foundation of Christian faith is the revelation of God's judging and redeeming work in Jesus Christ, who alone overcomes the sins of the world and gives life—life for real creatures in God's creation both now and in the age to come. A Christian approach to political responsibility must begin, then, with the judging and redeeming kingship of Jesus Christ. And there is no way to do that without recognizing that the one who was raised to sit at the right hand of the Majesty on high is the one in and through whom all things were created and the one who entered fully into the life of this age as a human to suffer death on the cross for the forgiveness of sins and to reconcile all things to God.

Political Community, Government, and Citizenship

The kind of politics and government for which Christians should be working, therefore, is the kind that unfolds from the responsibility God gave humans from the beginning to govern and develop God's creation with justice and loving care. Because of sin, that kind of political life also now entails government's restraining and retributive responsibilities, but the purpose of restraint and punishment is to make possible the healthy and just functioning of the political community. That kind of politics and government is part of what Christ's redemption of creation again makes possible. Political life exists as one kind of organized human community, the kind that is to establish and administer a just public-legal order for the good of all citizens and residents. Government officeholders in a political community bear responsibility to legislate, execute, and adjudicate public law for the common good, and they do so as citizens bound by the same laws that bind everyone else. In a just political community, there is no right for some humans to lord it over other humans. Those who would aspire to become governing officials, therefore, should be trained in the art of governance, the art of public service, the art of statecraft. As in other spheres of life, officers of government should be servant leaders, that is, public servants. And the politics of such a community must be organized around the participation and representation of citizens who also bear a responsibility for the common good.

The roots of this idea of a creation-grounded political community, structured under the rule of law, reach back at least as far as the covenantal framework of Deuteronomy 17:14–20, which we discussed in chapter 1. The kind of ruler that God wanted Israel to choose was one "from among your own people" who was not out to accumulate power and wealth, or to lord it over fellow Israelites, or to "consider himself better than his fellow Israelites." Moreover, the one who governed was to be subject to the laws of the covenant like every other Israelite. This order for Israel was not supernatural in character, in the sense of being at odds with the created responsibilities of humans. Rather, the order God prescribed for Israel was what human government should look like. God's covenant with Israel was restorative, renewing, and redemptive of the image of God as God intended humans to live with one another.

The biblical account of Christ's patient and merciful governance of creation is what leads to the conclusion that a just political community should be structured constitutionally (covenantally) in accord with what I've called "principled pluralism." This means, among other things, government's responsibility to recognize and protect each person and each legitimate human vocation, institution, and organization. Most of human social life is *not* political in character; most of our institutions and organized activities are neither departments of government nor created by the political community. Part of the limit of government's jurisdiction, therefore, is to be found in the reality of human relationships and associations that are not subdivisions of the political community. Doing justice to the multiple rights and responsibilities of persons and nongovernmental institutions is what we might say is government's responsibility to uphold "structural pluralism."

A second kind of pluralism that government should uphold is what we might call "confessional pluralism." As long as God sends rain and sunshine to the just and unjust alike, political communities should treat all citizens—all members of the political community—on an equal civic basis without giving special privilege or negative discrimination to any of them because of their religious commitments. The political community is a community of citizens, not a community made up only of those who share the same faith. Confessional pluralism, too, should, as a matter of principle, be part of the constitution of a political community.

One of the implications of a creation-based view of political life is that it puts the responsibility for shaping and governing political life squarely on the shoulders of men and women. Governing authority is not something that descends unnaturally or supernaturally from God through an emperor or pope, to whom other humans are simply subject. Nor is governing authority something that originates de novo from autonomous individuals below. Rather, men and women in their generations bear inherent responsibility to develop just means of public governance by virtue of their created likeness to God. Humans are neither self-sufficient creators of political life nor merely subjects of those who have power to lord it over them. Government and citizenship go hand in hand as constitutive elements of political community upheld by the gracious creator.

The art of governing, to use Althusius's words, is the art of political *symbiosis*, the art of shaping a community of public law that does justice to all members of the community. That is why the art of statecraft requires wisdom. Wisdom comes from searching out the ways of creaturely existence, including the art of governing justly. Political life is one of the ways we learn to walk with God in the course of learning to walk with one another. To do that requires real schooling in wisdom, which is what the wisdom literature of the Bible shows us.

Finally, in drawing together some of what we've learned in the foregoing chapters, a comment is needed on the meaning of "secularization." The first and now prevalent meaning of secularization arose in connection with Enlightenment humanism. It is the belief that religion should be confined to church life so that the so-called secular world can come into its own. From an Enlightenment point of view, it was a good thing for the Catholic Church to lose moral and legal authority over earthly life because that made possible the liberation of individuals from the church and other forms of authoritarianism. Reason should gain the upper hand over myth, superstition, and dogma. The goal of secularization in this sense is to free up individuals so they can shape their lives rationally and without unwanted subjection to ecclesiastical, social, and economic authorities. Secularization means the liberation of secular life from religious bondage. Secular now means "nonreligious," or "free from religion," or independent, self-contained, and self-sufficient, independent of the church and of God.

There is a second way to think of secularization, however, which is more constructive from a biblical point of view. It begins with the recognition that all of reality is directly related to, and dependent on, God. From this point of view, there is nothing secular in the sense just defined. All of reality is related to the creator of all. The medieval view of life was shaped too strongly by Neoplatonic and Roman imperial ideas of hierarchy, which distorted the biblical view of creation and the diversity of human responsibilities. Among other things, the medieval view turned the ecclesiastical authorities into the mediators of Christ's authority over everything on earth. The constructive idea of secularization, therefore, calls for "de-ecclesiasticizing" our understanding of society, which means recognizing that a church or churches do not hold preeminent authority over all other relationships and institutions on earth. But instead of suggesting that life outside the churches should thereby be dissociated from God and the institutional church, the second idea of secularization urges a recovery of the understanding that every arena of human responsibility is directly related to God and directly accountable to God rather than being related to God only indirectly through the mediation of the church. Christ is Lord of all, but church institutions under Christ are not the lord of all on earth.

This idea of "de-ecclesiasticization" goes hand in hand with the recognition that the people of God in Christ—the body of Christ—are more than an ecclesiastical institution. Ecclesiastical institutions represent, among other things, the organized gathering of the Christian community for worship and for celebration of the sacraments; for preaching, teaching, and fellowship to strengthen the whole body through the hearing of God's Word; for celebrating their faith union with Christ in anticipation of God's sabbath rest—the creation's seventh-day fulfillment; and for mutual encouragement to continue in the service of God and neighbors in every vocation and sphere of responsibility. As members of the body of Christ, Christians should see themselves as responsible to work together in the service of God and neighbors in all that they do. Understanding the body of Christ as more than an ecclesiastical institution can keep us from seeing our lives in this world as merely an exercise in waiting for the next life to begin. It can keep us from dividing life between the sacred, which is related to God, and the secular, which is not related to God. The Christian life is not only *a way of worship*, a way of engaging in ecclesiastically organized practices, but also *a way of life* in which Christians offer up everything they are and have in service to the creator, redeemer, and Lord of all things. To pursue such a way of life will often call for organized Christian efforts in diverse spheres of life so that the habits of repentance and forgiveness, of reconciliation and renewal, of discerning creational insights and working them out, can be nurtured and advanced in the nonecclesiastical as well as in the ecclesiastical arenas of responsibility.

Let us turn now to see what the view from this standpoint might mean for the exercise of our responsibilities as citizens and government officials today.

engagement
for what kind
of political
community?

What Is Government For?

You've heard the one-liners. "Fire this president and hire a new one," or "Government's number one job is to make sure people have jobs," spoken as if governing a country is like running a business enterprise.

Perhaps you believe there's another top job for the government, or another way of thinking about what government should do. Whatever the case, Americans tend to think in terms of what government should *do* rather than in terms of what the political community should *be*. In fact, the phrase "political community" that I have been using throughout this book sounds somewhat foreign to American ears. The closest Americans come to that terminology is when we speak of our *republic*. In fact, the word "republic" is a good one, for it draws attention to an organized institution or community that includes both citizens and government and refers to the political system of the United States as a whole.

The word "republic" comes from the Latin *res publica*, which means "public thing." Its identity contrasts with nonpolitical, nonuniversal institutions and organizations such as businesses, hospitals, universities, families, and churches. All of the latter, and many more besides, certainly participate in public life, but they are not parts of the political community in the way the Supreme Court, the military, the Environmental Protection Agency, and the fifty states of the republic are. It follows, then, that in order to understand what a government should *do*, we first need to know what a republic *is* or *should be*.

One of the reasons Americans are inclined to speak about what government should do without asking what the republic should be is our deep indebtedness to the liberal tradition of political thought that goes back to the English philosopher John Locke. (In the United States, conservatives and liberals represent different wings of this same liberal tradition.) The liberal tradition begins with the assumption that government is not natural for humans; we were not made for life in a political community. That's why Thomas Jefferson once said that the government that governs least governs best. Locke argued that government is created by a contract among free individuals when they decide they need government to protect their lives and properties. From a liberal/conservative point of view, a political community does not frame or constitute the responsibilities of citizens and government at the outset. Rather, the republic is constructed by, and exists to serve, the free, property-acquiring individuals who precede it. That is why libertarian liberals believe government should do nothing beyond protecting the life, liberty, and property of individuals. And that is why moderate liberals and liberal liberals are constantly arguing with one another over the additional things they want (or don't want) government to do to enhance the freedom and equality of all individuals.

Individual Americans and both profit-making and nonprofit organizations all want the government to do (or not do) certain things to benefit them. The major political parties, which help support candidates for elections, are not built on philosophies of what the republic should be but on a collection of things their supporters want government to do. Furthermore, the parties today have little power to bind candidates to election platforms on the basis of which the candidates promise to legislate after they are elected. Without disciplined and programmatic political parties that can be held accountable for their promises, citizens are left to vote for individual candidates on the basis of one or two issues or because of a preferred personality. Both before and after elections, diverse interest groups ranging from the National Rifle Association to Wall Street banks, from agribusinesses to Bread for the World, from insurance companies to aerospace industries, from pro-life and pro-choice coalitions to pro-environment and antiregulation coalitions (all with permanent offices in Washington) show up on Capitol Hill to lobby legislators on behalf of their constituents. As a consequence, legislators are pushed to become brokers of multiple interests rather than public servants held accountable by a national electorate for the republic's long-term well-being. Questions about justice for the body politic hardly get raised.

One of the reasons it is so important to expose this characteristic of the American republic is that most Americans, including Christians, simply assume that the liberal/conservative, interest-group-brokering mode of governing is the epitome of democracy. Interest-group politics provides the context—sets the table—for political engagement. But this understanding of political life offers no criteria for assessing the just and unjust condition of the republic and its long-term well-being as a political community. It is a serious mistake for citizens to accommodate themselves uncritically to such a system.

The Monopoly of Force vs. Christian Pacifism

Consider, for example, the question of whether a republic (or any political community) must monopolize the use of force as part of its very constitutional identity. Before it is possible to decide whether a particular use of force is just or unjust, we need to know whether the political community must be constituted with the right to make those decisions. With that question in mind, look at the contrast Robert Kaplan draws in his book *Warrior Politics* between a Christian ethic and the kind of ethic needed for real politics and government.[1] Kaplan, a highly acclaimed journalist and public-affairs scholar, contends that politics and government in the real world demand the use of force, which requires a "pagan ethos" because it cannot be sustained by a Christian ethos. Kaplan sides with Machiavelli, for example, who "preferred a pagan ethic that elevated self-preservation over the Christian ethic of sacrifice, which he considered hypo-critical."[2] The virtue Machiavelli had in mind was public virtue, says Kaplan, "whereas Judeo-Christian virtue is more often private virtue."[3] Kaplan allows that there can be an "overlap" of Christian and pagan virtues, in part because of the influence of Cicero and Plutarch on the Christian West, and in part because Christians such as Cardinal Richelieu, Otto von Bismarck, and Reinhold Niebuhr became realistic about politics. "What all these men were groping for," says Kaplan, "was a way to use pagan, public morality to advance—albeit indirectly—private, Judeo-Christian morality."[4] Nevertheless, progress in the world of real politics has come about as a result of "the evolution from religious virtue to secular self-interest."[5]

The main problem with Kaplan's argument is that he fails to recognize the important influence of Christianity in shaping the legal and governmental in-stitutions of the West and beyond. And that influence came about in part through struggles over questions about the just and unjust use of force, lead-ing to constitutional definitions and limitations of political communities and their governments. In other words, there is evidence in political life today of much more than a private ethical influence derived from Christianity. Kaplan shows almost no recognition of the Christian contribution to the differentiation of society and the process of structuring constitutional political communities whose governments bear responsibility for retributive justice as well as dis-tributive justice. A Christian ethos is not restricted to the nonpolitical spheres of personal responsibility. Kaplan pushes aside the idea of a Christian public ethos by presenting an easily dismissed cardboard figure of Christianity. That, he thinks, will give him the *ethical* backing necessary to support the harshest use of force by the American government to get what it wants in the name of its own survival and "secular self-interest." We must reject Kaplan's argument and his misrepresentation of Christianity.

Having raised the matter of government's use of force, let's turn to the arguments of some leading Christian pacifists who object to all use of force. These figures would seem to represent the very ethos that Kaplan is so anxious to dismiss. If a political order is constituted on the basis of a right to monopolize the use of force, say certain pacifists, then political life is not compatible with the Christian way of life. Their argument is that Christians are supposed to live entirely in accord with Christ's love and not accommodate themselves to a way of life built on violence, greed, and self-love. The most articulate representatives of this view of political life today are Stanley Hauerwas and Richard Hays, both of whom teach at Duke University's divinity school, and the late John Howard Yoder.

Hauerwas urges Christians to concentrate on *being* the church, which he believes is a polis in its own right with its own nonviolent form of community. The church, he argues, should be understood as a counter-polis, an alternative political community. "While the church clearly is a polity, it is a polity *unlike* any other insofar as it is formed by a people who have no reason to fear the truth. . . . For as Christians we are at home in no nation. Our true home is the church itself."[6] "The gospel is political," he continues. "Christians are engaged in politics, a politics of the kingdom. Such a politics reveals the insufficiency of all politics based on coercion and falsehood, and it finds the true source of power in servanthood rather than domination."[7]

Hauerwas and his associates go beyond the older Anabaptists who accepted the legitimacy of government's use of force as a God-ordained institution. But the Anabaptists of the sixteenth century believed that Christians should not participate in government for that very reason. In their view, God is at work in two ways in the world: inside the perfection of Christ and outside the perfection of Christ. Hauerwas, Yoder, and Hays, by contrast, question the legitimacy of any use of force, including force used by governments. In interpreting Romans 13, for example, Yoder speaks of God allowing or using government but not ordaining or establishing it. "Paul was simply arguing that the Christians in Rome should not rebel even against a government which threatened to mistreat them. . . . The state is not instituted, i.e., established, but rather accepted in its empirical reality, as something that God can overrule toward His ends."[8] This means, as Yoder sees it, that "the Christian is called not to *obey* the state, which would imply actually receiving from the state his moral guidance, but to *be subject*, which means simply that he shall not rebel or seek to act as if the state were not there."[9]

Pacifists such as Yoder do not recognize a distinction between illegitimate violence, such as the act of a murderer, and use of force by governments to restrain and punish those who use violence to obtain their ends. All use of force, from Yoder's point of view, is illegitimate even though God somehow uses such violence (by murderers or by governments) to achieve divine ends.[10] Therefore, rather than merely urging Christians not to hold a government office, these particular neo-Anabaptists call government itself into question in the light of the norm of nonviolent love. They want Christians to think in a different way about political life itself.

The attempt to approach politics in this way pits the polis of the church against the violent, fallen, nonchurch political systems of this age, somewhat like Augustine pitted the city of God against the earthly city. The church should live in the love of Christ in anticipation of the day when all earthly governments (established because of sin) disappear and the peaceful, loving city of God appears in its fullness. The difficulty Augustine faced with this contrast was that it did not answer the question of how Christians should live on earth in association with non-Christians until the day of God's final judgment and fulfillment of creation. And today's pacifists continue to face the same difficulty.

The deeper problem here, it seems to me, is with the idea of the political community as an illegitimate antagonist of Christ and of the church as an alternative polis. The simile of the church as polis is misleading. The church throughout the world is a community of faith that lives as witness to, and in anticipation of, the full revelation of the kingdom of God. It is not an alternative mode of organizing everyone (Christians and non-Christians alike) into territorial communities of public governance. The church may be like a political community in some respects, just as the church is like a family, a school, a vineyard, and a sheepfold. But the church is not a republic; it is not an earthly political community, or family, or school.

The work of Hauerwas and others is evidence of the difficulty of arriving at a normative approach to Christian political engagement if one does not recognize the creational basis of political life. From the neo-Anabaptist perspective, any normative, ethical, Christian judgments about political institutions must come either from outside modern states (i.e., from the city of God or from the church) or from within the sinful matrix of those self-loving, violent political entities. As a consequence, the only legitimate political community is the church, and every political community that is not the church is ethically illegitimate. There is no help from this point of view in understanding what an earthly republic (a political community that includes everyone within its territory) should *be* and how it should be governed in tune with God's patient and long-suffering governance of creation through Christ.

The neo-Anabaptists offer no more help than Kaplan in clarifying what a political community of citizens should be. From Kaplan's point of view, engagement in political life requires a pagan ethos, so Christians had better stay home or become realistic in the political arena. From the neo-Anabaptist point of view, engagement in political life also requires a pagan ethos, so Christians had better stay in their churches.

What Kind of Constitution?

If we take our point of departure from the standpoint established in the preceding chapters, we come to a view of political life quite different from Kaplan and the neo-Anabaptists. If we assume that governments should be the servants of their political communities and that a government's responsibility depends on what the political community should *be*, then we need to look closely at the meaning of political constitutions, that is, at the way political communities are constituted. In this regard, some of the best features of the American republic are found in its *constitutional* character. A written constitution may or may not correspond to the actual organization of a given polity, and some well-constituted political systems, like that of Great Britain, do not have written constitutions. But what a constitution does, or should do, is to articulate the normative purpose and limits of the political community and its government.

Roots of the constitutionalizing process can be found in the biblical tradition of covenantal obligations, in particular the subordination of rulers to the law of God, as well as in the biblical teaching that humans are sinners and that government itself must be held accountable in ways that help to restrain it from unjust practices. Roots can also be found in the heavy emphasis on law in the Roman republican and imperial traditions, particularly in the development of the *jus gentium* and private civil law. The struggles between church and empire up to the end of Christendom pushed both sides to try to constitutionalize their institutional authority. Evidence of this is found in the Justinian law codes, in the Roman Catholic Church's canon law, in the law systems of cities and medieval estates, and in the arguments of the conciliar movement. In Britain particularly, the struggles of feudal lords against kings that produced the Magna Carta, the rights of Englishmen, and the houses of Parliament also fed into American constitutionalism.

Several features of the United States Constitution (drafted in 1787, ratified by all the states by the end of 1788, and made operational in 1789) allow us to reflect on what makes a constitution good, mediocre, or poor. The American Constitution is good in distinguishing the responsibilities of three branches of government. Yet the way that was done has led to a number of questions and complaints. Many checks and balances on the federal government were built into the Constitution to inhibit hurried lawmaking and the concentration of power, but those inhibitions have often frustrated responsive and timely lawmaking. The US Constitution is also good in its articulation of certain civil rights of individuals that are to be protected by the federal government. The Constitution starts from the premise that individuals have an identity and bear responsibilities that the government may not abrogate. The Constitution also shows that the federal government's authority and jurisdiction is a grant from the states, which are the prior source of governing authority and retain their own constitutionally limited jurisdictions and responsibilities. This last characteristic, however, brings us to several factors that are problematic about the American Constitution.

The fact that the federal government was established to be a servant of the states, which wrote their own constitutions on the basis of 150 years of colonial experience, came about because the original thirteen states saw themselves as the primary polities or political communities. The federal Constitution was not written to create a government to serve a national political community directly. The rebels against King George III did not want a strong central government. In fact, their first federal compact (the Articles of Confederation) was too weak to support the Revolutionary War effort. The second attempt, which produced the existing Constitution, established a stronger, but still weak, federal government. The bias toward state governments coupled with suspicion of a central government explains why all the members of Congress—in both House and Senate—are elected on a state or local-district basis. The founders did not want congressional legislators to be elected on a nationwide basis by a nationwide constituency. Even the president was to be elected by state-chosen electors in an electoral college, not by a direct popular vote. The Constitution granted to the federal government two basic jurisdictional responsibilities: defense and the regulation of interstate commerce. The federal government was supposed to have a very limited role in the republic, the name of which is the United *States* of America, not the United People of America, or the National Democratic Union of America.

From a wider historical point of view, a federal political system can be seen to have many merits, particularly for a large country or for a union of diverse states, such as the European Union (which is not yet a fully integrated federal political community). Canada, post–World War II Germany, and a number of other countries, including small ones like Switzerland, also have federal systems or elements of federalism. The difficulty with the American system, now that the country has grown so large both in population and geography, is that matters of nationwide concern can get lost in limbo or be managed very poorly.

That is what happened with slavery, which was upheld by the 1789 Constitution. When tensions over slavery intensified to the breaking point, not only economic and social interests divided the country; the states themselves were divided, and Congress was unable to function as a national deliberative body to resolve the constitutional injustice. Of course, it might have been the case that even with a nationally representative Congress, conflict over the slave system would have led to civil war. But the states-based political system certainly showed its weakness at that point, and subsequent battles over states' rights and the responsibilities of the federal government have continued to this day.

It is even clearer now than it was when the Constitution's thirteenth through sixteenth amendments were adopted after the Civil War that the federal government has very limited powers to govern what is now a nationally integrated political community. Whether one thinks in terms of economic mobility, education, technology, the interstate highway system, Social Security, immigration, banking, health care, or the environment, it is now the case that Congress, the president, and the federal court system have great difficulty governing a nationally integrated polity, in large measure because of the outdated Constitution. Contemporary conservatives are correct that the federal government often looks like it is overreaching the limits of its original jurisdiction. But when the federal government or courts do push against their constitutional limits, they are typically trying to deal with nationwide legal conflicts or with pressing national issues that are not being dealt with adequately by the states acting within their own jurisdictions.

With respect to government's constitutionally authorized monopolization of the use of force, at least three current problems expose serious weaknesses in the US Constitution. One is the fact that the federal government was assigned the responsibility of national defense only, while the states retained all domestic policing responsibilities. The later creation of the FBI and the CIA were designed to fit the original constitutional restrictions. The FBI would deal only with national criminal matters and not interfere with the policing responsibilities of the states. The CIA would deal only with international dangers and not interfere with the FBI or the states. Yet with the intensification of responses to international terrorism and the creation of a new federal department of homeland security, the lines between the responsibilities of the CIA, FBI, and state law enforcement have blurred. Yet no change in the Constitution has been made to clarify the confusion, nor have Congress, the president, and the courts rewritten laws to show in clear detail how current operations can be held accountable within constitutional boundaries.

The second problem is that in the past decade the federal government has increasingly turned to the use of drone aircraft to target enemies or suspected enemies of the United States, even in countries with which the United States is not at war. Moreover, as of this writing in 2013, the drone operations are being run by the CIA, which is not part of the defense department, and the CIA conducts these operations largely in secret. Not only are there definite questions about the justice of the use of drones—whether they meet any criteria of justifiable warfare—but also there are questions about the accountability of the president and the CIA for such operations that fit nowhere clearly in the framework authorized by the Constitution.

The third problem is that there has been ambiguity from the beginning about the constitutional authorization of state and federal monopolization of the use of force. The courts today interpret the Constitution's Second Amendment as protecting individual ownership of guns, whereas the amendment's context was the protection of the right of states to organize militias. Therefore, the federal and state governments do not fully monopolize the use of force. In recent years, the number of killings of innocent victims by private individuals using guns—even assault rifles and rapid-firing handguns—has become so serious that most Americans are now aware of a crisis. But it is a crisis that is not being addressed by efforts to amend the Constitution.

Thus, the argument we have been making that governments of political communities should be authorized, with ample constitutional accountability, to monopolize the use of force in order to protect the innocent and punish evildoers must be directed critically toward the ambiguities, inner tensions, and injustices of the American constitutional system as it is currently operating.

What we are confronting here, in other words, are not simply problems of legislative, executive, or judicial mismanagement by unqualified public officials. Nor is it that there are simply too many liberals or too many conservatives in Congress. Serious problems exist because of the constitutional structure of the federal republic itself. That is part of the reason that paralysis and discord in Congress have been growing for the past two or three decades.[11] Representatives in the House and the Senate have difficulty reaching agreements sufficient to deal with long-range issues of taxes and spending, immigration, homeland security, health insurance, and environmental protection because they are brokering state, national, and interest-group pressures. Moreover, in many cases they are trying to frame laws without clear constitutional mandates or guidelines.

Another problem with the Constitution is that, for the most part, it articulates only the rights of individuals and states. I have laid great stress in this book on the fact that political communities exist in relation to various nonpolitical organizations and institutions. A constitution that specifies the nature, jurisdiction, and responsibilities of a political community and its government should also constitutionalize "structural pluralism," as we've called it. Many of our American debates and court battles at the national level are over education, marriage and the family, church-state relations, freedom of association, labor and management, and many more, which cannot be dealt with adequately on the narrow basis of individual rights. This means that many associational and institutional entities are overlooked or reduced (in legal arguments) to the rights of the individuals who make up families, schools, churches, and businesses.

Of course, part of the reason for the Constitution's "thinness" in regard to nonpolitical institutions is that it presupposes the "thickness" of the states as full-fledged political communities. Most of what is left of the rich inheritance from the common-law tradition remains at the state level, and the states bear original jurisdictional responsibility for family life, education, health, welfare, property law, and corporate law. But to remind ourselves of the breadth of state jurisdictions is to emphasize again the limited tools and authority (a few constitutional amendments about due process and equal treatment) with which the federal government has to work in dealing with substantive issues that belong to the original jurisdictional responsibility of the states.

The liberal tradition emphasizes limited government, but its idea of "limited" is that government should not take any more power than necessary from free individuals. And what those limits should be cannot be pinned down because there is no inherent identity of the political community that helps to clarify the kind and amount of power that government needs in order to exercise its responsibility to uphold justice for all. Under our Constitution, if proper procedures of representative government are followed, and if Congress, the president, and the Supreme Court agree on the laws that are made, the outcome will be the law of the land. But in the eyes of many, the outcome will show the exercise of either too much government or too little government.

This brings us back to the point that if Christians are to engage constructively in political life, we need to think not only in terms of discrete issues but also in terms of constitutional identity and work for reforms that will bring about a more just republic. What are the responsibilities of a republic (including those of both its citizens and its governments) that flow from its institutional identity, in contrast to the responsibilities of individual persons and nonpolitical institutions? What should government do to exercise its responsibility properly, sometimes in cooperation with other institutions, and what should it *not* do because that would be to overreach its jurisdiction and exceed its responsibilities?

The Common Good as Political Norm

Up to this point, we have used the phrase "common good" to talk about the life of a republic characterized by public justice. It is a phrase used often in the social teachings of the Catholic Church and by those who want to emphasize the solidarity of citizens in the political community. Yet the phrase "common good" is not politically specific and is also used by nonpolitical organizations and institutions. We want to argue, therefore, that if the common good is to be recognized as a normative standard for the political community, it needs to be qualified more specifically by the norm of public justice.

When the phrase "common good" is used by family members, university administrators, labor union leaders, or any number of others who bear responsibility for a particular community or organization, it means something quite different than when it is used by government officials. It is also apparent that the common good of a nonpolitical institution does not constitute the common good of everyone in a political community. Where the phrase is most fitting, then, is in reference to political communities, such as the American republic. To say this, however, raises some important questions of a constitutional nature.

If the common good refers to a universal good or to what is good for the most extensive and inclusive community humans can organize, does that imply that the political community needs to dissolve all other goods into itself for the sake of a truly *common* good? Not at all. In the light of everything we've said about the plural structure of society, it is not possible for a totalitarian state to be just or to serve the common good. To reject political totalitarianism, however, raises the question of whether there can be any *common* good that is, at the same time, restricted in some way. That is precisely what we are proposing. The normative demands of justice on a political community require the recognition and protection of all human responsibilities, most of which are not held in common by all citizens. The common good, in other words, refers to the good of a public community that can be realized only through the simultaneous affirmation of the diversity of nonpolitical responsibilities in a differentiated society.

Historically speaking, the struggle to advance or protect the common good shows that what is at stake is the relation of the political community to what is not political. Securing the commons for the good of all does not dissolve everything that is not shared in common but instead draws people together in the common *public* purpose of upholding justice for all. Central to the realization of the common good, in other words, is the establishment and maintenance of public justice. Giving to each its due, or doing right by each person, institution, nonhuman creature, and the environment, is thus constitutive of the common good. If, in the course of history, a political community is not constituted as a community of public justice in this way, it cannot realize or justly serve the common good.

Different Views of the Common Good

What do humans hold in common? Surely from a biblical perspective the *commons* is God's entire creation, the good of which only God can oversee and assure. That is why the Bible's portrayal of human responsibilities is set in the grand covenantal context of God's relation to the whole creation (Gen. 1–2; Ps. 8; Acts 17:24–31), and that is why no one other than God the creator-redeemer can be the ultimate reference point of human authority and responsibility (Exod. 20:1–11; Deut. 5:1–15; 1 Cor. 15:20–28). This is why God's covenant with Israel mandated that the chosen people serve no other gods and why the early Christians refused to acknowledge the Roman emperor as the divine-human concentration point of all authority on earth.

Yet, if we recognize that the macro-commons is God's single creation, we also need to recognize that human responsibilities are many. And that is why we insist on the need to distinguish between the kind of human community that exercises responsibility for the common good and every other kind of community and institution. However, the case for structural pluralism is not generally recognized in the West today, where individualist and collectivist views of life predominate. Consider, for example, the contrasting but not entirely contrary views of Alan Gewirth, a University of Chicago philosophy professor, and Michael Novak, a Catholic thinker and senior scholar at the American Enterprise Institute in Washington, DC.

Gewirth believes he can establish the idea of community and the common good on the basis of the autonomy of rational individuals. His individualist point of departure is the idea of universal human rights: "Each human must respect the rights of all the others while having his rights respected by all the others, so that there must be a mutual sharing of the benefits of rights and the burdens of duties."[12] The requirement of mutual respect, says Gewirth, amounts to a principle of solidarity. "By the effective recognition of the mutuality entailed by human rights, the society becomes a community. So the antithesis between rights and community is bridged."[13] From my point of view, the moment of truth in Gewirth's argument is that the modern, differentiated political order is, among other things, an institution of public-legal rights protection. However, Gewirth, with a debt to Locke, believes that the "community" is built on the mutual recognition of individual rights by individuals; a society *becomes* a community through the mutuality recognized by individuals. But Gewirth provides no basis for distinguishing the political community from any other institution that rights-bearing individuals might construct. Politically speaking, in other words, no community exists except the "mutuality of rights"; and that mutuality, with its sense of solidarity, depends on the willingness of each individual to accept the burden of duties toward other individuals.[14] Consequently, in Gewirth's thinking, there is no basis for the specification of a defined and limited political commons—a genuine political community—even though the enforcement of rights protection presupposes a specific authority that can, when necessary, impose its will on supposedly autonomous individuals.

The initial point of departure for Michael Novak is quite different from that of Gewirth. Novak starts not with the rights of individuals but with a Catholic vision of the transcendent destination of the human person: "God is the universal common good not only of humans but of all created things."[15] The dignity of the person is to be found in each person's responsibility before God, and that calls for the exercise of each person's practical rationality. When a person acts "with reflection and choice—acts, that is, *as a person*—the personal good and the common good tend to coincide," says Novak.[16] The person is more than an individual, and cooperation in love leads to the creation of various kinds of institutions. Novak admits, however, that there is "a serious problem in learning what the common good is," because the modern tendency, he believes, has been to reduce the person to either a "self-enclosed individual" or an "unfree collectivism."[17] He is especially opposed to the tendency toward collectivism through which an institution assumes power to decide, from the top down, what the substantive common good of all persons should be.

The strength of Novak's argument comes from his recognition that the common good cannot be achieved if everything that is uncommon is eliminated or reduced to a single collective good. He wants full recognition of the nonpolitical associations and communities of human life that also manifest the flourishing of responsible persons. Yet in his desire to avoid collectivism and totalitarianism, Novak nearly, if not completely, eliminates the political community as an authoritative institution qualified by the norm of public justice. "Not by politics alone is the common good publicly promoted," he writes.[18] It is almost as if Novak fears that any authoritative public body responsible for the commons will inevitably try to act in an omnicompetent, totalitarian fashion, violating the responsibilities of free persons. Instead, he defines the political community in a narrow, procedural way that sets out rules for individual and associational interaction in freedom. The political common good, consequently, is something he believes can materialize almost unintentionally and indirectly from the actions of responsible persons rather than through the direct actions of government in the political community. This is much like Adam Smith's idea of how the "common wealth" is achieved, namely, as an indirect result of individuals seeking their own economic interests in free exchange.[19] "In sum," says Novak, "the new concept of the common good pushes us beyond a simple reliance upon authority that defines for all the substantive good, and turns us instead toward achieving the rules that make an open society possible."[20]

Novak accepts the differentiation of society into various kinds of institutions and associations because they legitimately express the practical responsibility of free persons. But he does not see that the political community has a differentiated responsibility of its own. An authoritative—but nontotalitarian—public-legal integration of citizens in a republic does not fit in Novak's scheme of things. He tries to marry the liberal political tradition with Catholic political thought that has roots in Thomas Aquinas, but liberalism appears to triumph in the attempted synthesis. While he does not want to subordinate government to ecclesiastical authority, he speaks with Augustinian overtones of politics being subordinate to the eschatological fulfillment of human life. The complete common good cannot be achieved in this age, he says, and that is why the common good cannot be achieved "by politics alone."[21]

Gewirth is correct, I believe, that sharing in the burdens of achieving human rights for everyone is part of what constitutes political responsibility. And Novak is correct that the ultimate or comprehensive common good of all people in all respects cannot be achieved through politics. But neither of these positions is adequate to answer our questions about the constitution of a political community. If we agree that the protection of human rights is part of that responsibility and that politics is not everything, we are still left with the question of whether a territorial community of citizens under government can exist as a political community with its own limited, normative identity and responsibilities.

In a world of conflicting human aims and ideals, in which violent aggression is always a threat, there can be no successful attempt to uphold the common political good apart from governmental institutions authorized to draw up, enforce, and adjudicate public law. Any enforced order that is neither just nor recognized as legitimate by those subject to it will tend toward authoritarianism, totalitarianism, or anarchism. Real debates about the common good, therefore, must be about the good and just order that ought to be enforced, and that is where all the questions about the specifiable identity and limits of the political community come in.

Every quest for the common good—for a well-governed community of peace, mutual support, just treatment, and the exercise of responsibility by all citizens—has its roots, I believe, in our creaturely identity as the image of God with responsibility to cooperate with one another in developing and governing the earth. The possibility of realizing the common good in any society in the world today requires the exercise of a particular kind of public-legal responsibility that is differentiated from, and impartial toward, every other kind of associational, institutional, and personal responsibility. In other words, the historical differentiation of the political community—the *res publica*—from land ownership and economic position, from communities of language and ethnicity, and from racial and gender identities is required if justice is to be done to individuals and to all the legitimate institutions and associations humans have organized.

The Shrinking World

Finally, we must say a word about the constitution of political communities and the common good in relation to the growing interdependence of peoples throughout the world. Our world today is, for the most part, organized politically by territorial states, that is, by geographically defined political communities, each with its own government. However, many such states recognized by the United Nations are not mature and stable polities. They may lack adequate and just governments; they may be torn by internal conflicts and war that make them failed or failing states. Other states may be strong but highly unjust, without adequate protection for and representation of citizens, without an independent judiciary, or without enforceable limits to their power. And, of course, in all states, including the United States, there are injustices that require domestic (internal) reform. Consequently, the challenge of constituting just political communities is as urgent today as it has ever been.

Since World War I, however, the states of the world have been building more and more international organizations to try to deal with matters that affect them significantly but that transcend their ability and authority to manage by means of bilateral (one-to-one) or multilateral diplomacy and warfare. Just governance under law today demands more and more multilateral and transnational action to deal with regional and global concerns. We need only look at the reasons for the formation of the World Trade Organization, the World Health Organization, the European Union, the Organization of African States, NATO, the United Nations, and any number of other such organizations.

The driving force behind these efforts is not unlike the force that drove the original thirteen American colonies to seek confederation and then to organize into a federated republic. Within the federation, there are still states that have something of an internal identity as political communities, but they recognize that they are now part of a larger national polity, the United States, which is a more "universal political association," as Althusius would describe it. Increasingly, citizens of this world's diverse states are being forced to recognize that their interdependence economically, environmentally, and in other ways is calling for new ways of thinking about the common good that cannot be realized by the actions of separate states alone.

One need not jump immediately to the idea of a world government at this point, but that does not mean we may simply fall back on the assumption that justice can eventually and forever be done to the citizens of our various countries without new and better modes of international and transnational governance.[22] New kinds of political communities like the European Union may or may not represent the wave of the future. But if questions about what governments should *do* demand answers that depend on our knowledge of what political communities should *be*, then Christians around the world should be working together with increasing seriousness to help promote public justice at regional and global levels.

citizenship
as vocation

Citizenship: Burden or Opportunity

"The average American doesn't want to be educated; he doesn't want to improve his mind; he doesn't even want to work, consciously, at being a good citizen. . . . But there are two ways you can interest him in a campaign, and only two that we have ever found successful." One is to "put on a fight"; the other is to "put on a show."[1] That is the judgment not of some crank or naysayer but of the creator of American campaign politics, Clem Whitaker, seventy-five years ago.

Although many of us take for granted our status as citizens, we often act as if citizenship entails little more than obeying the law and voting in elections—if, that is, the election campaign draws us into a fight or puts on a good enough show. That, however, is a very restricted and even belittling view of citizenship. If the building of political communities is part of what God created us to do, then the exercise of civic responsibility represents a very high calling indeed. Citizenship requires an active role, not merely passive acquiescence to the status quo. However, what it means to be an active citizen is not obvious. Not everyone can be engaged full-time in politics or government, and if one has a family, a job, and responsibilities in an association, church, or parent-teachers organization, one can legitimately ask whether there is time to be an active citizen. Moreover, in the federal system of the United States, civic engagement can be very complicated because citizens and government function at local, county, state, and federal levels.

The first thing to say about the potentially burdensome task of citizenship, therefore, is this: don't think of it as an individual vocation. Political life is more a matter of what *we* do than of what *you* or *I* do. Of course, each of us bears responsibility, but exercising that responsibility meaningfully requires teamwork, a communal effort. Stop to think for a moment of how citizens obtain information about what is happening in their town, state, or nation. We depend on radio, television, newspapers, and the internet for news and commentary, all of which is generated by teams of reporters, writers, interviewers, researchers, and managing directors. Public officials are also tied into large networks of staff members, media consultants, legal advisers, and speechwriters. No one serving in an elected or appointed public office functions as a lone individual.

Partly because of the American emphasis on individual freedom and partly because of the Christian emphasis on personal moral obligation, American Christians tend to think in terms of "I" questions rather than in terms of "we" questions. That is, each person asks what he or she should do rather than what an organized group of citizens or the political community should do. It is no surprise, then, that individuals may resist the pressure to add the responsibility of active citizenship to their other duties.

This is one place where a Christian view of political life can make a valuable contribution. Starting with the realization that humans—male and female together—are created in the image of God and made for life in political community, we should be able to see citizenship as a corporate responsibility. Moreover, to recognize that those called into the service of Jesus Christ are a body—a community of faith and not a collection of individuals—helps us understand the meaning of joint and distributed responsibility in all areas of life. Christians, therefore, should see life in the political community as one of the arenas in which they have been called to serve in organized ways as stewards of justice and reconciliation for the sake of all their civic neighbors. Active citizenship oriented toward justice for all should be understood as an integral part of the Christian way of life, lived out as an expression of our prayer for God's kingdom to come and God's will to be done on earth as it is in heaven.

But how do we join in the kind of civic teamwork that can promote public justice? We do so by committing ourselves to public service for the common good, as discussed in the last chapter, and by learning how to engage politically to advance principled pluralism (structural and confessional) in public life, which we discussed in chapter 8. In saying only this much, we have already invoked the need for teamwork among citizens who share a distinctive vision of public life. How can a constructive approach from that point of view be developed without the full-time efforts of political writers, researchers, civic educators, policy formulators, leadership trainers, and public officials? It can't be! It requires organized efforts that cost money as well as time, including the full-time work of some people. All of this is needed if we are to fulfill our civic vocation.

Young people need to be educated in an atmosphere pervaded by a constructive view of citizenship. The Christian view of life that underlies this understanding of human responsibility needs to be grasped and absorbed. Teamwork to accomplish this does not require activism from everyone on a weekly or even monthly basis. Some may become full-time laborers at an educational or think-tank level; others may work as part-time promoters, fund-raisers, and coordinators of local events. Most will be those who read and listen to the news and analysis produced by other team members. Many will contribute financially to support the cause and encourage friends and colleagues to consider the ideas, policy arguments, and proposals put forward by those doing the full-time political and governmental work of research, writing, speaking, and strategizing. Organized efforts along these lines will not only make it possible for many citizens to vote with greater wisdom and insight but will also encourage the development of people's abilities to converse and debate with other citizens winsomely and with adequate knowledge and good arguments. In the long run, it will help prepare better-trained leaders for government service.

Everyone has been created for civic engagement. Christians have no privileged status or special qualifications to exercise this kind of creaturely responsibility, and they certainly have no right to lord it over other citizens or push them aside. As we've emphasized, Christ called his followers to serve their neighbors in keeping with creation-order norms and with the patience, mercy, and love he is now exhibiting in drawing the creation toward the full revelation of the city of God. The task of civic engagement is a matter of working to open up pathways of justice in every dimension of a republic's life and to contend with fellow citizens through frank discussion, thoughtful debate, and cooperation or noncooperation over a full range of policy issues and the process of government.

The kind of citizenship Christians should exhibit, therefore, is the kind that can help to clarify the distinctive art of statecraft and help to strengthen the political community for the common good. The art of governing and the art of citizenship go hand in hand in the building of a community of citizens confident that justice can be assured for all. This is a very complex art, developed over generations. It requires maturity, insight, and dedicated service to the body politic. It is an art that cannot be practiced very well by individuals acting separately and without historical knowledge or experience. It requires the work of organizations that coordinate a wide variety of skills, wisdom, and expertise.

This leads directly to the question of how those with a commitment to the common good of a political community should try to influence government. Should it be solely by voicing their views in the media? Should it include lobbying and other efforts to influence those in power? Should it include attempts to gain elected office through involvement in a political party? I believe that the representation of citizens in offices of government is one of the most, if not *the* most, important modes of civic engagement. Electoral representation is the direct and critical link between the vocation of citizenship and the responsibility of governing. Therefore, we need to look more closely at the requirements of an electoral system.

What Should an Electoral System Provide?

To ask what electoral representation should mean for citizenship is to become conscious of how important the public character of a political community is. In many newly formed democracies, people do not yet have sufficient experience to act as citizens of a *res publica*. Their ethnic, tribal, linguistic, or confessional identity often remains their primary social identity. So when elections are first held, those elected may aim first to exploit the opportunity of holding office to secure benefits for their ethnic or cultural group. Elections by themselves, in other words, do not assure the existence of a just political community. A sense of shared citizenship and dedication to justice for all in a public community typically takes a long time to develop, and, of course, it requires a growing confidence among all the people that justice can be done.

Despite the long history of democracy in America, where now African Americans, women, and adults of every religious, social, ethnic, and class background are finally eligible to vote, there is still too weak a sense of what constitutes the shared commons. Americans are frequently divided over what they think government should *do* in circumstances where they do not have a widely shared commitment to what the republic should *be*. That is why, in many instances, elected representatives to Congress act primarily to promote the interests of their states or electoral districts, or of a particular interest group—agricultural, banking, insurance, or some other. Interest-group brokering, however, functions as a very weak and inadequate means of lawmaking, even if it is supported by regular elections.

This drives us to the deeper question about representation. The liberal tradition views elections as an extension of self-government, believing it would be best if each individual could govern himself or herself. But once free individuals have contracted to create government, they have given up part of their autonomy to those who govern on their behalf. Voting, therefore, amounts to choosing someone to represent me, my autonomy, my property, my interests. Yet this is a modern, liberal view of representation. Ancient Roman and Chinese emperors claimed the right to rule because they *represented* God or a mandate from heaven. Medieval Catholic popes claimed to *represent* the authority of Christ, and that's why they believed their authority on earth should be recognized as supreme even over governments.[2]

With the historical development of political communities as constitutional institutions in which all citizens bear some responsibility, a new understanding of representation became possible. From this point of view citizens can and should participate more directly in a joint effort with their government to build the political community, a common good that should be characterized by public justice. Officials are to serve as the chief stewards or trustees of the *res publica*. And in that respect, governing officials can be recognized as stewards of God's gifts and callings for public life that inhere in humans as the image of God.

With this in mind, how does the American system of electoral representation stack up? What kind of grade should it get in a comparative evaluation of electoral systems? In my view, there are at least six ways in which the American system is weak and in need of reform.

1. This huge republic of more than three hundred million people has only one nationally elected public official—the president. Even though the Congress as a whole is jointly responsible for federal governance, no senator or representative is elected nationwide with accountability to citizens of the country as a whole. James L. Sundquist once explained that since all members of Congress are elected by districts, "Congress as a whole is not accountable to the people as a whole. Each voter can act to throw out one rascal, but the others are beyond reach. . . . Thus the Congress is in a very real sense an irresponsible body, beyond control by the voters, whatever their mood."[3]

2. One consequence of the first weakness is that national political parties are almost powerless to mold national agendas that can bind their elected members of Congress after an election. The party structures that exist perform a very small percentage of the work necessary for meaningful representation in a modern democracy. Today's political parties, says George Will, are "mere money-raising and money-distributing operations, and not even the most important raisers and disbursers."[4]

3. Individuals who win elections in our system each represent a voting *district* rather than a constituency of supporters who all voted for the winning candidate. This means that as many as half or more of the voters in a voting district find themselves represented by individuals they did not vote for and whom they wish were not representing them. Thus, the already weak link between citizens and their elected officials is further weakened by a decidedly antipathetic attitude of some citizens toward their members of Congress. Moreover, evidence suggests that this antipathy is easily transferred to Congress as a whole and is not confined to particular representatives.[5]

4. Most voters have so little positive connection with their representatives that they feel alienated from the political process generally. In fact, in federal elections over the past few decades, around 40 to 50 percent of the eligible voters have not bothered to vote. Even among those who have voted, most know little about the officeholder who represents the district in which they live. "Most Americans," says W. Lance Bennett, "experience elections as empty rituals that offer little hope for political dialogue, genuine glimpses of candidate character, or the emergence of a binding consensus on where the nation is going and how it ought to get there."[6]

5. Elected representatives, identified with political parties that are too weak to hold them accountable and representing districts where half or more of the voters are apathetic or antipathetic, are officials who function essentially on their own rather than as members of committed national party teams. This is true both in the running of their campaigns and in the way they serve in elected

office. This makes concerted congressional action on behalf of the national common good even more difficult to achieve. This is a large part of the reason for repeated stalemates in Congress despite the many urgent challenges that confront the country.

6. The most influential political connections the president and most senators and representatives have are with interest groups, not with national parties or supportive voters in their districts. This holds true both for the conduct of business in their government offices and for the conduct of election campaigns and the fund-raising necessary for those campaigns. Will says that governments have always responded to interests, but the word "respond" is far too benign to capture the truth about political reality. "The modern state does not merely respond to interests, it generates them and even, in effect, organizes them."[7]

One of the long-term consequences of the deficiencies just noted is that most of the citizens who do choose to engage in civic action at the national level put most of their time and money into the interest-group pressuring game, or they move into protest movements, marches, and litigation in the courts. Less and less civic action materializes in the form of mature, public-interest debate during and after election campaigns among competing political parties offering meaningful programs. In sum, our predicament is this: Americans—as citizens of the nation—are not represented in a way that allows them to fulfill their public-interest responsibilities; parties are too weak to connect voters to those who win elections; and interest-group brokering has displaced the work of public-interest statecrafting to the point that more and more citizens realize that the republic does not have an accountable government in Washington.

Countries other than the United States may have stronger or weaker (or even nonexistent) electoral systems, but in every situation citizens need to be vigilant in looking for ways to improve electoral systems for the sake of strengthening representative government and vibrant citizenship. Otherwise, our vocation as citizens is degraded and frustrated. In the face of the deficiencies just noted in the American electoral system, let's consider an approach to electoral reform that emerges from a broader view of the vocation of political responsibility that we've been advancing thus far.[8]

Strengthening Citizenship through Electoral Reform

The kind of electoral system devised by most democracies in the world is one that allows almost every vote to count, not just those of the majority in winner-takes-all voting districts. That system is characterized by some form of *proportional representation*, or PR for short.[9] The principle inherent in PR is that all citizens should have the opportunity to be represented by those for whom they vote. While there are many ways to design an electoral system with a greater or lesser degree of PR, one way for the United States to initiate this kind of reform in a historically realistic fashion would be to slightly alter the method of electing members to our House of Representatives. Under current law, population determines the number of seats in the House of Representatives allotted to each state. For the entire country, a numerical proportion is calculated between the number of House seats (435) and the total US population. Each seat is supposed to represent roughly the same number of people. Once that number is determined, each state knows how many representatives it may have, based on its population. Each state then carves up its territory into the number of districts corresponding to the number of House seats it may fill. Each of those districts becomes a single-member election zone to be represented in Congress by the candidate who wins a majority (or plurality) of the votes cast in that district's House election. This system typically encourages competition in each district between two candidates who try to win at least 50 percent of the votes. The winner of the majority of votes wins all, and the loser, even if he or she wins 49 percent of the votes, is eliminated.

In place of that system, the PR reform proposal I am suggesting would turn each state into a *single, multimember district* from which the state's allotted number of House seats would be filled by means of PR. For example, if one of the states is allotted twenty seats in the House of Representatives, then under PR a variety of political parties could each run a team of twenty candidates in an election that would cover that whole state as a single district. If the Democrats were to win 40 percent of the statewide vote, they would get eight seats in the House, not more or less. If the Republicans were to win 45 percent of the vote, they would get nine seats in the House, not more or less. If a Green Party, a Libertarian Party, and a Rainbow Coalition Party were each to win 5 percent of the vote, each would get one seat in the House, not more or less.

In this kind of election, not only would nearly every vote count—with minority as well as majority parties gaining representation—but nearly every voter would be represented by the party he or she actually voted for. The Democrat team of eight representatives would represent all who voted Democrat, no matter where they lived in the state. The Republican team of nine representatives would represent all who voted Republican. The one Green, Libertarian, and Rainbow Coalition representatives would represent all who voted Green, Libertarian, or Rainbow Coalition. This would begin a much stronger connection between voters and the representatives they elect. It would also open the way to other benefits. For example, PR allows groups of citizens, even small groups, to gain representation through the electoral process without in any way inhibiting a genuine majority from winning control of the House. Instead of some citizens giving up at the start because they think their votes will not count (since under the current system many votes do not count), they could instead be motivated under PR to work together to organize parties that could win a percentage of the House seats at election time. They would not have to win a majority of votes in a single district to assure representation for themselves. They would, however, have to work together to develop meaningful principles and programs and good candidates sufficient to convince a sizable group of citizens across the state to vote for their program and candidates.

The central value of PR is to make genuine representation possible—to connect voters and elected officials with one another in an accountability structure that keeps attention focused on the public interest. Those who are elected by means of PR are tied closely to the members of their party. Every candidate is part of a team that continues to function after the election. The party will continue to shape and direct the principles, programs, and policies of its representatives. Since each candidate who wins election represents his or her party, each will continue to be closely watched, guarded, and held accountable by that party. The way to bring about accountable, deliberative government is to make it possible for citizens both to deliberate seriously (as citizens and not merely as members of interest groups) and to hold accountable the representatives they elect to continue that deliberation in Congress.

The PR reform suggested here would help to achieve this goal by forcing a change in the way parties actually develop and function. Parties in PR systems have to work to define themselves very precisely and clearly in contrast to one another. Under PR, candidates trying to be all things to all people and therefore saying as little as possible about what they will do in office do not gain victory. Rather, parties win representation only in proportion to the number of votes they win, and no party is able to "take all" by winning only 51 percent of the votes. Voters are free to vote for the party they really believe in rather than being forced to choose between the lesser of two evils. Under PR, voters gain the opportunity to learn what they are voting for, and if they do not like what they see in one party, they can vote for another party or work to start a new one. No party will be able to benefit from being fuzzy and noncommittal. PR for the House of Representatives would open the way to more meaningful electoral competition.

Each party in this system would also be pushed to define what it plans to do on a wide range of national concerns. It would have to show why its program and platform are best for the country as a whole. Some citizens, interested in only one issue, might try to organize a party around that single issue, but over time, relatively few voters would cast their ballots for a party whose candidates have nothing to say on all the other issues that come before Congress. Another more comprehensive party would very likely adopt the same stance on that issue and thereby marginalize or eliminate the single-issue party.

Furthermore, if interest groups wanted to exercise influence in the political arena, they would have to deal with citizens from the start, at the party level where citizens are defining and organizing their platforms and agendas. Interest groups would no longer be able to buy up candidates individually before elections or wait until after the election to pressure individual representatives when they arrive in Washington. Citizens, in other words, would be able, under

PR, to exercise greater control of their representatives from start to finish and thereby deal with various interest-group pressures both prior to and following elections. Disciplined parties would have no desire to send lone rangers to Washington only to watch them become interest-group brokers outside of the party's control.

This, it seems to me, is the only fundamental way to get to the bottom of current problems associated with campaign financing and interest-group control of candidates and representatives. As long as citizens have no direct way to support the representatives in whom they place their confidence, they will feel powerless to hold accountable those who do win elections. Only by putting civic and electoral authority in the hands of citizens who can hold representatives accountable will it be possible to subordinate private interest groups to the civic work of shaping law in the public interest.

Once the conduct of elections under PR shift from the buying and selling of individual candidates to campaign debates among disciplined parties with clearly articulated legislative agendas, citizens would be much more likely to get involved in evaluating different party programs and helping to shape them from the inside. With respect to a national legislative agenda, each party would want to maximize its strength nationwide. Representatives from the Republican Party in Illinois, for example, would want to work closely with Republicans from other states right from the start, not just after their elected representatives from all the different states arrive in Washington. In fact, the initiative for organizing parties and party programs would most likely gravitate to the national level. Democratic, Republican, and other parties would have to organize nationally and map out consistent and coherent strategies for their House campaigns in all the states. Integral, comprehensive, and distinctive national programs would be developed by each national party and then put before the electorate by the branches of that party in each state. Any party that could demonstrate nationwide coherence and strength would have an advantage over parties that could not demonstrate that capability. Americans would finally have the possibility, through national parties, of holding Congress more accountable to the national common good.

Another consequence of the emergence of national parties would be the appearance of a greater number of national political leaders. Each party would, in essence, put forward its best people for election. The most outstanding leaders of each party would, of course, have to win election in a particular state. But leaders of that kind, whether elected from Texas, California, or Pennsylvania, would be leaders of nationwide parties with national agendas.

Once the benefits of PR in the House of Representatives became apparent, the door would very likely open to other significant reforms. One such reform could be a shift to a two-stage election of the president. The first stage would allow all eligible parties to put a presidential candidate on the ballot. If in the first stage one candidate were to win a majority of the votes, there would be no need for a runoff. However, if no candidate were to win a majority in the first stage, then the second round would see a runoff between the top two vote getters in the first round. The winner of the second round would then become the president. This method would have the advantage of allowing voters to vote their conscience in the first round. They would not be wasting their vote by voting for the candidate they really believe in but who would not be expected to come in first or second place. They would not have to limit themselves to choosing between the lesser of two evils. Moreover, the number of votes received even by minor-party candidates in the first round could have a big impact on the thinking of the candidate who finally wins the presidency, as happened when Ross Perot won 19 percent of the vote in the 1992 presidential election. First-round votes would send important signals. At the same time, the certainty of arriving at an electoral conclusion at the end of the second stage would mean that consideration of a wide variety of candidates at the first stage would not create instability in the system.

Criticism of Proportional Representation

Several objections to PR are raised by Americans. Let's consider one of them, namely, that under PR too many parties might come into existence and cause legislative instability if no party were to gain majority control of the House. In response, I suggest that a greater number of parties might be precisely what the United States needs if the views of its citizens are more diverse than can be represented by a two-party system. Would it not be better, in other words, for Americans to be able to see in the members of Congress exactly how diverse the body politic is rather than being misled and frustrated by the impression that the Democrats and Republicans adequately represent the nationwide polity? More parties in a system that allowed for better and truer representation could bring greater rather than less stability to our system because it would generate greater voter confidence in elected representatives and in the political system as a whole. The real question is whether the present system is any longer really stable.

We also must be careful not to compare apples with oranges. A system of PR tends to create parties that are more disciplined and coherent, each with a definite program and philosophy. Even if six or eight parties gained significant representation in the House, and even if none of them held a majority of seats, the process of negotiation and accommodation among them would likely be less chaotic and more purposeful than is the case under the current system. Why? At present, majority control of the House by Republicans, for example, gives a superficial impression of coherent, majority-party control. Yet given the nature of our undisciplined parties and the interest-group influences on individual committees and representatives, the process of negotiation typically involves far more than six or eight groups or camps. Seldom do all Republicans or all Democrats vote as one, without dissent.

In addition, most countries that employ a system of PR typically establish a threshold, which is a certain percentage of votes that any party must win in order to be able to gain representation. In other words, there is a relatively simple way to avoid the problem of subjecting the House to the onslaught of too many very small parties. A typical threshold is 5 percent, which means that a party must win at least 5 percent of the votes cast in the contested electoral district in order to gain a seat in the legislative assembly.

Finally, it is important to notice that evidence gathered over time from the experience of other democracies shows that PR by itself is not the cause of government instability.[10] Instability of government typically has more to do with the governing system and the political culture than with the electoral system. There is no need, for example, to consider changing to a parliamentary system from America's three-branch system of government with its independent executive (the president). As long as the American president is elected independently to head the executive branch of government, then PR in the House of Representatives would never lead to a situation where a government cannot be formed.

Under the electoral system proposed here, Americans would, in all probability, witness the rise of a variety of strong nationwide parties serving to represent nearly every voter (and not just voting districts) in Congress. A greater number of national leaders, working with party teams, would give nearly all citizens a voice in political debate. Interest-group politics could gradually be demoted to second place behind genuine party politics. And citizens could begin to experience direct representation in a more deliberative Congress. In all probability, voter turnout would increase, while demand for real statecraft over interest-group brokering would grow, as interparty negotiations and accommodation proceeded in Congress. By means of such a system, the unity of the republic's national political community could be reconciled with the representation of the true diversity of the nationwide citizenry. The pluralism of political convictions would be respected and channeled through real competition into shared responsibility for the national commonwealth that belongs to all citizens. This reform would facilitate both structural and confessional pluralism by doing greater justice to the structure of the electoral system and assuring room for the equal, proportionate treatment of the political convictions of all citizens. This is something Christians should be able to advocate as a matter of principle.

A sound electoral system is only one part of what is needed to promote stronger citizenship. But it is one of the most important parts. If we are serious about encouraging Christians to contribute to a more just political community and world, then the reform of the American electoral system is an example of what could be done to strengthen the civic vocation and the representation of all citizens.

family, marriage, and education

The United States and many other countries around the world today are highly complex societies consisting of different kinds of relationships, organizations, and institutions that are relatively free to shape their own distinctive identities and purposes. Families, churches, businesses, scientific and artistic organizations, universities, newspapers, book publishers, and thousands of nonprofit organizations all follow their own courses, acting not as departments of government or as the delegated programs of an established church. Parents in a home bear responsibility for their children, and children grow up learning they are accountable to their parents. Employers and employees, teachers and students, friends and neighbors all bear distinct types of responsibility defined by the peculiar character of their relationships and institutions. Consequently, the just and equal treatment of citizens in a political community cannot be achieved if the law does not recognize that individuals are always *more than* citizens.[1] How then should public law take into account the full breadth and complexity of human experience? Or, to ask it in a different way, how can government do justice to citizens (political creatures) who are always more than members of a political community and who are not, in fact, autonomous individuals, but thoroughly *inter*dependent social creatures?

Some of the most important public policy issues in any society always revolve around the questions of government's relation to nongovernmental institutions, organizations, and interpersonal relationships. In a liberal-minded country like the United States, the tendency is to focus on the rights of individuals in relation to government and to overlook the identities and responsibilities of institutions. There are fundamental protections of individuals that certainly must be upheld. But there is more to life and the law than individual rights and freedoms. The limits of an individualist perspective are especially apparent when it comes to a consideration of the core institutions in any society, namely, family, marriage, and schooling.[2] Christian political engagement must address the constitutional and public-policy relationships to these institutions.

The Family

Let's enter the discussion of these concerns at a natural starting point, namely, with the birth of a child in a family. Starting here is not to ignore the fact that many children grow up in broken homes or without adequate parenting, particularly in places where war, famine, and disease leave countless orphans in their wake. Nor should we ignore the fact that families are shaped by the societies in which they live. Nevertheless, newborns typically enter the world completely dependent on their families (or on part of a family or a family substitute). The birth experience—even when involving high-tech medical assistance—is a newborn's experience with his or her mother and (one hopes) father, siblings, and an extended family. A newborn enters the world and begins to mature from within an all-encompassing and intimate social setting—mother, child, and immediate family. Every bodily function, every experience inside and eventually outside the home, is experienced by the infant in the family or through the mediation of the family.[3] That is why the family is generally thought to be the seedbed of society, the basis of any social order, the key to almost everything else humans can do in schools, businesses, and political life.

The legitimate process of social differentiation, which we have been affirming in this book, does not contradict the largely undifferentiated experience of an infant in the family. Healthy social differentiation demonstrates the peculiar truth that mature people can handle *multiple* responsibilities as expressions of their *singular* personal identity. Spouses in a marriage are always and everywhere married to one another even when separated in space, but each is also more than a spouse. Parents of children are always and everywhere parents, but each is also more than a parent. A woman who is a wife and mother might also be a journalist, a church member, a student, and a citizen at the same time. None of those differentiated roles or experiences is reducible to the others, and none allows for the reduction of the others to itself. Problems arise only with schizophrenia or multiple-personality disorder or with people who have so compartmentalized their lives that they lose awareness of their identity as whole persons with many roles and responsibilities.

Hindrances to healthy social differentiation make for another story, however. In a differentiated society, a family whose husband and father refuses to allow the wife and mother to function in any role other than wife and mother is not thereby strengthening the family unit but hindering the development of the woman's full personhood.[4] A state that tries to build a unified civic community by trying to exercise omnicompetent control over the whole of society is not creating a more integrated and equal society but is violating the nongovernment responsibilities that belong to people and is thereby undermining their capability and willingness to contribute to public life.

The point is this: the healthy (normative) differentiation of society opens the way to a multiplicity of responsibilities that are mutually compatible with, not mutually exclusive of, one another. And it takes the full range of social responsibilities to express the richness of what it means to be mature humans. A person can hold or exercise multiple responsibilities simultaneously precisely because none of them is exhaustive of the human person, none of them demands the entire life of a person, and none may lay claim to an undifferentiated, omnicompetent authority over all others. The other side of this coin is that any differentiated institution or association that tries to exercise authority beyond its competence will inevitably interfere with other institutions and responsibilities.

The single anomaly here might appear to be the family. I have just argued that infants and young children experience (or should experience) all of their early life from within the context of family life. Yet if the family itself is but one differentiated social institution among many, and if the family does not bear omnicompetent authority over its children and all of society, how may it function in such an all-encompassing way for children? The key factor that dissolves the apparent anomaly is the difference between young children and adults. The family, from the standpoint of the parents and the rest of society, is only one differentiated institution among many, and therefore healthy parenting entails rearing children toward adult maturity for life in an open, differentiated society, not for slavery or stunted growth within the confines of a closed family, clan, autonomous plantation, or totalitarian state.

Nevertheless, within the limits of their differentiated authority, parents should be recognized as the *principals* (having legal principalship) in the rearing of their children from birth to the age of majority (legal adulthood).[5] The experience of children from birth through infancy and childhood, in other words, ought to be recognized as an experience that legitimately develops from within the family, *by way of parental guidance*, toward participation in a complex social world. Bearing responsibility as a mature person in a diversity of social spheres generally becomes possible, however, only if that person can grow into such responsibilities from out of the early childhood experience of a wholesome, all-connecting family bond (or close family substitute). To be truly human in maturity, in other words, is to be able to experience life as an integral whole even though the wholeness manifests differentiated complexity.

It follows, then, that public policies that aim to improve the life of children should always aim to strengthen family life and parental responsibility for children. No other differentiated institution, including the political community, should be allowed to displace parental responsibility for child rearing. Governments certainly should guard the lives of all citizens, including children, from any molestation or threat to life. Thus, public intervention into highly dysfunctional homes to protect children (or spouses) from abuse should be considered part of the proper task of government, not an illegitimate interference in family life.[6] But from this point of view, child abuse is not a legitimate part of child rearing; it actually represents parental violation of their child-rearing responsibility. Healthy child rearing involves the oversight and nurturing of children from the newborn's undifferentiated experience in the beginning through to majority independence.

This is the context in which to make the argument for the protection of the unborn. There will inevitably be circumstances (such as danger to the life of a mother) in which an abortion may be warranted, but those circumstances should be seen as exceptional. Public law ought to be grounded constitutionally in the presumption that human life originates and develops in families from conception through to adult maturity. Only in the framework of liberal thought does one begin with supposedly autonomous individuals and then play off one individual (the mother) against another (the not-yet-born child). Only from an individualist perspective does one try to deal with the highly important concerns of women's health and autonomy by legally disconnecting a pregnant woman and the father from the unborn child by defining the unborn as not a human person and thus without a right to be protected. Of course, a child in the womb is not a person like an adult, a six-year-old, or even a newborn child. But the unborn is nothing other than human, with the meaning of its life dependent on the family bond. It is thus, first of all, the family that public policy should be concerned to protect, enhance, and encourage in the exercise of its responsibilities. The unborn and young children are not isolable from the family context, and to try to isolate them legally as separate entities in order to conform to liberal individualist assumptions is to disregard the family as an institution constitutive of human identity.

All of this means something distinct for children and adults. For children it means that the law should *not* recognize parentlike authority in anyone other than parents or guardians. In the case of schooling, for example, where young children will be under the tutelage of teachers who serve *in loco parentis*, it should be the parents themselves, not government, who act as the *principals* in placing their children in schools. For adults, however, no differentiated institution should be allowed to act toward its members—its employees, citizens, students, customers, or clients—*as if* it had all-embracing, parentlike authority over them. Politically speaking, all tendencies toward a paternalistic or maternalistic state are dangerous. Public policies that require schools, for example, to function as homes, day-care centers, job-training centers, and private police forces are misguided.

At the same time, however, the interdependence of persons and institutions in a differentiated society shows that child rearing is not something parents can accomplish without support and encouragement from the outside. Political communities should recognize that the future of healthy citizenship depends on healthy parenting and educating of children. It is good and just public policy for a government to provide income-tax deductions for the care of dependents, subsidy for the cost of basic education, support of medical care, and so forth. All of this is in keeping with the nurturing of a healthy and just political community in which family life, child rearing, education, and health care should not depend on a family's wealth, religious confession, or racial identity.

Same-Sex Marriage?

There are many important questions related to marriage that we will not address here, such as what constitutes a healthy marriage? When is divorce justified? How should Christians interpret biblical texts that deal with equality and headship in marriage, with polygamy and monogamy, and with the ways marriage reveals something about the relation of the bride of Christ to her bridegroom? The focus of our concern is with the way marriage, in the United States at least, should be recognized in public law. Governments and the law do not create marriage, but they need to recognize its identity in order to give it proper treatment under the law.

Likewise, there are many important questions about homosexuality that we will not take up here, such as whether a homosexual orientation is natural or learned. Is homosexual practice a healthy or unhealthy form of sexual expression? Does the Bible condemn homosexual practice and if so what are the implications for Jews, Christians, and Muslims? Our attention will be focused instead on the question of how public law should respond to those seeking recognition of same-sex partnerships as marriages.

From the start, I am taking for granted that every person in a political community should receive equal treatment and protection under the law. Governments should uphold the dignity of every person and protect them from abuse and threats to life and property regardless of a person's color, religion, wealth or poverty, sexual orientation, marital status, or any other distinction. This means that government should not abridge or permit the infringement of any person's right to life, liberty, speech, association, and religious practice. This means, among other things, upholding those rights for persons who believe that religion is foolishness, or that Islam is superior to Christianity, or that monogamy is old-fashioned, or that there is a difference between healthy and unhealthy sexual practices. Likewise, many distinctions must be made if the law is to uphold and protect the civil rights of all. Children are not adults; modes of speech or association that endanger life are not the same as those that protect life; the marriage bond is different from a commercial contract; membership (as student or faculty member) in a university is different from membership (as a citizen) in a political community; and so forth. These and many other kinds of distinction are part of the structural and confessional diversity of human society. Free and open debate, including political and legal contention, about these matters is essential to a healthy political community. The question on which we want to focus our attention is how public law should identify and deal justly with marriage and whether it is just for the law to identify and treat same-sex partnerships as marriages.

On June 26, 2013, the US Supreme Court handed down two rulings, each by a 5-4 decision, on the matter of same-sex marriage. One concerned a California ballot initiative, known as Proposition 8, which amended the state's constitution to define marriage as a bond between a man and a woman. Proposition 8 passed by a majority of votes in 2008 and thus became part of California's constitution. That took place subsequent to a ruling by the California Supreme Court affirming that same-sex unions deserved the same recognition as heterosexual marriages. Those events led to legal disputes and appeals that went all the way to the US Supreme Court. The high Court, however, decided that the parties to the dispute did not have legal standing before it. In other words, the case as presented should not have reached the Court, and the Justices voted 5-4 to "vacate" and "remand" it, sending it back to California for resolution. Proponents of same-sex marriage in California immediately revived their quest for equal protection on the basis of the earlier ruling by the California Supreme Court while opponents of same-sex marriage countered that the statewide vote of the majority in support of the constitutional amendment—Proposition 8—meant same-sex partnerships should not be recognized as marriage.

The second case decided by the Supreme Court on June 26 concerned a law passed by Congress and signed by the president in 1996 called the Defense of Marriage Act (DOMA), which said that only heterosexual unions should be recognized as marriages under federal law. In the years that followed, however, twelve states decided to recognize same-sex unions as marriages. It is important to emphasize here that from the beginning of the republic marriage law has always been a matter of state jurisdiction. The federal Constitution says nothing about marriage. The case before the Supreme Court had come from New York, one of the states that had legalized same-sex marriage. The issue at stake concerned Edith Windsor whose same-sex marriage partner, Thea Spyer, had died and left her estate to Ms. Windsor. However, the IRS (with the force of DOMA behind it) refused to grant her the tax benefit that would have gone to the deceased's husband. The Court ruled that since states have jurisdiction over marriage, DOMA was unconstitutional in denying equal treatment to same-sex marriages in states that recognize them. An unstated implication of the ruling seemed to be that DOMA is constitutional with respect to states that have not legalized same-sex marriage.

As one can see from these two cases, the Supreme Court seemed to be advancing the cause of same-sex marriage, as its advocates claimed at the time. Yet the two cases were more about federalism and equal treatment of citizens under civil rights laws than they were about the identity of marriage as such.

Does this mean, therefore, that the future of the legal definition of marriage will remain a matter for the states to decide, with some states accepting and others rejecting same-sex marriage? Perhaps, but perhaps not.

On the one hand, the Supreme Court declared DOMA unconstitutional because it illegitimately intruded on New York's jurisdiction over marriage law. On the other hand, however, the majority opinion, written by Justice Kennedy, states, "The Constitution's guarantee of equality 'must at the very least mean that a bare congressional desire to harm a politically unpopular group cannot' justify disparate treatment of that group" (p. 20 of the majority opinion in United States v. Windsor, 570 US ___ [2013]). As Justice Scalia pointed out in his dissent, the Court's decision overruled DOMA as "'a deprivation of the liberty of the person protected by the Fifth Amendment of the Constitution' . . . that it violates 'basic due process' principles, . . . and that it inflicts an 'injury and indignity' of a kind that denies 'an essential part of the liberty protected by the Fifth Amendment'" (p. 17 of Justice Antonin Scalia's dissenting opinion).

This language suggests that the Court overruled DOMA because Congress and the president, in enacting the law, expressed an illegitimate (unconstitutional) aim of injuring a particular group of individuals, namely, same-sex married partners. But which was primary in the Court's DOMA decision, upholding the sovereignty of New York (and other states) in determining marriage law or guaranteeing that individuals throughout the United States should not suffer injury from discrimination under federal civil rights laws? There may not be a clear answer to that question in the ruling, but an answer might come in the future when, for instance, a same-sex couple married in New York moves to Kansas and sues that state in federal court on the grounds that Kansas does not recognize same-sex marriage and thus inflicts injury and indignity on the couple in violation of their civil rights. Will the Supreme Court then decide that federal civil rights law trumps state sovereignty where states do not recognize same-sex marriage, or will the Court uphold the right of states to decide what constitutes marriage in their jurisdictions?

It is clear from these Supreme Court decisions that the Justices were relying on the primary tool they had at their disposal, namely, civil rights law. And typically, civil rights law can overrule any matter in a state's jurisdiction if a case can be made that what is at stake is not, first of all, the identity of marriage, or a university, or a religious institution but the federally protected civil rights of individuals. But what about the identity of marriage in distinction from the civil rights of individuals? Has any argument been made about substantive marriage law—about the identity of marriage—in contrast to arguments about civil rights? This question takes us back to the states where state constitutions, legislatures, courts, and/or popular ballot initiatives have the jurisdiction to decide what should be recognized as marriage. Yet what we discover at the state level, as at the federal level, is that almost every argument offered in support of same-sex marriage has been an argument for equal and nondiscriminatory treatment of individuals who want their same-sex partner-ships to be recognized as marriages.

Early in 2005, for example, California Supreme Court Judge Richard Kramer stated that California's ban on same-sex marriage was unconstitutional because it appears "that no rational purpose exists for limiting marriage . . . to opposite-sex partners."[7] But what passed for "rational purpose" in his estimation? May a legal tradition that has stood for thousands of years be declared to have no rational purpose after only a few decades of opposition to it? Judge Kramer stated that an appeal to tradition in support of heterosexual marriage is no stronger than earlier appeals to tradition in support of a ban on interracial marriage. However, the ban on interracial marriage was based on racial discrimination and was not concerned with the heterosexual identity of marriage. Until very recently, societies almost everywhere have recognized heterosexual marriage as having a distinct identity and a rational purpose related to establishing bonds for family life and social order arising from marriage's potential for procreation and child rearing. The primary historical disputes over marriage have been about polygamy and monogamy, not about same-sex and opposite-sex marriage. Jews, Christians, Muslims, and those of other faiths have recognized the institution of marriage as natural or divinely established with creation. To be sure, a long tradition is no guarantee of its truth and justice, but a decision to change what the law has recognized as marriage demands more than a civil rights argument in support of individual freedom and equality.

In recent decades, however, a different attitude toward marriage has emerged, rooted in the liberal tendency to see all relationships as created by the individu-als who participate in them. A growing number of people, including many who believe marriage should be between man and a woman, think of marriage as a partnership established by two people for sexual and other kinds of companion-ship. Marriage is thus being reconceived as a relationship of mutual commitment where sexual difference is no longer necessary as a defining characteristic. The conception of marriage is changing from an institution that a man and a woman enter, to a commitment individuals make to love each other in ways they deem appropriate. This development has been aided, of course, by new technolo-gies of birth control and extrauterine embryo development and implantation as well as by growing acceptance of the legitimacy of adoption by same-sex couples. If two men or two women can create a family by adopting children (if they want them), or by drawing on sperm and egg donors and employing surrogate mothers, then there no longer appears to be a "rational purpose" for excluding same-sex couples from the circle of those permitted to create families. And if marriage is reconceived as an intimate partnership that any two people can establish, then the identity of marriage as an exclusively and distinctively heterosexual union can be discarded by legal decree.

These developments raise many legal as well as social and moral questions about both marriage and the family. If, for example, marriage is what two individuals, or a popular majority in a state, are free to call it, then why should three or more partners not have a right to call their bond a marriage? If marriage is a matter of individual choice and no longer about an institution's identity, then on what legal grounds could a court or a majority of legislators argue that their refusal to recognize polygamy (either heterosexual or homosexual) inflicts no injury or indignity on polygamists? If the argument is made that homosexual as well as heterosexual marriage must be monogamous because monogamy is part of the American tradition, how can such an appeal to tradition be allowed to stand? If marriage is grounded in the right of individuals not to be discriminated against in their choice of a partner, then what rational purpose is left for denying civil rights protection to those who want to join with more than one partner in marriage?

Insofar as governments want to encourage enduring friendships and bonds of love and commitment that would make possible the sharing of benefits formerly enjoyed only by heterosexual marriage partners, there are many ways to change the laws governing health care, social security, inheritance, and taxation to achieve those purposes without using marriage as the means to that end. Moreover, if such bonds are going to be encouraged, then there should be a further widening of the law to allow two or more persons who have no intention of engaging in sexual relations to benefit from joining a bond of mutual care that they do not consider a marriage or a family. If such people are denied the social and economic benefits that flow to heterosexual and homosexual partners, won't they experience their exclusion as the infliction of legal injury and indignity in violation of their civil rights?

The burden of my concern here arises from the conviction that the civil rights protection of individuals is not a sufficient basis for dealing with the institutional identities and rights of marriages, families, schools, churches, and business corporations. Individuals should certainly enjoy the protection of their civil rights, including freedom of speech, association, and religious practice as well as access to a fair trial, the right to vote, and equal treatment under the law. However, marriages, families, and many other institutions are not reducible to the individuals who exercise responsibility in them. The farther our society moves in the direction of believing that human relationships of all kinds are nothing more than contractual constructs by autonomous individuals, the more we will find that the wide variety of institutional identities and obligations so important to the dignity of persons created in the image of God will sink away into the morass of competing rights claims with no one left to adjudicate them but judges in the courts.

Justice for Schooling

Let's turn now to a third crucial matter of public-legal concern that involves at least three institutions. There are two fundamental legal principles that have structured education law in the United States for most of its history. One is that parents are the legal *principals* in the education of their children. The second is that government is the *principal* in the education of citizens. Early in American history, the first principle predominated and different kinds of schools were organized to serve the needs of parents and their children. Gradually, however, more and more localities and states began to operate on the basis of the second principle, starting with Massachusetts and New York. The two approaches did not run into much conflict until local and state governments began to require and fund schooling for all children. The subsequent conflicts and the ways governments have tried to resolve those conflicts open a window on crucial issues of structural and confessional pluralism that are fundamental to a just republic.

In the 1840s, when large numbers of Catholic immigrants began to settle in Boston and New York, Catholic leaders requested public funding for their schools similar to the public financial support that was at that time going to the common schools of the white Anglo-Saxon Protestant (WASP) majority. In response to those requests, officials in New York City established the New York Public School Society to oversee schooling decisions that would be appropriate for the public. That society determined that public funds for schooling ought to go only to "nonsectarian" schools and not to "sectarian" schools. It was a decision that essentially granted a public-funding monopoly to the common schools of the majority with an open invitation to Catholics to send their children (at no cost) to those schools so they could become properly Americanized.[8]

The New York Public School Society's decision established a pattern that has continued to this day, a pattern that has been adopted throughout the country. It was built on two presumptions. The first was that the majority of the people (who were WASP at the time) had every right to monopolize publicly funded schooling for the purpose of strengthening the moral unity of the whole society. That is what "nonsectarian" meant. The word did *not* mean "nonreligious" because the common schools regularly read from the King James Bible, taught religious ethics, said prayers, and in general fostered a WASP way of life among the students. The word "sectarian" referred, without saying so, to Catholic schools, for they read a different version of the Bible, taught children that their supreme authority was the pope, and did other "un-American" things. The Catholic schools would receive no public funds and would thus be kept outside the mainstream of American life. They could remain open, but only in private at private expense. Of course, in slave states, no schooling at all was offered to slave children, and that was only one part of the much larger story of the injustice suffered by slaves in the United States.

Catholics were free to set up their own schools, and parents were free to send their children to those schools if they chose to do so, but as citizens they were also obligated to pay taxes to support the government-run schools. Before long, other state governments, following the lead of Massachusetts and New York, adopted this approach, recognizing two ways that parents could educate their children with government approval: either by sending them to the publicly funded common schools or by sending them to so-called sectarian schools. The public schools belonged to the majority through government ownership and operation. The private schools belonged to those who established them on a private, nongovernment basis. Parental principalship continued to be honored, in part, because parents were allowed to send their children to either the public schools or the private schools.

This inequitable system was firmed up in federal law when the US Supreme Court ruled in 1925 on a case from the state of Oregon. Oregon had attempted to outlaw Catholic schools entirely, and the court ruled (in *Pierce v. Society of Sisters*) that parents could not be denied the right to choose religious schools because their children "are not mere creatures of the state." Yet even though that decision confirmed the principalship of parents in the education of their minor children, it did nothing to overcome the inequity involved in the government's monopolization of tax income for its schools alone. From my point of view, this legal framework of American schooling, which continues largely intact today, violates both structural and confessional pluralism. A resolution of the inequity can be found only by upholding the principalship of parents and requiring that government give equal treatment to all students and all schools to which their parents choose to send them.[9]

As we argued above, parents in the family bear chief responsibility for rearing their *children*. That involves much more than educating them, but when it comes to decisions about schooling, the parents should be able to choose the school they prefer without any inequitable treatment of their children by the government or other parties. As soon as schools enter the picture, another social structure with its own differentiated calling comes to the fore. Teachers in schools educate *students*. Schools are not families, and teachers do not raise students as their children. But neither do schools focus only on the minimum requirements that governments might establish for basic civic education. Schools typically offer educational riches (such as music, art, and a range of sciences and humanities) that far exceed the basic requirements governments may have in mind for what is essential for self-control, employability, and civic responsibility. Nevertheless, there is every reason to acknowledge that the differentiated institution of the political community has its own legitimate interest in the basic education of every young *citizen* so that none of them is denied access to opportunities in the wider society.

Thus, it is evident that minors should be viewed from at least three vantage points when it comes to their education and maturation: as *children* in homes, as *students* in schools, and as *citizens* in the political community. And it is precisely government's responsibility to see that justice is done to all three of these institutions in order that youngsters receive their due as children in families, students in schools, and citizens of the political community. Indeed, children "are not mere creatures of the state."

The second important ingredient here is confessional pluralism. If government is to uphold the First Amendment freedoms of families and schools, it has no right to impose a penalty or an advantage on one faith or on one type of association. It was fundamentally unjust for the WASP majority in the 1840s to approve public funding only for the schools that taught their way of life while disallowing public funding for schools that taught a different way of life. That was the equivalent of an establishment of religion and discrimination against one kind of school in favor of another kind of school. If public justice is going to characterize the education policies of government, then nondiscriminatory and equitable treatment should be assured for all families and schools without regard to the faiths on which they are built.

Why have Christians, among others, been willing to accept the inequitable system of schooling that the United States has upheld since the 1840s? In part, it is because the majority has, by and large, been more interested in upholding the American way of life than in upholding public justice for diverse institutional structures and views of life. Protestants through much of the nineteenth century promoted many anti-Catholic causes. Their civil-religious vision of America was not only antimonarchical but also anti-Catholic. At the same time, their distinction between "nonsectarian" and "sectarian" gradually became identified with the distinction between secular and sacred, between state and church, between public and private. Today, as a consequence, the supposedly nonsectarian public schools are no longer WASP in character, and all private schools (whether religious or not) are treated as undeserving of equitable funding from the public treasury. The inequitable structure remains even though the religious ideologies have changed.

This general accommodation to the nonsectarian/sectarian division in schooling is supported by a view of life that thwarts public justice for all, for it reveals a deeply religious commitment that is given public-legal privilege (establishment) over other views of life. Listen carefully to the following profession of faith by commentator Ellen Willis:

> I believe that a democratic polity requires a secular state: one that does not fund or otherwise sponsor religious institutions and activities; that does not display religious symbols; that outlaws discrimination based on religious belief, whether by government or by private employers, landlords or proprietors—that does, in short, guarantee freedom from as well as freedom of religion. Furthermore, a genuinely democratic society requires a secular ethos: one that does not equate morality with religion, stigmatize atheists, defer to religious interests and aims over others or make religious belief an informal qualification for public office. Of course, secularism in the latter sense is not mandated by the First Amendment. It's a matter of sensibility, not law.[10]

Indeed, Willis is correct that belief in a secularized public arena is not mandated by the First Amendment. To the contrary, the First Amendment declares that there should be no legal infringement of the free exercise of religion. Yet Willis, like so many others, insists that the only religions that should be fully protected by the First Amendment are highly privatized ones that are willing to accept the government's establishment of a secularized view of life in the public arena. She wants courts and legislators to *establish* the faith of secularism as a matter of public sensibility.

Part of what makes Willis's language work is her unexamined supposition that there is nothing religious or confessional about her own profession of faith. Her language depends on readers sharing her deeply held belief that "religions" as she defines them are separable, private matters. But her argument hides her own faith commitment even if she is not conscious of it. For her way of life can be upheld only if her view of life is granted a monopoly over the common life of the political community. Willis's conviction manifests the same characteristics as the nineteenth-century WASP belief that its self-declared nonsectarianism was religiously neutral. I believe, to the contrary, that a political community—the American republic—should recognize and protect the plural structure of society and the confessional diversity of the American public. The Constitution's First Amendment should be taken for what it says, not for what has been read into it. The First Amendment does not call for public secularity and the privatization of religion any more than it grants to a majority the right to decide which of the confessional viewpoints among the people should be eligible or ineligible for special treatment under the law.

From a principled pluralist point of view, we read the First Amendment to say that religious free exercise must be protected in all areas of life and that the establishment of religion can be avoided only by giving equal treatment to all citizens, not granting the privilege of establishment to any religion or ideology. The First Amendment's nonestablishment clause does not mean "no aid to religious groups"; it means no establishment of any religion or religiously equivalent institution or confession. If the convictions of citizens, whether Christian or secularist, whether Jewish or Muslim, guide them to educate their children in keeping with their deepest convictions and ways of life, then government has no authority to discriminate against some of them or to establish one of them. Confessional pluralism should be upheld as a matter of principle by recognizing that the religions of many Americans are ways of life and not only ways of private worship. The Constitution as many read it guarantees its citizens the free *exercise* of their religions, not merely freedom of conscience or freedom to associate privately to educate their children as "sectarian" citizens.

Confessional pluralism for schooling should be coupled with structural pluralism. Government should begin by doing justice fully, not partially, to parental principalship in education. Schools chosen by parents should be recognized as differentiated social institutions in their own right and not as extensions of the family or as departments of state. The government's legitimate concern should be to require a certain level of education for all citizens and to help make that possible by funding the schooling of all children, implemented by fair and non-discriminatory treatment of all families and all schools. If 55 percent of parents choose schools that present themselves as secular and nonsectarian, then 55 percent of the public funding should go to those schools either directly or via student vouchers. If 15 percent of parents choose Catholic schools for their children, then 15 percent of public funding should go to those schools on the same terms. Moreover, most states now recognize home schooling and various kinds of charter schools. Each mode of education requires just and equitable treatment within the framework proposed here. The government does not have to own or operate any schools in order to require, for example, (1) that every student must achieve a certain level of proficiency in English, math, history, and science; (2) that every school must be transparent in making known its philosophy of education, its governance structure, its curriculum offerings, and the test scores of its students on one or another standard testing measure; and (3) that every school provide adequate and appropriate education for students with disabilities (which would be supported by proportionately greater public funding). Many other details of government's education policies would need to be worked out to assure that equal opportunity and justice for all students is being upheld. It is not the aim of this book or of this chapter to do that. But the principles of structural and confessional pluralism are the foundation on which government should act.

Schooling has always been one of the most important and most controversial matters in modern societies. Today, that is even more the case in our complex, globalizing societies. Christian citizens ought to be vigorously engaged in promoting nondiscriminatory public support for the education of all young people. Out of concern for everyone created in the image of God and for the just treatment of all our neighbors, we should act with the conviction that there is no justification for patterns of schooling that contribute to unemployment, religious discrimination, and inequitable burdens on many families, particularly those who are poor. Justice for schooling demands government's adherence to principled pluralism as a central pillar of the common good. Thus, in this as in many other areas of public policy, new modes of Christian political engagement are urgently required.

economics
and the environment

To exercise our civic responsibilities with the aim of promoting a just political community, we need to give high priority to economic life and the environment. These are two of the most important arenas of policy dispute throughout the world today. At the outset, we must come to grips with deeply held beliefs about free markets, free trade, limited government, and economic growth that have exerted such great influence in the United States and internationally. Many of the assumptions that have undergirded economic policy in recent decades are now being called into question because of the increasing frequency of international crises such as the financial collapse that began in 2008, causing the greatest economic and political upheaval since the Great Depression.

Two of the most frequently repeated phrases in the discussion of politics and economics in the United States are "free enterprise" and "free markets." These are hallmarks of a liberal society, which is built, in part, on the idea that individuals should be free to own property and to buy and sell products and services in open markets. Yet freedom does not mean anarchy to most entrepreneurs, consumers, and capitalists, who want government to protect and encourage their pursuits. But does everything about human life and politics ultimately boil down to individual freedom, economics, and free markets? Most of us typically distinguish the economy from families, schools, nonprofit organizations, and personal relationships. Is that a mistake? Or are all of these really just functions of "the economy"?

We have been arguing that government exists within and for a political community, which is more than a market. Government is not a reflex of individual freedom but an office of responsibility within a political community, such as the republic of the United States. To properly exercise its responsibilities, government must certainly do justice to everything related to economic needs, organizations, production, and commerce. Yet the political community does not exist simply as an adjunct to free markets and private property. Consequently, a distinction we will work with in this chapter is the following: economic activities related to business, commerce, and employment are those qualified or distinguished by an *economic purpose*, while the activities related to government and citizenship in a political community are qualified or distinguished by the *purpose of upholding public justice for the common good of all*. We will also be assuming that the people involved in both economic and political life are always more than economic and political creatures.

In this chapter, I will attempt to frame the question of how the political community should do justice to economic responsibilities in the larger context of a complex society. To do this it is first necessary to look briefly at the great influence of John Locke and Adam Smith on American political and economic culture.

John Locke, Adam Smith, and Liberal/Conservative Economics

John Locke (1632–1704) is the primary source of what is generally referred to as the liberal tradition, which includes both conservatives and liberals in the United States.[1] For Locke, all humans were created by God in a state of equality, "without subordination or subjection" to one another.[2] Moreover, God gave "the world to men in common," and they are to make the best use of reason to enjoy life (134). In Locke's view, however, there is no divinely appointed responsibility for "men in common" to manage and *govern* the earth and all that is in it. What is shared in common among individuals is the Maker's law of nature, "which teaches all mankind who will but consult it that, being all equal and independent, no one ought to harm another in his life, health, liberty, or possessions" (123).

The meaning of the word "common" for Locke is that each person shares the same rationality and liberty and is subject to the same law of nature. That which is universal, in other words, is the law of individual freedom, not a law that holds for common responsibilities. "The natural liberty of man is to be free from any superior power on earth, and not to be under the will or legislative authority of man, but to have only the law of nature for his rule" (132). As a consequence, the only way a common interest or common project can come up for rational consideration is through agreed-upon action of free individuals. Before such action can take place, however, individuals are already appropriating things around them for their personal use. They have begun, in freedom, to mix their labor with their natural environment and thus to make it part of themselves. Locke puts it this way:

> Though the earth and all inferior creatures be common to all men, yet every man has a property in his own person; this nobody has any right to but himself.

The labour of his body and the work of his hands, we may say, are properly his. Whatsoever then he removes out of the state that nature hath provided and left it in, he hath mixed his labour with, and joined to it something that is his own, and thereby makes it his property. It being by him removed from the common state nature hath placed it in, it hath by this labour something annexed to it that excludes the common right of other men. For this labour being the unquestionable property of the labourer, no man but he can have a right to what that is once joined to, at least where there is enough and as good left in common for others. (134)

Furthermore, Locke continues, "the taking of this or that part [out of the state of nature] does not depend on the express consent of all the commoners" but becomes "my property without the assignation or consent of anybody. The labour that was mine, removing them out of that common state they were in, hath fixed my property in them" (135). One critic has called Locke's perspective "possessive individualism."[3]

Locke begins, in other words, with a picture of free persons doing work independent of any political or legal context (other than the law of nature) and apart from any environmental concern or obligation. He does recognize one moral limit to what a person may rightfully possess: there must be "enough and as good left in common for others." If we ask whether there is anything for which individuals bear *joint* responsibility either in the development and use of their possessions or in the protection of themselves and their own properties, Locke answers that there is indeed a major institution that transcends individual freedom and private possession. But it comes later as a creation by the free individuals who have already become property owners. That institution is the civil government. Government is not something ordained by God above or as a condition of individual liberty. Individuals are not *naturally* political. They were not created for political community. Rather, government comes later when free individuals decide to establish it by a mutual contract to protect their lives and properties (184).

The limit to freedom that individuals are willing to accept arises from the desire to avoid a limit they do not want to accept, namely, "the invasion of others" into their lives and properties. The equal freedom of others is what gives birth to fears and insecurity. Free but fearful and insecure individuals thus decide to establish an umpire to protect each of their lives and properties from others (168–83). That umpire is what Locke calls civil government, and the creation of government is what establishes political society. No political society can exist, says Locke, "without having in itself the power to preserve the property and, in order thereunto, punish the offences of all those of that society . . . where every one of the members hath quitted his natural power, resigned it up into the hands of the community in all cases that excludes him not from appealing for protection to the law established by it" (163).

The responsibility of government for political society, in other words, arises by delegation from the original self-government of individuals. There is no other commons or human community for which government bears a prior responsibility. In fact, the authority of the government is a mere extension of each person's self-government, much like property becomes a person's possession as an extension of his or her own self-possession. In one sense, then, we can say that for Locke there is no such thing as *public* authority or *public* government but only the consolidation of many private self-governments into a common or compound self-government (164). Nevertheless, in the establishment of government, individuals do give up some of their autonomy; they quit at least some of their natural powers and resign them up into the hands of the community.

The importance of this point both for interest-group politics and for environmental protection cannot be overemphasized. Each person gives to the government the power to punish offenses against the law of nature, which are offenses against any person's freedom and private property, and yet that governmental power is, in an important sense, merely the extension of each person's original power to execute one's own judgments that are now to be made through one's representatives, who are an extension of individual liberty and property. This act of creating political society, says Locke, is what takes individuals out of the state of nature and into a commonwealth. The government of the commonwealth is thus "a judge on earth, with authority to determine all the controversies and redress the injuries that may happen to any member of the commonwealth; which judge is the legislative, or magistrate appointed by it" (164). The government thus has genuine power and is supported by the obligation that each member of the society must now yield to the majority determination of what the law should be (169). Yet no rational person would enter into a political society that did not have as its purpose to support and protect each individual's life and property (186).

Entirely foreign to Locke's thinking—and to liberalism to this day—is recognition of the political community as the original, institutional context of government's obligations, of government's offices of responsibility and accountability to uphold public justice for the common good. To have standing before the law in a liberal society, individuals must have a life- or property-interest that government has been created to protect. Consequently, a broad-based, society-wide ecological concern would have to rise to a level of such importance for a large number of property owners that a majority of legislators would agree that it deserves the attention of civil law. But legislation to protect the environment in the interest of the majority would have to be written and passed time and again, in case after case, and not once and for all, because government's mandate always comes back to the protection of private property, life, and liberty, not to the protection of a political community's hypothetical common good.

John Locke was essentially a political philosopher who built his idea of civil society on the basis of individual freedom, labor, private property, and economic exchange. Adam Smith (1723–1790), however, gave his attention directly to "the wealth of nations"[4] and argued that markets for free exchange were crucial for a nation that wanted to expand its wealth. Smith believed that governments cannot engineer economic progress and wealth directly. But if governments will legalize entrepreneurial freedom and free exchange, then the prosperity of society as a whole and the improvement of the condition of everyone will come about *indirectly* by the guidance and coordination of an "invisible hand," a kind of divine, providential enforcer of the natural law.

Some critics, like Duncan Foley, criticize Smith for failing to show how market freedom of that kind can indirectly generate the common good.[5] Foley refers to this problem as "Adam's fallacy" because, for Smith, the government is supposed to remain largely passive in regard to the supposed transmutation of multiple self-interested acts into the larger public good—the "common-wealth." While it may be true that market capitalism generates many more private goods, it does not guarantee that everyone in society benefits equitably from that prosperity, says Foley.

The libertarian response to the idea of Adam's fallacy is to insist that there is no fallacy. If the conscience of free individuals compels them to reach out privately to assist neighbors in need, then that is laudable and in keeping with individual freedom, but social-service philanthropy is not government's job. In fact, governmental benevolence can get in the way of market disciplines that are necessary for economic efficiency and growth, and without the latter, there will not be much wealth generated to benefit the larger society. At the other end of the spectrum, the response of liberal liberals to Adam's fallacy is to say that government should fulfill two kinds of economic responsibility: one is to keep the marketplace as free as possible for the pursuit of economic self-interest so that more and more wealth can be generated; the second is for government to extract by taxation some of the wealth produced through private enterprise to provide safety nets for individuals who don't benefit as much from, or are hurt by, the capitalist system.

What is missing from the views of both libertarian liberals and liberal liberals is the recognition that a political community has an identity and purpose of its own different from that of a mere umpire of economic markets. Consequently, when governments do act on a wider range of activities, as they inevitably do, there are always those on the right who say government has gone too far in interfering with market disciplines and freedom, and those on the left who say government hasn't done enough to overcome economic inequalities so all individuals can share in growing prosperity. Commentator Sebastian Mallaby tries to resolve this opposition from a standpoint in the middle, reminding his American readers that we live in a *mixed* economy, that is, a *single* economy that mixes private and public enterprises. The more developed a society becomes, the more public goods citizens want, not all of which can be produced by free enterprise. Public goods, says Mallaby, are "the things that government produces:

security (from criminals and terrorists), clean air and water, food and medicine whose safety is guaranteed by regulators, public education, and so on."[6] Yet, says Mallaby, we need to remember that "free markets do a lot of jobs better than government," so we should not hesitate to "embrace growing government," but we should "be ruthless about making government and markets more efficient. If your private-sector engine is shrinking relative to your public-sector vehicle, you need to root out every design flaw that threatens to slow you down."[7]

In Mallaby's view, American society, or the American way of life, is one big public vehicle with a private-sector engine. That engine-driven vehicle—America—must do everything possible not to slow down economically. Government and private enterprises are partners in one grand venture of promoting economic goods and growth as speedily as possible. In Mallaby's faith-based picture of reality, there is no significant difference in the institutional purposes of government and business. The two are partners in the same great cause of the market society's quest for constantly expanding prosperity that fuels the progress of freedom. The political community, in this case, has been reduced to, or reconceived as, an economic marketplace. Our highly differentiated society is reduced to an undifferentiated, single-engine vehicle whose aim is ever expanding prosperity.

A "Responsibilities Economy"

In contrast to the liberal/conservative view of economic and political life, I believe we should start with the conviction that the political community is a public institution with its own reason to exist. Economic life should then be approached from the perspective of a "responsibilities economy." The debates between libertarian liberals and liberal liberals do not allow for a proper recognition of the many types of human responsibility that exist in a differentiated society. Yet that recognition is exactly what is necessary if we are to understand how the diversity of economic responsibilities relate to all the other responsibilities we exercise. Most important for our purposes is to understand how justice can be done to all of them, including those that are economic. The way a government serves its citizens, who are also parents, children, students, educators, scientists, artists, doctors, lawyers, employers, and employees, is by recognizing and doing justice to the structural diversity of society—thus "structural pluralism."

The word "responsibility," when we speak of a "responsibilities economy," means at least two things that should be held together. First, the word suggests an *ability* to take initiative, make judgments, and act with intention. The second suggests *accountability*, answerability, where a person or organization bears an obligation of some kind. The first connotation is accented when we say that a child is now able to tie her own shoes and therefore can exercise that responsibility herself. The second connotation comes to the fore when a parent tells a child to take care of his bedroom and make his bed or else there will be consequences. When we speak of responsibility or responsibilities in what follows, we will most often be conveying both connotations at the same time—both capacity and obligation, both capability and accountability.

Why should we enter a discussion of economic life through a consideration of responsibilities? One of the most important reasons is to remind ourselves that the "economy" and "the market" are not entities that exercise responsibility; they are not accountable, answerable subjects. To speak of the economy as if it is something that acts to determine our fate or to call us to action is to see ourselves as mere cogs in a wheel rather than as persons responsible for our actions in organizations as well as individually. To speak of "the economy," in other words, is to speak of an abstraction; it refers to an aggregate of all economically relevant activities carried out by a large number of responsible persons and institutions.

In addition, many types of responsibility are not economically qualified. Educating a student may be essential to all kinds of future employment and economic benefits, but the art of teaching and the work of learning have their own meaning that is not reducible to economic categories. Loving one's children may contribute significantly to their self-confidence, security, and patience as they grow up, helping them to become excellent employers and employees, but the meaning of parent-child love is not reducible to an economic category. Worshiping God may lead communities of the faithful to build houses of worship, publish prayer books, and pay for broadcasting, all of which may lead to employment for construction workers, book producers, and makers of broadcasting equipment. But worship has a heart-deep meaning in its own right that is not primarily economic in character.

It is also quite evident that most individuals in developed societies such as ours exercise a variety of responsibilities *simultaneously*. Today, one person might be an autoworker, a union member, a husband, a father, a church deacon, a member of the volunteer fire department, a consumer, and a citizen, all at the same time. Another might be a real estate developer, a wife, a mother, a consumer, and a citizen, all at the same time. Some of these responsibilities are characteristically economic or economically qualified, while others are not. How, then, can we distinguish them?

Think for a moment about the kinds of responsibilities we ordinarily associate with the market economy, such as making and selling furniture, cell phones, televisions, automobiles, children's toys, and millions of other things. There are also economic services that produce nothing—no things—but that satisfy customers who are willing to pay for an insurance policy, a haircut, leaf raking, counseling, and banking services. Although not all human capabilities are employed in the production of goods and services, even the activities we typically associate with economic life are very different in kind and depend on different capabilities, motivations, and aspirations.

Much of the talk about wealth creation today, says economist John Kay, stresses financial reward as the "mainspring of innovation," but those who talk this way are "apparently unaware that material gain was not even at the back of the minds of those who invented computers, discovered antibiotics or created green revolution crops."[8] According to Kay, "Young people looking towards the world of work should understand that the greatest reward from a job is the satisfaction of doing it well." Even in the business world, says Kay, those who are most successful in the long run "are people who are passionate about business—whose aspirations are to bring new products and services to market, to serve customers better, to motivate their staff to greater efforts."[9] In that respect, a businessperson is not significantly different from a professor or a priest. The reason for pursuing the line of work each person has chosen is because of what that work means to them, how it meshes with their talents and sense of calling. In complex, highly differentiated societies such as ours, there is an economic dimension to everything we do, even if it plays only a minor or indirect role in some activities and employments. At the same time, there is more to life, even in the world of business and markets, than "the economic."

Differentiated yet Interdependent Responsibilities

Michelle Singletary, a commentator on money and finance, tells the following story. For years, she, like many Americans, had no qualms about thinking of herself as a "consumer." "To be a consumer is equivalent to being a good American," she writes. "We use the word consumer when referring to ourselves even when the topic isn't about consuming."[10] But one day she realized this was a mistake because it greatly reduces the way we understand ourselves and distorts the way young people grow up and prepare for life. "More children go shopping every week than read, go to church, participate in youth groups, play outdoors or spend time in household conversation," she commented. Even our national holidays "are celebrated by shopping." What Singletary realized through self-discovery is that humans cannot properly be labeled by only one of the responsibilities they exercise. We all consume resources, goods, and services, but consumption, particularly in the market-measured way we often think of it, is not the defining characteristic of human identity.

To think about human responsibilities in this way drives us back to more basic questions about human identity and the meaning of life. If we are not merely *homo economicus* (economic creatures), then what else are we, and where do economic capabilities and ambitions fit into the larger scheme of things?[11] Amartya Sen, a Nobel Prize–winning economist, argues that poverty, measured as "lowness of income," is not the best way to understand poverty. Income is an *instrumental* factor that can be one means of keeping or lifting people out of poverty, but the more important measure of poverty is the "deprivation of human capabilities." Capability deprivation, he argues, is *intrinsic* poverty.[12] The meaning of human life is found in realizing and exercising one's capabilities, not in gaining wealth. Income is a means to more important ends. "There is a danger," writes Sen, "in seeing poverty in the narrow terms of income deprivation, and then justifying investment in education, health care and so forth on the ground that they are good means to the end of reducing income poverty. That would be a confounding of ends and means." The goal should be to enhance human capabilities rather than to aim at increased income. Enhancing "human capabilities also tends to go with an expansion of productivities and earning power. That connection establishes an important indirect linkage through which capability improvement helps both directly and indirectly in enriching human lives and in making human deprivations more rare and less acute."[13]

Sen's distinction between the "instrumental" and the "intrinsic" lends weight to the argument we've been making. Yet we need to take a further step. Why should we want to enhance human capabilities? Why should humans have freedom to live lives they "have reason to value," as Sen puts it?[14] For Sen, the answer is found in the intrinsic value of human freedom. Others might say the reason is that humans have a right to be happy, to experience the joy of exercising one or more responsibilities. Still others will reason that the greater the number of people who can live lives they value, the greater will be the collective good of society in terms of stability, peacefulness, economic growth, and long-term endurance. All of these reasons may be valid, but they still don't answer questions about who we are, what it means to be human, and why we should prefer stability, peace, wealth, and the fruitful exercise of our capabilities.

A biblical view of human nature identifies capabilities, freedom, happiness, responsibility, and social well-being as dimensions of what it means to bear the image of God, enjoying life and coming to know ourselves through serving God and neighbors. Capabilities, properly developed, are part of our human calling to develop and govern the earth to the glory of God. Human capabilities, like life itself, are gifts from God, and, in their proper exercise through cooperation with one another, we come to know what it means to be human and why we exist. The reason, from a biblical point of view, for wanting each person to be able to develop his or her capabilities is to make possible the maturation and enrichment of everyone for the greater fulfillment of human life. Each person whose capabilities go undeveloped and who is unable to exercise responsibility represents a loss for everyone and a dishonor to God.

The answer to poverty, therefore, is in many ways the same as the answer to wealth. Humans need to work together in order to experience the rich and diversified meaning of life for which God has created us. The gain of more income by individuals can have instrumental value if it grows from and goes hand in hand with the mutual development of human talents and capabilities.

But if economic life is organized in ways that aggravate and perpetuate the capability deprivation of some persons, then it fosters intrinsic poverty that negatively affects all of us, including those who may be wealthy as measured by their income.

Having said this much, we must be careful not to assume that wealth, profit-making, and shopping are necessarily expressions of greed and self-seeking that lead inevitably to the mistreatment of other people and the degradation of the environment. The evils of greed and selfishness can be found in the world of buying and selling, of investing and profit seeking, to be sure, but they can also be found in churches and universities, in research laboratories and government agencies because humans act selfishly in every arena of life. Economic life and its institutions, therefore, are not evil villains in contrast to the supposedly moral activities of other practices and institutions. Our question about how to understand economic life and political economy from the viewpoint of human responsibilities is thus a question about how to exercise healthy and constructive productivity, trade, wealth creation, and the employment of the talents and capabilities of everyone.

With that in mind, consider for a moment the oft-repeated term "self-interest." Typically, self-interest is used in contrast to a proper regard for others. We may think of economic agents as "purely self-interested" people in contrast, for example, to those engaged in volunteering, philanthropy, or social service. Self-interest is bad; philanthropy is good. However, there is a big difference between self-interest and selfishness. The biblical command to love our neighbors is worded "love your neighbor as yourself." A proper *self*-regard and *self*-care is thus an essential, constructive human responsibility. It is not selfish for people to take time to eat, sleep, bathe, and care for themselves. What the biblical injunction implies is that the proper love of our neighbors is intertwined with proper love of self, and that we should learn to give ourselves to others in truly loving and caring ways. Looking to the well-being of our neighbors is essential to the realization and fulfillment of all of us as creatures made in the image of God. Proper self-interest, such as care for one's own family, or for one's own business, is certainly legitimate and does not have to be worked out selfishly and unjustly. True self-interest is deeply intertwined with the love of neighbors and their love for us. A proper self-interest leads to or spills over into service, creativity, industry, empathy, cooperation, and philanthropy.

A just political community is one that will recognize and encourage entrepreneurial talent, production and commerce, free markets for the exchange of goods and services, and the creative development of economically qualified organizations of diverse kinds. It will do this as part of its public-legal recognition and protection of responsibilities of all kinds. Government should act as more than a means to economic ends, but it should not treat economic activities as merely a means to its political ends. A just political community will promote a balanced and just "responsibilities economy."

Economics and the Environment

Against the backdrop of the discussion above, it should be easier to understand why any organized effort to advance environmental protection in a liberal society like the United States must position itself as one interest group among others in an interest-group brokering process. In other words, environmental protection depends on the strength of interest groups that will make that concern their chief cause. One of the reasons for this is that the natural environment and the ecological commons have no standing before government and the courts in a liberally constituted political system. Only individuals, corporations (as legal "persons"), and governments with their various interests have standing. Thus, in the political process of interest-group bargaining, environmental groups must compete with business, labor, agricultural, and energy interests, to name only the most prominent ones.[15] And quite often because of the perpetual drive for economic growth, long-term environmental concerns take a backseat to "progress."

A contemporary illustration of the tension between economic ambition and environmental concern is the use of the new technology called "fracking" (hydraulic fracturing) that makes it possible to obtain oil and gas locked in subterranean rocks. But as economics commentator Martin Wolf points out, quoting from a study in the November 2011 *Scientific American*, "'horizontal fracking requires enormous volumes of water and chemicals. Huge ponds or tanks are also needed to store chemically laden "flowback water" that comes back up the hole after wells have been fractured.' A single shaft requires 2m to 4m gallons of water and 15,000 to 60,000 gallons of chemicals. It is little wonder that critics allege the new technology threatens severe pollution of groundwater and is for this reason, an environmental nightmare."[16]

Is there no alternative, then, but for governments to allow economic production and marketing to set the pace until environmental dangers build up to the point where citizens feel compelled to protest and lobby governments to halt or regulate one industry or another? Should citizens have to choose sides: either jobs or the environment, either cheaper food or the environment, either adequate energy supplies or the environment, either economic growth or environmental protection?

In contrast to the liberal tradition, I believe the natural environment of human society should be given foundational, even constitutional recognition from the start. If we acknowledge that the natural environment—a vast array of diversified creatures with their own identities and value—is part of God's creation and sustains human life, then the environment itself needs to be taken into account when we consider the responsibilities God has given us. And, in fact, that is precisely what the biblical story—slighted by Locke—does. From the first pages of the Bible, we learn of God's commission to humans to "work [the garden] and take care of it" (Gen. 2:15). Humans bear a stewardship obligation to God to care for the earth and one another. Furthermore, when God gave commandments for human flourishing on earth, the sabbath principle was central: "Six days you shall labor and do all your work, but the seventh day is a sabbath to the LORD your God. On it you shall not do any work, neither you, nor your son or daughter, nor your male or female servant, nor your animals, nor any foreigner residing in your towns" (Exod. 20:9–10). Human labor, from the biblical point of view, is not an extension of each person's self-possession but rather an expression of human responsibility to God under creation-wide conditions for the common good. In other words, attached to the possessions that belong to any person or family is a stewardship requirement, namely, that everyone, *even the animals*, must rest every seventh day. God directly commands that there should be a day of rest for every creature, for they all belong to God. Consequently, the human owner's possessions carry with them a condition: no work for either humans or animals on the sabbath. All of this is part of the biblical message that no one is the absolute owner of anything, even of oneself. God is the owner of all things; humans are only stewards of what belongs ultimately to God.

When God gave Israel more elaborate commandments about their responsibility for the land, the sabbath principle was extended. Not only humans and animals must rest; the land itself must rest. "When you enter the land I am going to give you," says the Lord, "the land itself must observe a sabbath to the LORD. For six years sow your fields, and for six years prune your vineyards and gather their crops. But in the seventh year the land is to have a year of sabbath rest, a sabbath to the LORD. Do not sow your fields or prune your vineyards. Do not reap what grows of itself or harvest the grapes of your untended vines" (Lev. 25:2–5). The pattern of rest here was built in as an encumbrance, a kind of zoning regulation, as a *basis* for human community. Calvin DeWitt sees the sabbath principle as one of three basic ecological principles articulated in the Bible. The other two are earthkeeping and fruitfulness. To keep the earth (Gen. 2:15) means to "make sure that the creatures under our care are maintained with all their proper connections." To heed the fruitfulness principle means that humans may eat and use the earth's fruits but must not destroy its ability to continue to be fruitful.[17]

This is all part of the biblical story that Locke ignored when he offered his own account of creation. Locke's god simply turns over the world to autonomous individuals for their individual appropriation. Locke's creatures have nothing to fear except the potentially violent threats from other autonomous individuals. Each is the lord of his or her own possessions, defined as that which each person has mixed his or her labors with. From the biblical point of view, by contrast, humans must above all fear the Lord who gives life and holds humans accountable for the way they exercise their stewardship of God's creation, including the animals and the land. And God speaks to Israel not as a collection of self-possessing individuals but as a community with a common land, common responsibilities, and a law that has the sabbath principle built right into it.

Most Americans now recognize intuitively, if not in a critical and reflective way, that human freedom and the use of different kinds of property for economic growth cannot flourish or be sustained for future generations unless justice is done to water, air, land, plants, and animals. The environmental movement has been built on that intuitive insight, which deepens as people become dissatisfied with pollution of all kinds. Nevertheless, the dominant influence of liberal thought in our political, legal, and economic tradition still guides the American approach to environmental protection.[18] That is why I am emphasizing that justice for both people and nonhuman creatures requires a change at the foundations and not only at the level of lobbying tactics and year-by-year legislation. What we need is not merely a few more government regulations or a little more federal expenditure here and there to satisfy environmentalists. We need a fundamentally different perspective on *government's* responsibility for the well-being of the commons, a perspective that arises from a different picture of human responsibility than the one we find in Locke's creation story and in Smith's view of wealth creation.

Environmental protection can best be thought of as a stewardship obligation or an encumbrance on citizens generally and on any owner or user of property, similar to the way zoning works in a town or city and the way civil rights protection works in all employment decisions. Homeowners and business owners do not hold unqualified rights to their private property and the resources they buy, use, and sell. Homeowners in my town may not set up a commercial or industrial business on property that is zoned residential. The simple fact is that property ownership is encumbered with various stewardship obligations from the start.

Of course, many aspects of environmental health and well-being cannot be known until social development, productivity, commerce, and scientific advances make us aware of ecological limits and emerging or potential environmental degradations. But it would make a great difference if the political community agreed from the start that any change in environmental conditions would trigger government's action to protect the environment and its sustainability. The first principle of public law should not be the protection of private property and free markets but the proper recognition and identification of every person and nonhuman entity so that each can be given its due, so that justice can be done to all of them, including individuals, families, markets, entrepreneurship, private property, air, water, and other natural resources. If, as history unfolds, people discover that an earlier law misidentified or failed to do justice to the true character of a person, institution, or natural thing, then revision of the law should be a requirement, not an option. The precondition for this principle is that a constitutionally established government should be recognized as bearing the responsibility to uphold environmental soundness just as it is responsible to uphold civil rights protection and national defense.

The argument we've offered for a responsibilities economy and justice for the environment does not lead automatically to public-policy recommendations to deal with the host of economic and ecological issues that governments face day by day. But if we want to arrive at a just framework of protection and regulation, or a just tax policy, or a just trade policy, or anything else that bears on economic life and the environment, it will make a very significant difference if we start with principled pluralist assumptions rather than liberal or socialist assumptions. It will make all the difference in the world if we believe that humans are created in the image of God with the calling to be good stewards and just viceroys of God's creation.

politics
in one world

The Changing Locus of Sovereignty

Once upon a time in world affairs, a few ambassadors, a few trading companies, and a few armies made almost all the connections that existed among the peoples of the world. Today's technologies of communication, travel, and transportation allow hundreds of millions of people, representing millions of organizations, to interact with one another across borders as quickly and almost as easily as they interact with people in their own countries. Trade and diplomacy are now dominantly multilateral, and the networks are so dense and intricate that they depend on a growing number of international organizations for the management of their affairs. Many business corporations are multinational, with major offices and production facilities in different parts of the world. There can be little doubt that the world of supposedly sovereign states—distinct political communities—is changing radically. It is not so much that states are disappearing but that the nature of international intertwinement and global shrinkage is demanding of them an exercise of responsibility they can no longer adequately achieve on their own.

It is useful to look at these developments from the perspective of international law. For the most part, people everywhere depend on laws made by tribal, local, and/or national governments. These include laws for marriage, ownership, commerce, public health, crime, and much more. Healthy and stable governments are needed to make, enforce, and adjudicate those laws. But what happens when a growing body of law is needed for international trade, or to regulate atmospheric pollutants, or to deal with terrorists, or to determine when an international body of police or military forces should go into a region of conflict (such as the Middle East, North Africa, or Afghanistan/Pakistan) to try to stop the conflict and protect innocent people? The need for these types of international law has been growing rapidly as the world shrinks, warms, flattens, and endures war and genocide. Yet there is no transnational government to initiate and enforce such lawmaking. That means states, international organizations, and nonstate organizations often feel compelled to take action to deal with problems beyond their range of competence, sometimes making matters worse. It also means that some crises will continue to grow because existing states and international organizations cannot agree, or are very slow to agree, on what to do.

Economic and Civil-Society Globalization

From an economic point of view, the shrinking, flattening world is increasingly familiar to a wide public even if no one can understand its complexities. Americans, for example, are aware that most of their clothes, electronic devices, and children's toys are made in China, Korea, Japan, or Vietnam. Many of the jobs that once existed in the United States have moved elsewhere. We also realize, at least in some dim sense, that rising oil and gas consumption all over the world has, for all practical purposes, created a single global energy market.

Perhaps the most difficult thing for Americans to adjust to is the fact that their economy is increasingly being shaped and conditioned by the initiatives of other countries and by corporations and investors from other parts of the world. American civil-religious nationalists are offended if not angered by this evidence of the loss of American sovereignty and global preeminence. Optimists look on the bright side of economic globalization: more jobs, more goods, more services for more people, including more poor people. The pessimists notice the millions of people who are not benefiting from the process and stress the negative consequences of ever increasing industrial growth and global shrinkage: climate change, environmental degradation, conflicts over limited resources, sweatshop labor conditions, the concentration of power in a few large multinational companies, and more. The views of both optimists and pessimists push the question of responsibility to the fore. Who is responsible for what? Where does state sovereignty reach its limits? Are we at the stage today where new kinds of governance structures are needed to establish and uphold international public justice?

Beyond economic integration and growth are other dimensions of human interdependence that receive less attention. The world, after all, is being shaped not only by states, international government organizations, and business and commercial corporations. People throughout the world educate their children, worship gods, pursue scientific and philosophical inquiries, make music, write poetry, take action to serve neighbors in need, develop widely diverse cuisines, create popular culture, engage in competitive sports, and communicate increasingly via the internet. We cannot possibly understand what is going on in these spheres of life if we look at the world only through political and economic spectacles.

Think of the work of scientists. Many of us may still imagine that American scientists are working to keep the United States in the lead scientifically, technologically, and militarily. We take pride in the number of Americans who win Nobel Prizes in contrast to the number of winners from other countries. But science was never a nationally circumscribed mode of human endeavor. And today we are witnessing the expansion of international networks of scientists cooperating in the study of space, the environment, particle physics, and human diseases.

Some writers argue that the consequence of a shrinking world is homogenization or "flattening," but we might better think of the world as an arena where new valleys and peaks are emerging in a culturally diverse and institutionally differentiating world that is also, simultaneously, becoming more integrated. Flattening may be taking place to the extent that the work of scientists is communicated more quickly and uniformly throughout the world and that scientific methods and studies can be shared more extensively across all borders. But it is also true that we are now discovering more and more species of plants, insects, sea creatures, birds, and animals, as well as becoming aware of the serious rate of species extinction. We are learning about new kinds of medical treatments in different cultures and about types of knowledge that Western sciences ignored or never obtained by their methods. In all of these respects, the world is expanding, not shrinking; it is becoming more undulated, creviced, and peaked rather than flattened. And in the realms of science, the arts, medicine, religious institutions, schooling, and more, we participate in types of human activity that are not primarily defined by political or economic boundaries and purposes.

The Question of Governance

Looking to the future, the challenge is to figure out how to promote just governance for the common good of all peoples. What will it take to respond to this challenge? In some parts of the world, what is needed most is sound governance capable of overcoming tribal conflicts or oppression by unaccountable dictators or both. In other parts of the world, the most urgent need is for regional cooperation among several states. In other places, the need is for governments capable of establishing independent courts, a just system of representation, and accountable bureaucracies that provide fair and equitable treatment for citizens of diverse ethnic and religious identities.[1]

At the international level, the challenge seems far greater in part because of the complexity of the world's peoples and cultures and because of the difficulty of creating international and transnational governing structures that can assure a greater degree of justice. After all, it is not obvious that creating a larger, more authoritative international governing institution or a new kind of transnational state (which the European Union might someday become) will mean that the peoples of the world (or of Europe) will automatically experience more justice. Good government at any level is something that must be achieved and demonstrated, not merely wished for. It is something that requires adequate accountability as well as support from the governed. And just governance at a transnational level cannot be achieved by eliminating lower levels of government. To the contrary, just governance at a higher level requires strong agreement among peoples and nations about the relationship between levels of government, from the lowest level up to the highest.

An assessment of what constitutes just public governance must take into account the actual conditions and changes occurring in the world. The greater the differentiation and development of nonpolitical spheres of life and the greater the economic, technological, military, environmental, and informational interdependence of peoples and states, the more urgent the question of transnational justice and governance becomes. As Michael Sandel puts it: "In a world where capital and goods, information and images, pollution and people, flow across national boundaries with unprecedented ease, politics must assume transnational, even global, forms, if only to keep up. Otherwise, economic power will go unchecked by democratically sanctioned political power. Nation-states, traditionally the vehicles of self-government, will find themselves increasingly unable to bring their citizens' judgments to bear on the economic forces that govern destinies."[2]

However, Sandel, as well as Michael Walzer, is leery of any type of centralized government in the world that would, in Walzer's words, lack the "capacity to promote peace, distributive justice, cultural pluralism, and individual freedom."[3] We should think in terms of "dispersing" rather than "relocating" sovereignty, writes Sandel. "The most promising alternative to the sovereign state is not a cosmopolitan community based on the solidarity of humankind but a multiplicity of communities and political bodies—some more extensive than nations and some less—among which sovereignty is diffused. Only a politics that disperses sovereignty both upward and downward can combine the power required to rival global market forces with the differentiation required of a public life that hopes to inspire the allegiance of its citizens."[4]

For Walzer, even the idea of a "federation of nation states" is too uniform and centralized because it would probably "make its peace with material inequality" and would be too oligarchic. A global federation would more likely "be reached and sustained by pressure from the centre than by democratic activism at (to shift my metaphor) the grass roots," says Walzer.[5] He proposes something looser and more pluralistic than a global federation, namely, "the familiar anarchy of states mitigated and controlled by a threefold set of nonstate agents: organizations like the UN, the associations of international civil society, and also regional unions like the European Community."[6]

Walzer, however, does not adequately distinguish governmental from non-governmental organizations. If there is not to be a single global federation, then undoubtedly, as is now the case, the stronger states will have greater control of the UN, the European Community, the World Trade Organization, and other regional and international civil society organizations. The most important normative question is about how governments can promote justice for both individuals *and* nongovernmental institutions under law, rather than about how people and nongovernmental institutions can thwart anarchy and centralization.

Ultimately, the questions about politics around the world today are about norm-responsiveness, that is, about how well actual governments and societies respond to the demands of justice. The answers to these questions will not be found simply by noting that liberal democracy is better than totalitarian communism, or that democracy leads to greater happiness and prosperity for more people than does dictatorial government. People need to experience justice in the laws, regulations, and institutions of their governments. They need to see justice being done to them and their neighbors as citizens and in their capacities as family members, educators, businesspeople, laborers, scientists, artists, and members of different communities of faith. Humans certainly cannot perfect or save the world through global government. In our sinfulness, we might do just the opposite, for we continue to demonstrate our ability to create unjust political systems and to destroy millions of people and other creatures through the powers of government, particularly when our countries are at war. But the question of transnational governance cannot be dismissed.

Can the Use of Force Ever Be Justified?

These concerns bring us once again to the age-old question that Augustine, Aquinas, Calvin, and other Christian leaders have been compelled to address: Is there a just way to use force for the sake of justice and peace? Do the great love commandments—to love God above all and our neighbors as ourselves—ever permit the use of force? Isn't it inevitable that even the official use of force for a good cause will violate the love commands and do more harm than good? Isn't it foolish to imagine that higher levels of government can achieve a greater degree of justice than national, local, and tribal governments, which have done so much harm through acts of violence over the centuries? Isn't government's use of force part of the problem rather than part of any solution in the quest for public justice?

In earlier chapters, we commented briefly on the pacifist arguments of John Howard Yoder, Stanley Hauerwas, and Richard Hays, who do indeed argue that violence of every kind is destructive and that Christians should not look to different levels of government to help them respond to the Bible's love commands. For most of Christian history, they argue, Christians have failed to recognize that the only grounds for the use of force are to be found in a pagan ethic. Hays, for example, devotes a central chapter of his book *The Moral Vision of the New Testament* to a discussion of violence.[7] His argument depends, however, on an equivocal use of the word "violence." When he asks, "Is it ever God's will for Christians to employ violence in defense of justice?"[8] the question is rhetorical. His use of the word "violence" connotes an unloving, unjust use of force that injures someone else. How could God call Christians to commit such harmful, unloving, and unjust acts in the name of justice?

If Hays had phrased his opening question differently to ask, "Is it ever God's will for unjust acts of violence to be met with just punishment?" he would have begun to put biblical language on the table, particularly the language of Romans 12 and 13. He might have identified and distinguished various biblical terms, such as the Greek words *ekdikesis* and *ekdikos*, which have the retributive connotation of a *response* to a prior act of harm. Words like "retribution" and "punishment" have a different meaning than the words "murder" and "act of violence" initiated against someone by a private party. The Bible speaks clearly of just retribution for unjust acts, but it does not speak of God commanding murder or the initiation of harm against one's neighbor. In other words, more than one word is needed to express the different meanings of acts that employ the use of force, such as murder, revenge, punishment, penalty, and so forth.

With regard to one meaning of "violence," Hays is quite right about New Testament teaching. The people united through faith in Christ have not been called to a mission of advancing their cause by stepping on and destroying others. Nor did Jesus tell his disciples to build the Christian community as a territorial polity that would need to defend itself by means of force. But is that it? What responsibility should Christians bear in their civic capacities in the service of fellow citizens, whether Christian or non-Christian? Hays argues simply that Christians should not participate in the use of force. He admits that no text in the New Testament says explicitly that Christians may not hold the office of a military or police official; nevertheless, he judges that "the place of the soldier within the church can only be seen as anomalous."[9] Under Christ, therefore, there is, in Hays's view, no place for a public ministry of justice of the kind that political authorities render. Any soldier who fights in a war or any judge who passes judgment (perhaps capital punishment) on a violent criminal is committing an unjust act of violence contrary to the Christian way of life. Consequently, there is no possibility of developing a *Christian* public ethic for a government's monopolization and use of force.

That is why Hays reads Romans 12–13 the way Yoder does.[10] Hays, like Yoder, believes that Christians may not hold the human office of government that Paul discusses in Romans 13 because God appoints (or allows) the governing authority to use force in exercising vengeance. From Hays's viewpoint, Paul in Romans 12 is following Jesus, while Paul in Romans 13 is apparently falling back on older traditions and modes of reasoning that are not fully compatible with Jesus's teaching. In fact, this contrast would appear to drive the incompatibility between "turning the other cheek" and "vengeance" all the way back into the Godhead. On the one hand, Jesus, the incarnate Son of God, calls Christians to live as a community whose members should not hold any office that exercises forceful retribution. On the other hand, "outside the perfection of Christ," God the Father establishes or permits officials to exercise a measure of God's vengeance (unjust vengeance?) on evildoers.

In contrast to Hays, the view of government I am presenting requires definite and severe strictures of a constitutional nature on governments, in keeping with their responsibility to do justice. It is in this regard that Christianity has made one of the most significant contributions to government and the structure of political communities. If a political community may rightfully monopolize and use force only for the purpose of upholding justice for all, then it may not, on any terms, be the kind of community whose government uses force arbitrarily or to satisfy the selfish ambitions of its leaders and people. The task of government, on biblical terms, is a modest one, a humble duty of administering public justice for the common good, always limited in its domain of competence. The proper exercise of government's authority under law will help to protect the innocent, settle differences without resort to violence, and preserve peace so that humans will be able to fulfill the wide variety of responsibilities God has given them.

The restraint and punishment of those who harm the innocent and endanger public peace will be a necessary function of governments as long as unjust acts persist during the present age sustained by Christ's patient, long-suffering governance of creation. Today, some of the most urgent questions we face about the restraint and punishment of injustice are about acts that reach beyond the jurisdictions of local police forces and national governments. Are international courts and coalitions of national military forces sufficient for this? Who bears responsibility to thwart and defeat terrorists or to hinder and turn back states that take unjust military action? One can understand the skepticism of Hays and his associates about the just use of force by governments. I have written in criticism of the US government's entrance into and prosecution of wars in Afghanistan and Iraq, arguing that the wars have violated most, if not all, of the just-war criteria.[11] Today, serious questions of justice are being raised, as they should be, about America's shift to the use of drone aircraft to kill suspected enemies in any part of the world, an operation run by the CIA, not even by the military.[12] But the unjust acts of governments do not disqualify the institutions of government and political communities any more than unloving acts of spouses or parents disqualify the institutions of marriage and family. The violations of justice and love become evident only in the light of the normative standards of justice and love that call us to account before God and one another. The question at stake here is at least as old as Augustine, and it has to do with whether political life is something that belongs to the creaturely life of humans and is normed by high standards of justice. Hays and Yoder cannot agree that governments are legitimate even if established only to restrain and punish evildoers. Therefore, they can offer no criteria for distinguishing between government's unjust use of force and its just use of force, whether at the domestic or at the international level.

In order to think normatively about international politics and government, Christians should begin with the conviction that this world is God's creation. We should neither fear the increasing global interdependence of peoples nor give up working politically for the world's just governance at all levels. From that point of view, some kind of transnational federal or modified federated structure, built on the rule of law with constitutional definition and democratic accountability, would appear to be a normative necessity, especially when it comes to clarifying the proper aims and limits of governments' monopolization and use of force. For governments to protect the innocent and to restrain and punish lawbreakers justly—giving all their just due—they must have constitutional authority (under law) to monopolize and use force in keeping with articulated norms of justice. The urgent need for a just-war and just-policing ethic at all levels of governance is and will remain with us. Christians today, working together across all national boundaries, should be debating, refining, and helping to implement the constitutional terms of just governance.

Religions as Ways of Life

With all the experience of globalization in the last two or three decades, perhaps the least understood dimension of it has been the role of religions.[13] We have indicated from the start our conviction that religions are ways of life and not merely ways of worship. And it is evident that religions such as Christianity, Islam, Hinduism, nationalism, scientism, and materialism are global forces today.

John Kay, an economics professor and columnist for the *Financial Times* of London, once commented, "Environmentalism offers an alternative account of the natural world to the religious and an alternative anti-capitalist account of the political world to the Marxist. The rise of environmentalism parallels in time and place the decline of religion and of socialism." Environmentalism, in other words, has become a kind of religion, or a stand-in for religions. Businesspeople, says Kay, should respond to the rise of environmentalism as they would to "other forms of religious belief. Business leaders do not themselves have to believe its doctrines. Indeed we should be wary if they do: business linked to faiths and ideologies is a sinister and unaccountable power."[14]

On one count, I believe Kay is correct to say that for many people modern ideologies such as environmentalism have displaced Christian and other religious ways of life. Environmentalism, like socialism and other isms, can function as an all-encompassing frame of reference and way of life. Yet Kay apparently believes that all religions and ideologies are dangerous or at least sinister if joined to business. He wants businesspeople to avoid such dangers and stick to sound business judgments. He imagines that religions and religious isms should be shunted off to the side so they won't interfere with secular life. However, Kay seems unaware of the degree to which many people have turned business, the market, profit, capitalism, and economics into a modern religion, as Robert Nelson believes they have done.[15] Religion, when thought of as cultic, ceremonial, and theological practices led by religious leaders, may indeed be one among many kinds of activity—such as business, science, and sport—in which some people engage. But we must not count as *unreligious* those ways of life that integrate and drive whole communities and cultures even when they make no reference to a transcendent or mysterious source of life. Secular religions such as environmentalism, but also capitalism and nationalism, can become the deepest motivating drives of a society or of large sections of it, working in competition and sometimes in cooperation with one another.

Consider China today. Many people refer to communist China as godless, or at least as controlled by godless communism. Traditional religious practices certainly are controlled tightly in China. Like many educational, scientific, and media organizations, churches must meet strict registration guidelines. Many groups that cannot accept the strictures operate secretly, underground, for as long as they can. Is it correct, then, to identify China as a nonreligious, secular, communist system that happens to restrain or oppress religions? No, that is not quite accurate, for it keeps us from seeing the *religiosity* of China, the nation, as a whole.[16]

China's leaders are subtly at work today, for example, trying to revive admiration for, if not veneration of, Confucius, as Richard McGregor has reported.[17] The religious zeal that characterized the communist regime of Mao Zedong (from 1949 to 1976) led the leader to attack Confucius as an outdated drag on the communist transformation of China. Mao destroyed the temple that honored Confucius in the ancient philosopher's hometown of Qufu. As a comprehensive wisdom for life, Confucianism was perceived as a major roadblock to Mao's plan to radically transform China into a communist society. It may be surprising, then, to realize that Mao's attempt to build a new kind of society based on his own wisdom put him in a position similar to that of earlier Confucian emperors. Mao adopted a role like that of the ancient Son of Heaven (the emperor), who was empowered by the Mandate of Heaven to establish a harmonious Confucian social order. For Mao, the new religion would be Chinese-communist nationalism.

Among the problems China now faces, decades after Mao, is a weakening moral fabric. The current way of life that China's leaders have authorized is dedicated to ever increasing economic growth, which also justifies personal quests for wealth. As has happened in the West, where consumerism and the all-out push for economic growth can undermine moral obligations and social solidarity, so in China there is a similar tendency at work. The government senses that its moral authority is weaker than Mao's and much weaker than the authority once enjoyed by the emperors who nurtured strong Confucian moral bonds with the people. To be able to keep pushing an agenda for China's growth, the political leaders want to regain something like the mantle of benevolent and enlightened moral authority that once united the people with their leaders.

What I've just described is nothing less than a government-led religious way of life, and that is where the new attention to Confucius comes in. As McGregor writes, Confucius can be seen by the authorities to serve as "an important antidote to organized religion, especially Christianity, which is growing rapidly in China. At a time when Chinese leaders fret about rampant capitalism and a parallel 'collapse in values,' they prefer any spiritual vacuum to be filled by a quasi-state religion framed around Confucius rather than a potentially dangerous import." There is no room, in other words, for two (or more) ultimate authorities and comprehensive ways of life to coexist in the same place at the same time. A Confucius-blessed, communist-capitalist way of life ordained by a government that subordinates every other way of life to its own is nothing less than a civil-religious way of life with totalitarian Chinese-nationalist characteristics.[18]

Consider one more example. According to Omer Faruk Genckaya, a professor at Bikent University in Turkey, "secularism is the most defining element of the establishment of the republic. It is a kind of religion in Turkey that is as important as Islam."[19] Vincent Boland comments, "The idea of secularism as religion is a paradox, but it helps to explain the singular notion of what Turkish secularism actually means."[20]

Turkey is one of the most important places in the world today in which to observe the dynamism of religions (secularism included) competing to shape society and government down to their very root. It is a country of more than seventy-four million people, most of whom (more than 90 percent) are Muslim. Yet its state structure, established by Mustafa Kemal Ataturk in 1923, has been until recently absolutely secular, which means that it excluded all Muslim practices—even the wearing of headscarves—in the affairs of government and in much of the economy and education. Ataturk had reason in 1923, after the collapse of the Ottoman Empire, to worry about the stability and success of an Islamic state in such a large and populous territory. Taking a cue from French *laicism* (secularism), which had forcefully displaced public Christianity in France, Ataturk set out to define government and citizenship in terms of secular nationalism instead of Islam and to force Islamic practice into a narrow private realm.

In many respects, Ataturk was successful beyond all expectations. Secular nationalism was taught so well in schools and enforced so strongly that it became the driving force of the public way of life. Not everyone converted to the new secular-nationalist religion, but most people accommodated themselves to its requirements enforced by secularist elites, especially the military. Yet, we might ask, isn't the privatization of Islam a contradiction in terms? Muslims believe in a God who transcends all human political authority and governs all of life.

It might be one thing for Muslims to be forced to accommodate themselves uncomfortably to a regime that disallows full public expression of Islam, but to demand of all citizens that they accept public secularism as a matter of faith is another thing altogether. In fact, since 1923, many forms of rebellion and resistance to Turkey's secularism have arisen among the people, but none was able to change the system. Whenever they thought it necessary, the military would put down rebellions, oust governments, and make clear to everyone that force was on the side of "Kemalism"—political secularism.

Over time, however, and particularly in the past two decades, popular Muslim movements have addressed the needs of the middle classes and the poorer communities in Turkey's cities, villages, and countryside, needs that were not being met by the increasingly complacent elites. Leaders among the common people focused on jobs, health care, and other services; their efforts were expressive of obligations incumbent on the Muslim faithful. Before long, some of those leaders were elected to city councils and then to mayoral offices, and finally, through the rapidly expanding Justice and Development Party (the AKP), to the prime minister's office in 2002. The relatively new AKP, led by Recep Tayyip Erdogan, who became the prime minister and then president of the country, won the support of ordinary people—mostly faithful Muslims—who had not been served well by the secular nationalists.

This was something new in Turkey, a political party that did not hold to or insist on the ideology (religion) of secularism yet accepted the practice of democracy with no evident intention to establish Islam as the exclusive public religion. Erdogan and the AKP fostered economic growth, built up the infrastructure, and worked harder than any prior government to move Turkey toward entrance into the European Union and toward a greater role in the Middle East. The AKP demonstrated that it is not necessary for citizens *to believe* in secularism in order to enjoy full citizenship in the republic. In essence, the AKP is trying to put something new into practice, different from both monopolistic secularism and monopolistic Islam. We might call it public pluralism through which people of all faiths, including both secularists and Muslims, are able to carry out their ways of life. Will this new venture succeed and become the permanent constitution of Turkey? That remains to be seen.

Conclusion

Will any of the major ways of life that have the greatest influence in the world today become more powerful than all others? Will it be *nationalism*, in all its variegated colors, that comes to dominate? Or will free-market *capitalism* become the dominant religious driving force, since even in China capitalists can now be members of the Communist Party. If capitalism becomes the dominant way of life, it may be able to transcend and bring conformity to the world's many states that are losing some of their sovereign power and authority to global corporations. It certainly appears to be the dominant faith and hope of many economic globalists. However, if capitalism cannot draw the poor as well as the rich into its way of life, then divisions and conflicts will likely increase between wealthier groups who keep the capitalist faith and poorer people who turn against it.

Perhaps, however, we are about to enter a time when one of the older world religions—*Christianity* or *Islam*, for example—will become most influential and draw people together beyond their national and class identities to establish a framework for multicultural and multi-institutional community on a global level. Yet here too, the historical record of conflict and opposition among religious ways of life does not make one overly optimistic.

What seems more likely is that competing ways of life with different guiding faiths will continue to contend with one another for the hearts and habits of people, without one of them becoming dominant worldwide. Samuel Huntington's argument about the "clash of civilizations" builds on this possibility.[21] Yet Huntington's argument assumes, for the most part, that the clashes will be *between* civilizations, when, in fact, many of the strongest clashes are taking place *within* each of the civilizations he discusses. This is what we see in Turkey with the internal clash between Islam and secularism and in a milder way in places like the United States and Great Britain, between and among Christianity, secular nationalism, and capitalism.

There can be little doubt that the dominant ways of life in the world are not confined within national borders. Nationalism, capitalism, Christianity, and Islam, to take just four of the most vibrant shapers of societies and civilizations, are global forces. None has a monopoly over the shaping of life, but in most regions of the world, two or more of these are strongly contending with one another. American civil-religious nationalism and capitalism contend with each other and with the Christian, Jewish, and Muslim ways of life in the United States, Great Britain, and other Western countries.[22] Secularism contends with nationalism, capitalism, and Islam in Turkey. Nationalism and capitalism contend with Confucianism, Christianity, and Islam in China. And all of these ways of life are in contention at the UN, in the WTO, in NATO, and in other international forums and institutions.

The challenge facing people of every faith and every way of life today is global in scope; but this should not surprise Christians who profess that the creator, judge, and redeemer of all things is the God who rules all nations and calls people everywhere to repent and turn to the truth revealed in Jesus Christ. From a biblical point of view, the whole world is one world and it is God's creation. And the gospel of Jesus Christ goes out to the entire world. Christians should, in faithfulness to Christ, have no difficulty subordinating every responsibility they have (political, economic, familial, educational, and more) to the way of life of the kingdom of God. And yet the difficulties of living as faithful Christians are ever present. No Christian person or community is in a position to act self-righteously or to claim a position of special privilege or preeminence among fellow humans. In this shrinking, warming, flattening, warring world, people everywhere may legitimately ask, What does the Christian way of life have to offer by way of wisdom, justice, and love for the responsibilities of governance, child raising, economic development, science, technology, schooling, and everything else that pertains to life in this world? Words are not sufficient to answer that question. The response must come from the practice of a Christian way of life.

notes

Introduction

1. Quoted by Robert N. Bellah, "Religion and the Legitimation of the American Republic," in *Varieties of Civil Religion*, ed. Robert N. Bellah and Phillip E. Hammond (San Francisco: Harper & Row, 1980), 17.

2. Darryl Hart, *A Secular Faith: Why Christianity Favors the Separation of Church and State* (Chicago: Ivan R. Dee, 2006), 10.

3. Ibid., 12.

4. For Darryl Hart's political views in more detail, see his *From Billy Graham to Sarah Palin: Evangelicals and the Betrayal of American Conservatism* (Grand Rapids: Eerdmans, 2011).

5. Heba Saleh, "Moment of Youth: Egypt's New Activists," *Financial Times*, February 10, 2012, www.ft.com/intl/cms/s/2/6cf358a6-5207-11e1-a30c-0041feabdc0.html.

6. Bellah, "Religion and Legitimation," 6.

7. The following books begin to suggest the diversity of Christian approaches to American politics today: Ronald J. Sider, *Just Politics: A Guide for Christian Engagement* (Grand Rapids: Brazos, 2012); Kenneth J. Collins, *Power, Politics and the Fragmentation of Evangelicalism* (Downers Grove, IL: IVP Academic, 2012); Miroslav Volf, *A Public Faith: How Followers of Christ Should Serve the Common Good* (Grand Rapids: Brazos, 2011); Sandra F. Joireman, ed., *Church, State, and Citizen: Christian Approaches to Political Engagement* (New York: Oxford University Press, 2009); Catherine E. Wilson, *The Politics of Latino Faith* (New York: New York University Press, 2008); Cornell West, *Democracy Matters* (New York: Penguin, 2005); United States Conference of Catholic Bishops, *Faithful Citizenship: A Catholic Call to Political Responsibility* (Washington, DC: USCCB, 2003); Robert P. Kraynak, *Christian Faith and Modern Democracy: God and Politics in the Fallen World* (Notre Dame, IN: University of Notre Dame Press, 2001); Stephen L. Carter, *God's Name in Vain: The Wrongs and Rights of Religion in Politics* (New York: Basic Books, 2000); James W. Skillen, *The Scattered Voice: Christians at Odds in the Public Square* (Grand Rapids: Zondervan, 1990).

8. Martin Luther King Jr., "Letter from a Birmingham Jail," in *I Have a Dream: Writings and Speeches That Changed the World*, ed. James M. Washington (San Francisco: HarperOne, 1992), 96.

9. Ibid., 97.

10. Ibid., 94.

11. Sacvan Bercovitch, *The American Jeremiad* (Madison: University of Wisconsin Press, 1978), 8–9.

12. Ibid., 19. A notable recent edition of Alexis de Tocqueville's classic is *Democracy in America*, trans. and ed. Harvey C. Mansfield and Delba Winthrop (Chicago: University of Chicago Press, 2000).

13. There were, of course, diverse views among early American Quaker, Episcopalian, Presbyterian, and Puritan settlers, not the least of which was the view of Roger Williams, who wanted more freedom for religious dissidents and the individual conscience than the Massachusetts Puritans would allow. But Williams seems not to have taken complete distance from the idea of a "Christian" colony. See the recent biography by John M. Barry, *Roger Williams and the Creation of the American Soul: Church, State, and the Birth of Liberty* (New York: Viking, 2012).

14. A fine collection of American speeches and writings expressing the "new Israel" theme, beginning in the early colonial era and carrying through to the 1990s, is Conrad Cherry, ed., *God's New Israel: Religious Interpretations of American Destiny*, rev. ed. (Chapel Hill: University of North Carolina Press, 1998).

15. Harry S. Stout, *Upon the Altar of the Nation: A Moral History of the Civil War* (New York: Viking, 2006), 249.

16. Ibid., 459.

17. Andrew Michael Manis provides keen insight into the conflict between the white and black versions of the American civil religion in his study of Baptists in the South in the decade leading up to the civil rights achievements of the 1960s: *Southern Civil Religions in Conflict: Black and White Baptists and Civil Rights, 1947–1957* (Athens: University of Georgia Press, 1987).

18. Martin Luther King Jr., "I Have a Dream," in *I Have a Dream*, 101–6.

19. Stanley Hauerwas, *Christian Existence Today: Essays on Church, World, and Living in Between* (1988; repr., Grand Rapids: Brazos, 2001), 185. The best-known work of John Howard Yoder is *The Politics of Jesus* (Grand Rapids: Eerdmans, 1972).

20. Since the 1960s, warnings of America's decline and of God's judgment have increased, along with campaigns to recover America's original identity and mission. For an up-to-date, wide-ranging report and analysis of American declinism—economic, political, and cultural—see Edward Luce, *Time to Start Thinking: America in the Age of Descent* (New York: Atlantic Monthly Press, 2012).

Chapter 1 God's Kingdom Coming

1. Robert C. Tannehill explains, "Jesus' answer to the question about restoring the reign to Israel denies that Jesus' followers can know the time and probably corrects their supposition that the restoration may come immediately, but it does not deny the legitimacy of their concern with the restoration of the national life of the Jewish people." *The Narrative Unity of Luke-Acts: A Literary Interpretation*, vol. 2, *The Acts of the Apostles* (Minneapolis: Fortress, 1990), 15.

2. "Jewish hope," according to N. T. Wright, "was concrete, specific, focused on the people as a whole. If Pilate was still governing Judaea, then the kingdom had not come. If the Temple was not rebuilt, then the kingdom had not come. If the Messiah had not arrived, then the kingdom had not come. If Israel was not observing the Torah properly . . . then the kingdom had not come. If the pagans were not defeated and/or flocking to Zion for instruction, then the kingdom had not come." *Jesus and the Victory of God* (Minneapolis: Fortress, 1996), 223.

3. Ibid., 218.

4. N. T. Wright, *The New Testament and the People of God* (Minneapolis: Fortress, 1992), 375.

5. Wright, *Jesus and the Victory*, 216.

6. There has been much argument about whether the Heb. 2 passage, with its quote from Ps. 8 and reference to Gen. 1, is primarily about humans as created or about Jesus. Any disjunction, however, is a mistake because the passage is clearly about the Son of God who became human in Jesus. The passage is about humans having been created to govern the earth under God, a reality not yet fulfilled. But we *do* see Jesus, and the Jesus we see is the One who was made like his brothers and sisters, flesh and blood. In other words, the order of creation is the presupposition of what is said about Jesus here. For detailed background on the exegetical disputes, see Paul Ellingworth, *The Epistle to the Hebrews*, The New International Greek Testament Commentary (Grand Rapids: Eerdmans, 1993), 147–68.

7. The issue of taxation was crucial in Roman-controlled Israel of Jesus's day. For background on the forms of taxation and what they meant for the Jews, see Alan Storkey, *Jesus and Politics: Confronting the Powers* (Grand Rapids: Baker Academic, 2005), 211–28.

8. According to Gordon J. Spykman, Jesus's response came down to this: "Give to God what is rightfully his, namely, total and undivided allegiance. Then, under the sovereign claim of God's Word, give to Caesar what is justly his—no more, no less. By extension Christ's words lead us to conclude: Give also to parents, to church officers, to educators, to administrators in every sphere of life the respect which is rightfully theirs—remembering that all earthly offices and institutions have but a limited authority. God's authority alone is absolute and all-encompassing. Thus understood, Christ's rejoinder stands as a reaffirmation of that abiding norm which calls for differentiated tasks within communal relationships." *Reformational Theology: A New Paradigm for Doing Dogmatics* (Grand Rapids: Eerdmans, 1992), 283.

9. Eric Nelson has shown in *The Hebrew Republic: Jewish Sources and the Transformation of European Political Thought* (Cambridge, MA: Harvard University Press, 2010) how sixteenth- and seventeenth-century European Protestants used the passage in 1 Sam. 8 to argue for a republican form of government ("republican exclusivism") over against monarchy and mixed forms of government.

10. An outstanding book showing the connection between Deut. 17:14–20 and Psalms is Jamie A. Grant, *The King as Exemplar: The Function of Deuteronomy's Kingship Law in the Shaping of the Book of Psalms* (Atlanta: Society of Biblical Literature, 2004).

11. Quoted in ibid., 176.

Chapter 2 The Revealing Image

1. For critical reflection on this tension, thought by some to be a contributor to and evidence of the crisis of modernity, see, for example, Stephen Toulmin, *Cosmopolis: The Hidden Agenda of Modernity* (Chicago: University of Chicago Press, 1990); Herman Dooyeweerd, *Roots of Western Culture: Pagan, Secular, and Christian Options*, series B, vol. 3 of *The Collected Works of Herman Dooyeweerd*, ed. D. F. M. Strauss (Lewiston, NY: Edwin Mellen, 2003); Craig Calhoun, Mark Juergensmeyer, and Jonathan VanAntwerpen, eds., *Rethinking Secularism* (New York: Oxford University Press, 2011); Eric Voegelin, *From Enlightenment to Revolution*, ed. John H. Hallowell (Durham, NC: Duke University Press, 1975); Michael Polanyi, *Personal Knowledge: Towards a Post-Critical Philosophy* (Chicago: University of Chicago Press, 1958).

2. The views of Plato and Aristotle are developed in *Plato's Republic*, trans. G. M. A. Grube (Indianapolis: Hackett, 1974); *The Ethics of Aristotle*, trans. J. A. K. Thomson (New York: Penguin, 1955); and *The Politics of Aristotle*, ed. and trans. Ernest Barker (New York: Oxford University Press, 1946).

3. For a full discussion of Gen. 1–2 and the creation days, see my "The Seven Days of Creation," *Calvin Theological Journal* 46, no. 1 (April 2011): 111–39; and Henri Blocher, *In the Beginning: The Opening Chapters of Genesis* (Downers Grove, IL: InterVarsity, 1984), 15–134.

4. A detailed commentary on this passage can be found in Paul Ellingworth, *The Epistle to the Hebrews*, The New International Greek Testament Commentary (Grand Rapids: Eerdmans, 1993), 212–60.

5. Raymond C. Van Leeuwen, "Cosmos, Temple, House: Building and Wisdom in Mesopotamia and Israel," in *Wisdom Literature in Mesopotamia and Israel*, ed. Richard J. Clifford (Atlanta: Society of Biblical Literature, 2007), 67–90. See also J. Richard Middleton, *The Liberating Image: The Imago Dei in Genesis 1* (Grand Rapids: Brazos, 2005).

6. See Richard B. Gaffin Jr., *Resurrection and Redemption: A Study in Paul's Soteriology* (Grand Rapids: Baker Book House, 1978), 78–92.

7. Augustine, *City of God*, ed. Vernon J. Bourke, abridged ed. (Garden City, NY: Image Books, 1958), XIX, ch. 12, 454.

8. Ibid., XIX, ch. 15, 461.

9. Richard B. Hays, *The Moral Vision of the New Testament: A Contemporary Introduction to the New Testament* (San Francisco: HarperOne, 1996).

10. See "The Schleitheim Articles" (1527) in Oliver O'Donovan and Joan Lockwood O'Donovan, eds., *From Irenaeus to Grotius: A Sourcebook in Christian Political Thought* (Grand Rapids: Eerdmans, 1999), 631–37.

11. See Hans Boersma, *Violence, Hospitality, and the Cross* (Grand Rapids: Baker Academic, 2004), 235–61. Along this line, see also Alan Storkey, *Jesus and Politics: Confronting the Powers* (Grand Rapids: Baker Academic, 2005), 171–93.

12. See, for example, Hays, *Moral Vision*, 314–42; and John Howard Yoder, *The Politics of Jesus* (Grand Rapids: Eerdmans, 1972), 183–214.

Chapter 3 Citizenship in the Kingdom

1. A two-kingdom view from a contemporary Lutheran perspective is offered by Robert Benne, *The Paradoxical Vision: A Public Theology for the Twenty-first Century* (Minneapolis: Fortress, 1995). From a Reformed perspective, the two-kingdom idea is defended by David VanDrunen, *Living in God's Two Kingdoms: A Biblical Vision for Christianity and Culture* (Wheaton, IL: Crossway, 2010). See also VanDrunen, "The Two Kingdoms and Reformed Christianity," *Pro Rege* (March 2012): 31–38. In critique of VanDrunen and others who support a two-kingdom view, see Ryan McIlhenny, ed., *Kingdoms Apart: Engaging the Two Kingdom Perspective* (Phillipsburg, NJ: P&R, 2012).

2. VanDrunen tries to have it both ways. On the one hand, he argues that God rules all things in his Son and in that sense Christ is the single lord of all. On the other hand, he contends that "Christ exercises [his] kingly rule in a twofold manner," which sets up the two-kingdom idea ("Two Kingdoms and Reformed Christianity," 32, 35). VanDrunen bases his argument on a distinction between God's covenant with Noah, on the one hand, which expresses God's providence over life in this world but has nothing to do with eternal salvation, and God's covenant with Abraham, on the other hand, which is the beginning of salvation of the elect for eternity. Christ's "twofold kingship," as VanDrunen presents it, does not allow for a genuine unity of his kingship or of God's kingdom. VanDrunen's idea of God's providential upholding of this world and the idea of salvation in the next world are mutually exclusive.

3. See Kurt Rudolph, *Gnosis: The Nature and History of Gnosticism* (San Francisco: Harper & Row, 1983); Hans Jonas, *The Gnostic Religion*, 2nd ed. (Boston: Beacon Press, 1963); and N. T. Wright, *The New Testament and the People of God* (Minneapolis: Fortress, 1993), 435–43.

4. For detailed commentary on these passages, see Paul Ellingworth, *The Epistle to the Hebrews*, The New International Greek Testament Commentary (Grand Rapids: Eerdmans, 1993), 197–212, 580–86.

5. Our exploration of these implications for the normative constitution of a political community will come in part 3. By way of anticipation, we will refer to the two constitutional characteristics as "structural pluralism" and "confessional pluralism." They are introduced in James W. Skillen, *Recharging the American Experiment: Principled Pluralism for Genuine Civic Community* (Grand Rapids: Baker Books, 1994), 83–94. For readings from diverse nineteenth- and twentieth-century sources on social and political pluralism, see James W. Skillen and Rockne M. McCarthy, eds., *Political Order and the Plural Structure of Society* (Grand Rapids: Eerdmans, 1990).

Chapter 4 Constantine, Augustine, and the Fraught Future of "Christian" Politics

1. The text can be found in J. Stevenson, ed., *A New Eusebius: Documents Illustrative of the History of the Church to AD 337* (London: SPCK, 1965), 21.

2. On the nature and historical development of ancient political systems, see S. E. Finer, *History of Government*, vol. 1, *Ancient Monarchies and Empires* (New York: Oxford University Press, 1999).

3. See Acts 22:22–29 and Paul's continuing appeals that took him all the way to Rome (Acts 22–28). For more on Roman citizenship and governance, see Finer, *History of Government*, 1:411–41, 528–604.

4. Walter Ullmann, in *A History of Political Thought: The Middle Ages* (New York: Penguin, 1965; reissued in 1975 as *Medieval Political Thought*), presents a clear historical assessment of what he calls the two main theses about government that contended with one another from ancient times to the modern era: (1) the *descending* view (authority from the top with subjection to it by those below) and (2) the *ascending* view (authority arising from citizens below with government's subjection to the law above them).

5. F. Edward Cranz summarizes this point, with particular reference to Augustine, by saying, "Paul is engaged in a Christian transformation of an earlier Judaism; Augustine is primarily engaged in a Christian transformation of an earlier Hellenism" (Cranz, "The Development of Augustine's Ideas on Society Before the Donatist Controversy," in *Augustine: A Collection of Critical Essays*, ed. R. A. Markus [Garden City, NY: Doubleday Anchor Books, 1972], 383).

6. Ullmann, *Political Thought*, 17.

7. Ibid., 41.

8. Oliver O'Donovan and Joan Lockwood O'Donovan, eds., *From Irenaeus to Grotius: A Sourcebook in Christian Political Thought, 100–1625* (Grand Rapids: Eerdmans, 1999), 177.

9. See selections from Tertullian in ibid., 25–29.

10. See, for example, Michael Grant, *Constantine the Great: The Man and His Times* (New York: Scribners, 1993), 144–47.

11. For more on the two systems, see Ullmann, *Political Thought*, 19–44.

12. O'Donovan and O'Donovan, *Sourcebook*, 2.

13. Ibid.

14. Stevenson, *New Eusebius*, 391–92.

15. O'Donovan and O'Donovan, *Sourcebook*, 2.

16. Ibid., 70–71.

17. See the Vintage Spiritual Classics edition of *The Confessions*, trans. Maria Boulding (New York: Vintage Books, 1997), which includes a brief, annotated chronology of Augustine's life and times, xxvii–xxxvii.

18. For a reading of *The Confessions* as a journey that is more than merely autobiographical, and for more on the background and subtleties of the text, see Garry Wills, *Augustine's Confessions: A Biography* (Princeton: Princeton University Press, 2011).

19. There are many fine editions of Augustine's *The City of God*. I am using an abridged version, edited by Vernon J. Bourke (Garden City, NY: Doubleday Image Books, 1958), and excerpts in O'Donovan and O'Donovan, *Sourcebook*, 137–63.

20. See the compilation of texts edited by Henry Paolucci, *The Political Writings of St. Augustine* (Chicago: Henry Regnery Gateway Edition, 1962); and the interpretive essays by Herbert A. Deane, *The Political and Social Ideas of St. Augustine* (New York: Columbia University Press, 1963); and P. R. L. Brown, "Political Society," in Markus, *Augustine*, 311–35.

21. Augustine, *City of God*, XIV, ch. 4, 300–302; see also XIV, ch. 28, 321–22; and XV, ch. 4, 327–33.

22. Heaven, says Augustine, "will be the fulfillment of that Sabbath rest foretold in the command: 'Be still and see that I am God.' This, indeed, will be that ultimate Sabbath that has no evening. . . . And we ourselves will be a 'seventh day' when we shall be filled with His blessing and remade by His sanctification" (*City of God*, XXII, ch. 30, 543).

23. Ibid., XIX, ch. 17, 464.

24. For a good account of Augustine's distinction of time and eternity as it relates to the two cities, see Brown, "Political Society," 319–24; and Cranz, "Development of Augustine's Ideas," 362–65.

25. Augustine, *City of God*, XIX, ch. 17, 464.

26. Quoted in Paolucci, *Political Writings*, 153, from *City of God*, XIX, ch. 17.

27. Augustine, *City of God*, XIX, ch. 14, 459.

28. I am not suggesting that Augustine's faith in God as creator of all things does not shine through at many points both in *The City of God* and in his other books, sermons, and letters. He is explicit about this at many points when criticizing Neoplatonism and Manichaeism for not grasping the goodness of creation as it comes from God. Nevertheless, his reference point for discussing the meaning of life in this age is typically the sinfulness of fallen humanity. See Cranz, "Development of Augustine's Ideas," 357–58.

29. For an intriguing exploration of Augustine's struggle with the dualities of heaven and earth, soul and body, life and death, see Andrea Nightengale, *Once Out of Nature: Augustine on Time and the Body* (Chicago: University of Chicago Press, 2012).

30. On the Neoplatonic and other ideas that so greatly influenced Augustine, see Cranz, "Development of Augustine's Ideas," 347–52, 372–74. In the long run, says Cranz, "Augustine's synthesis is precarious. He has tried to harmonize two bodies of thought which are essentially disparate. He has tried to express his own Christian experience in a language which is basically alien to it" (352).

31. The hierarchical, natural order is articulated in many of Augustine's writings. See his phrasing, for example, in *City of God*, XIX, ch. 13, 456, and XIX, ch. 27, 481.

32. On Augustine's appeal to vestiges and semblances of the natural law for ordering the common life on earth, see Cranz, "Development of Augustine's Ideas," 359–60; and Deane, *Ideas*, 97–100.

33. Deane, *Ideas*, 95–96. See Augustine, *City of God*, IV, ch. 4, 88–89; Paolucci, *Political Writings*, 28–43.

34. Deane, *Ideas*, 148.

35. On the Donatists and Augustine, see Deane, *Ideas*, 172–220.

36. O'Donovan and O'Donovan, *Sourcebook*, 132, from one of Augustine's letters.

37. Paolucci, *Political Writings*, 206–7, from one of Augustine's letters.

38. Ibid., 214, from one of Augustine's letters.

39. Brown, "Political Society," 328.

40. In O'Donovan and O'Donovan, *Sourcebook*, 125.

41. Deane, *Ideas*, 164–65.

42. For an introduction to, summaries of, and selections from Augustine's writings on just war, see William R. Stevenson Jr., *Christian Love and Just War: Moral Paradox and Political Life in St. Augustine and His Modern Interpreters* (Macon, GA: Mercer University Press, 1987); Arthur F. Holmes, ed., *War and Christian Ethics* (Grand Rapids: Baker Book House, 1975), 61–83; Deane, *Ideas*, 154–71; and Paolucci, *Political Writings*, 162–83.

43. Augustine, *City of God*, XIX, ch. 7, 447.

44. Ibid., XIX, ch. 7, 447.

45. Holmes, *War and Christian Ethics*, 63.

46. Paolucci, *Political Writings*, 164.

47. Finer, *History of Government*, 1:439–40.

Chapter 5 From Augustine to the Splintering of Christendom

1. Johan Huizinga, *The Autumn of the Middle Ages*, trans. Rodney J. Payton and Ulrich Mammitzsch (Chicago: University of Chicago Press, 1996), 21.

2. Ibid., 20.

3. Harold J. Berman, *Law and Revolution: The Formation of the Western Legal Tradition* (Cambridge, MA: Harvard University Press, 1983).

4. The discussion that follows draws on Berman, *Law and Revolution*; Oliver O'Donovan and Joan Lockwood O'Donovan, eds., *From Irenaeus to Grotius: A Sourcebook in Christian Political Thought* (Grand Rapids: Eerdmans, 1999); Walter Ullmann, *A History of Political Thought: The Middle Ages* (New York: Penguin, 1965); Judith Herrin, *The Formation of Christendom* (Princeton: Princeton University Press, 1987); Christopher Dawson, *Religion and the Rise of Western Culture* (New York:

Doubleday, 1957); and Herman Dooyeweerd, *The Struggle for a Christian Politics*, series B, vol. 5 of *The Collected Works of Herman Dooyeweerd*, ed. D. F. M. Strauss (Lewiston, NY: Edwin Mellen, 2008).

5. For a recent treatment of this development, see Peter Brown, *Through the Eye of the Needle: Wealth and the Fall of Rome, and the Making of Christianity in the West, 350–550 AD* (Princeton: Princeton University Press, 2012).

6. O'Donovan and O'Donovan, *Sourcebook*, 169.

7. Ibid., 174.

8. Ibid., 175.

9. S. E. Finer, *The History of Government*, vol. 1, *Ancient Monarchies and Empires* (Oxford: Oxford University Press, 1997), 601–2.

10. Ibid., 603.

11. Ibid., 604.

12. Ullmann, *Political Thought*, 47.

13. Berman, *Law and Revolution*, 206.

14. O'Donovan and O'Donovan, *Sourcebook*, 232.

15. Ibid., 232.

16. Huizinga, *Middle Ages*, 247.

17. Berman, *Law and Revolution*, 207.

18. On this subject see especially Dawson, *Religion and the Rise of Western Culture*.

19. Berman, *Law and Revolution*, 168.

20. Ibid., 169.

21. Ibid., 169–71.

22. Huizinga, *Middle Ages*, 175.

23. Ibid., 177.

24. O'Donovan and O'Donovan, *Sourcebook*, 233–34.

25. Berman, *Law and Revolution*, 110–15.

26. Ibid., 222–23.

27. Ibid., 530.

28. Ibid., 223.

29. Ibid., 293.

30. Ibid., 285.

31. Ibid., 273.

32. The discussion of Thomas Aquinas that follows draws from Anton C. Pegis, ed., *Introduction to Saint Thomas Aquinas* (New York: Modern Library, 1948), with selected texts and an introductory essay by Pegis; F. C. Copleston, *Aquinas* (New York: Penguin, 1955); Marcia L. Colish, *Medieval Foundations of the Western Intellectual Tradition, 400–1400* (New Haven: Yale University Press, 1997), 265–302, 335–59; Dooyeweerd, *Struggle for a Christian Politics*, 27–44; O'Donovan and O'Donovan, *Sourcebook*, 320–61, with selected texts and an introduction by the editors. One of the texts of Aquinas excerpted by O'Donovan and O'Donovan is *On Kingship*, which some scholars now doubt was written by Aquinas; see their introductory essay (321).

33. Book Two of Aquinas's early work *Summa Contra Gentiles* focuses on creation and the Christian confession that God is the creator of all things. Yet it also shows Aquinas fully at work synthesizing biblical faith and Aristotle. See Saint Thomas Aquinas, *On the Truth of the Catholic Faith, Book Two: Creation*, trans. James F. Anderson (Garden City, NY: Doubleday Image Books, 1956).

34. O'Donovan and O'Donovan, *Sourcebook*, 331.

35. Ibid., 336.

36. Ibid., 353.

37. Pegis, *Introduction to Aquinas*, 614. See also the excerpt from Aquinas touching on this point in O'Donovan and O'Donovan, *Sourcebook*, 328.

38. Pegis, *Introduction to Aquinas*, 612. On Aquinas's view of the political order as natural and original, see Copleston, *Aquinas*, 229–32, and O'Donovan and O'Donovan, *Sourcebook*, 322–23.

39. Jean Porter, "The Common Good in Thomas Aquinas," in *In Search of the Common Good*, ed. Dennis P. McCann and Patrick D. Miller (New York: T&T Clark, 2005), 114. See further Jean Porter, *Nature as Reason: A Thomistic Theory of Natural Law* (Grand Rapids: Eerdmans, 2005).

40. O'Donovan and O'Donovan, *Sourcebook*, 339.

41. Porter, "Common Good," 115.

42. O'Donovan and O'Donovan, *Sourcebook*, 348.

43. Ibid., 360.

44. Copleston, *Aquinas*, 198.

45. Porter, "Common Good," 115.

46. O'Donovan and O'Donovan, *Sourcebook*, 326.

47. Pegis, *Introduction to Aquinas*, 653.

48. Ibid., 649. Copleston states Aquinas's position this way: "By the light of his own reason, therefore, man can arrive at some knowledge of the natural law. And since this law is a participation in or reflection of the eternal law in so far as the latter concerns human beings and their free acts, man is not left in ignorance of the eternal law which is the ultimate rule of all conduct. 'The natural law is nothing else but a participation of the eternal law in a rational creature'" (*Aquinas*, 214).

49. On Aristotle's view of war, see Aristotle, *The Politics of Aristotle*, ed. and trans. Ernest Barker (Oxford: Oxford University Press, 1958), 79, 285–86, 301–2, 317–22.

50. The summary that follows here is drawn from excerpts from Aquinas's works in O'Donovan and O'Donovan, *Sourcebook*, 354–55; and in Arthur F. Holmes, ed., *War and Christian Ethics* (Grand Rapids: Baker Book House, 1975), 102–17.

51. Copleston, *Aquinas*, 216–17.

Chapter 6 Nations, States, and Protestant Reformers

1. Christopher Dawson, *Religion and the Rise of Western Culture* (New York: Doubleday Image Books, 1957), 199. Dawson's classic is the published version of his 1948–49 Gifford Lectures.

2. Ibid., 194.

3. Ibid., 206.

4. Ibid., 198.

5. Marcia L. Colish, *Medieval Foundations of the Western Intellectual Tradition, 400–1400* (New Haven: Yale University Press, 1997).

6. Ibid., 334.

7. Ibid., 346–51. For excerpts from Fortescue's writings, see Oliver O'Donovan and Joan Lockwood O'Donovan, eds., *From Irenaeus to Grotius: A Sourcebook in Christian Political Thought* (Grand Rapids: Eerdmans, 1999), 530–40.

8. Martin van Creveld, *The Rise and Decline of the State* (Cambridge: Cambridge University Press, 1999), 104.

9. Ibid., 117.

10. See Walter Ullmann, *A History of Political Thought: The Middle Ages* (New York: Penguin, 1965).

11. O'Donovan and O'Donovan, *Sourcebook*, 391.

12. For excerpts from the writings of these figures, see ibid., 413–75.

13. Colish, *Medieval Foundations*, 340.

14. Ibid., 342.

15. J. N. Figgis, *Political Thought from Gerson to Grotius: 1414–1625* (1916; repr., New York: Harper Torchbooks, 1960), 66.

16. Ibid., 69.

17. Ibid., 73.

18. Harold J. Berman, *Law and Revolution: The Formation of the Western Legal Tradition* (Cambridge, MA: Harvard University Press, 1983), 29.

19. O'Donovan and O'Donovan, *Sourcebook*, 586. Page numbers in this section refer to this volume.

20. Figgis, *Political Thought*, 89.

21. Ibid., 89.

22. For texts from and history of the Anabaptists, see Michael Baylor, Quentin Skinner, and Raymond Geuss, eds., *The Radical Reformation* (Cambridge: Cambridge University Press, 1991).

23. O'Donovan and O'Donovan, *Sourcebook*, 634.

24. Ibid., 634.

25. Ibid., 635.

26. Ibid., 635–36.

27. John Witte Jr., *The Reformation of Rights: Law, Religion, and Human Rights in Early Modern Calvinism* (Cambridge: Cambridge University Press, 2007), 77.

28. Ibid., 50.

29. Ibid., 76.

30. Ibid., 58.

31. Ibid., 65.

32. Johannes Althusius, *The Politics of Johannes Althusius*, ed. and trans. Frederick S. Carney (Boston: Beacon Press, 1964), 69.

33. John Calvin, *Institutes of the Christian Religion*, ed. John T. McNeill, trans. Ford Lewis Battles (Philadelphia: Westminster, 1960), 1486–87.

34. Althusius, *Politics*, 54.

35. Ibid., 70, 74.

36. On Calvin's social, economic, and political thought and his involvement in Genevan society, see W. Fred Graham, *The Constructive Revolutionary: John Calvin and His Socio-Economic Impact* (Richmond: John Knox, 1971).

37. Calvin, *Institutes*, 1520.

38. Ibid., 1497.

39. Ibid., 1500.

40. Ibid., 1497–1501.

41. Althusius, *Politics*, 181–84.

42. See Theodore Beza, "Right of Magistrates," in *Constitutionalism and Resistance in the Sixteenth Century*, ed. and trans. Julian H. Franklin (New York: Pegasus, 1969), 97–140.

43. Ibid., 110–11.

44. Ibid., 130.

45. *Vindiciae contra tyrannos*, in Franklin, *Constitutionalism and Resistance*, 141–99.

46. Ibid., 174.

47. Althusius, *Politics*, 12. Page numbers in this section refer to this volume. For a detailed exposition of Althusius, see Witte, *Reformation of Rights*, 151–207.

Chapter 7 From the Reformation to Contemporary Engagement

1. For the very brief comments offered here, the primary reference is S. E. Finer, *The History of Government*, 3 vols. (Oxford: Oxford University Press, 1997). Two recent volumes that attempt a broad historical overview are Francis Fukuyama, *The Origins of Political Order: From Prehuman Times to the French Revolution* (New York: Farrar, Straus & Giroux, 2011); and Norman Davies, *Vanished Kingdoms: The Rise and Fall of States and Nations* (New York: Viking, 2012).

2. Finer, *History of Government*, vol. 2, *The Intermediate Ages*, 624.

3. Ibid., 625–26.

4. Ibid., 661.

5. Ibid., 660–61.

6. Finer, *History of Government*, vol. 3, *Empires, Monarchies, and the Modern State*, 1409.

7. Ibid., 3:1419.

8. Ibid., 3:1197–98.

9. Ibid., 3:1162–63. Compare the interpretation of Efraim Karsh, *Islamic Imperialism: A History* (New Haven: Yale University Press, 2006).

10. Finer, *Empires, Monarchies*, 3:1196.

11. Ibid., 3:1170–71.

12. Finer, *Intermediate Ages*, 2:806.

13. Finer, *Empires, Monarchies*, 3:1129–30, 1140–41. On Confucius (551–479 BC) and his influence on the culture and governance of China, see H. G. Creel, *Confucius and the Chinese Way* (New York: Harper Torchbooks, 1960); and T. A. Wilson, *On Sacred Grounds: Culture, Society, and the Formation of the Cult of Confucius* (Cambridge, MA: Harvard University Asia Center, 2002).

14. Finer, *Empires, Monarchies*, 3:1159–60.

15. Ibid., 3:1160.

16. Ibid., 3:1161.

17. For more on this idea, see Eric Voegelin, *The New Science of Politics* (Chicago: University of Chicago Press, 1952), 162–89, esp. 178–83.

18. See ibid., 110–32; Voegelin, *Science, Politics and Gnosticism* (Chicago: Henry Regnery, 1968); and Voegelin, *From Enlightenment to Revolution*, ed. John H. Hallowell (Durham, NC: Duke University Press, 1975).

19. See John Locke, *Two Treatises of Government*, ed. Thomas I. Cook (New York: Hafner, 1973); and Locke, *The Reasonableness of Christianity*, ed. I. Ramsey (Stanford: Stanford University Press, 1958).

20. On this subject see Walter A. McDougall's Pulitzer Prize–winning history, *Promised Land, Crusader State: The American Encounter with the World Since 1776* (New York: Houghton Mifflin, 1997).

21. In his book *Bad Religion: How We Became a Nation of Heretics* (New York: Free Press, 2012), Ross Douthat exposes the two religious streams in America: privatized religion, on the one hand, and nationalized civil religion, on the other (211–76). For a broader and deeper historical interpretation, see Mark A. Noll, *America's God: From Jonathan Edwards to Abraham Lincoln* (New York: Oxford University Press, 2002).

22. On this subject see Sacvan Bercovitch, *The American Jeremiad* (Madison: University of Wisconsin Press, 1978).

Chapter 9 Engagement for What Kind of Political Community?

1. Robert D. Kaplan, *Warrior Politics: Why Leadership Demands a Pagan Ethos* (New York: Random House, 2002).

2. Ibid., 52.

3. Ibid., 56.

4. Ibid., 109.

5. Ibid., 112.

6. Stanley Hauerwas, "The Servant Community: Christian Social Ethics," in *The Hauerwas Reader*, ed. John Berkman and Michael Cartwright (Durham, NC: Duke University Press, 2001), 378.

7. Ibid., 377.

8. John Howard Yoder, *The Christian Witness to the State* (Newton, Kans.: Faith and Life Press, 1964), 75. For a full discussion of Romans 13, also see Yoder, *The Politics of Jesus* (Grand Rapids: Eerdmans, 1972), 193–214.

9. Yoder, *Christian Witness*, 75.

10. For a biblical-exegetical argument to the effect that all violence, including the use of force by government, is morally illegitimate for Christians, see Richard B. Hays, *The Moral Vision of the New Testament: A Contemporary Introduction to the New Testament* (San Francisco: HarperOne, 1996), 317–46.

11. Sanford Levinson, a constitutional law professor, is the author of a new book that calls for the rewriting of the US Constitution: *Framed: America's Fifty-One Constitutions and the Crisis of*

Governance (New York: Oxford University Press, 2012). But Levinson does not, in my opinion, reach deep enough into the sources of the Constitution's weaknesses.

12. Alan Gewirth, *The Community of Rights* (Chicago: University of Chicago Press, 1996), 6.

13. Ibid.

14. Ibid., 93. Another liberal political philosopher, William A. Galston, does a better job than Gewirth of transcending individualism to account for and do justice to the complexity of social life: Galston, *Liberal Pluralism: The Implications of Value Pluralism for Political Theory and Practice* (Cambridge: Cambridge University Press, 2002).

15. Michael Novak, *Free Persons and the Common Good* (Lanham, MD: Madison Books, 1989), 30.

16. Ibid., 32.

17. Ibid., 34–35.

18. Ibid., 137.

19. See ibid., 83–87.

20. Ibid., 142.

21. Ibid., 121, 186–87.

22. For a recent historical exploration of the problems and prospects of world government, see Mark Mazower, *Governing the World: The History of an Idea* (New York: Penguin, 2012).

Chapter 10 Citizenship as Vocation

1. Clem Whitaker, quoted by Jill Lepore, "The Lie Factory," *The New Yorker*, September 24, 2012, 55.

2. On the subject of representation and its historical expressions, see Hanna Fenichel Pitkin, *The Concept of Representation* (Berkeley: University of California Press, 1967).

3. James L. Sundquist, *Constitutional Reform and Effective Government*, rev. ed. (Washington, DC: The Brookings Institution, 1992), 178–79.

4. George Will, *Restoration: Congress, Term Limits and the Recovery of Deliberative Democracy* (New York: Free Press, 1992), 92.

5. See, for example, Sundquist, *Constitutional Reform*, 177–82; and W. Lance Bennett, *The Governing Crisis: Media, Money, and Marketing in American Elections* (New York: St. Martin's Press, 1992), 185–86.

6. Bennett, *Governing Crisis*, 163.

7. Will, *Restoration*, 19. For an in-depth assessment see Robert G. Kaiser, *So Damn Much Money: The Triumph of Lobbying and the Corrosion of American Government* (New York: Knopf, 2009).

8. The following assessment of the American electoral system, with a proposal for reform, draws on chapter 8 of my *In Pursuit of Justice: Christian-Democratic Explorations* (Lanham, MD: Rowman & Littlefield, 2004), 129–46.

9. For an introduction to proportional representation (PR) as it might affect American politics, see Michael Lind, "A Radical Plan to Change American Politics," *Atlantic Monthly*, August 1992, 73–83; Douglas Amy, *Real Choices/New Voices: The Case for Proportional Representation Elections in the United States* (New York: Columbia University Press, 1993); Steven Hill, *Fixing Elections: The Failure of America's Winner Take All Politics* (New York: Routledge, 2002); and Kathleen Barber, *A Right to Representation: Proportional Election Systems for the Twenty-First Century* (Columbus: Ohio State University Press, 2000).

10. On this point, see Enid Lakeman, "The Case for Proportional Representation," in *Choosing an Electoral System*, ed. Arend Lijphart and Bernard Grofman (New York: Praeger, 1984), 46–47.

Chapter 11 Family, Marriage, and Education

1. This is the matter that Michael Walzer explores so fruitfully in *Spheres of Justice: A Defense of Pluralism and Equality* (New York: Basic Books, 1983).

2. Cf. Mary Ann Glendon, *Rights Talk: The Impoverishment of Political Discourse* (New York: Free Press, 1991), and William A. Galston, *Liberal Pluralism: The Implications of Value Pluralism for Political Theory and Practice* (Cambridge: Cambridge University Press, 2002).

3. For a valuable account of the continuing importance of the family for children, see David P. Gushee, "Rebuilding Marriage and the Family," in *Toward a Just and Caring Society*, ed. David P. Gushee (Grand Rapids: Baker Books, 1999), 499–530.

4. The importance of a strong family for children must not be played off against women's rights as if the two are incompatible. See Anne Carr and Mary Stewart Van Leeuwen, eds., *Religion, Feminism, and the Family* (Louisville: Westminster John Knox, 1996).

5. On the rights of the family, see David Wagner, "The Family and the Constitution," *First Things*, August/September 1994, 23–28.

6. See Jean Bethke Elshtain, "The Family Crisis and State Intervention: The Construction of Child Abuse as Social Problem and Popular Rhetoric," in *Power Trips and Other Journeys* (Madison: University of Wisconsin Press, 1990), 73–88, and Mary-Lou Weisman, "When Parents Are Not in the Best Interests of the Child," *Atlantic Monthly*, July 1994, 43–63.

7. Joe Dignan and Amy Argetsinger, "Calif. Judge Backs Same-Sex Marriage," *Washington Post*, March 15, 2005, www.washingtonpost.com/wp-dyn/content/article/2005/03/25/AR2005032509559.html.

8. On the history of conflicts over the public establishment of so-called nonsectarian schools, beginning early in the nineteenth century, see Charles L. Glenn, *The Myth of the Common School* (Amherst: University of Massachusetts Press, 1988); Diane Ravitch, *The Great School Wars* (New York: Basic Books, 1974); and James W. Skillen, Rockne M. McCarthy, and William A. Harper, *Disestablishment a Second Time: Genuine Pluralism for American Schools* (Grand Rapids: Eerdmans, 1982). Ravitch's latest statement of support for the system we are criticizing here can be found in her book *The Death and Life of the Great American School System* (New York: Basic Books, 2010).

9. For some of the background on what follows, see Charles L. Glenn, *The Ambiguous Embrace: Government and Faith-Based Schools and Social Agencies* (Princeton: Princeton University Press, 2000); Stanley W. Carlson-Thies and James W. Skillen, eds., *Welfare in America: Christian Perspectives on a Policy in Crisis* (Grand Rapids: Eerdmans, 1996); and James W. Skillen and Rockne M. McCarthy, eds., *Political Order and the Plural Structure of Society* (Grand Rapids: Eerdmans, 1991) (see chap. 3n5).

10. Ellen Willis, "Freedom from Religion: What's at Stake in Faith-Based Politics," *The Nation*, February 1, 2001, www.thenation.com/print/article/freedom-religion.

Chapter 12 Economics and the Environment

1. For an excellent introduction to and critique of liberalism, see David T. Koyzis, *Political Visions and Illusions: A Survey and Christian Critique of Contemporary Ideologies* (Downers Grove, IL: InterVarsity, 2003), 42–71, 124–51.

2. John Locke, "Second Treatise of Civil Government," in the Hafner Library of Classics edition, *Two Treatises of Government*, ed. Thomas I. Cook (New York: Hafner Press, 1973), 122. Page numbers in this section refer to this volume.

3. See C. B. MacPherson, *The Political Theory of Possessive Individualism* (Oxford: Oxford University Press, 1962).

4. Adam Smith's most famous book is *The Wealth of Nations*, first published in 1776. A recent paperback republication by Barnes and Noble (2004) is edited by C. J. Bullock with a new introduction by Prasannan Parthasarathi. Two new takes on the old question can be found in David S. Landes, *The Wealth and Poverty of Nations: Why Some Are So Rich and Some So Poor* (New York: W.W. Norton, 1998); and Daron Acemoglu and James Robinson, *Why Nations Fail: The Origins of Power, Prosperity, and Poverty* (New York: Crown, 2012).

5. Duncan K. Foley, *Adam's Fallacy: A Guide to Economic Theology* (Cambridge, MA: Belknap Press of Harvard University Press, 2006).

6. Sebastian Mallaby, "Capitalism: The Remix," *The Washington Post*, December 4, 2008.

7. Ibid.

8. John Kay, "What Tesco Knows and Woolies Forgot," *Financial Times*, January 7, 2009.

9. Ibid. Joseph Schumpeter distinguished between the prospect of making money and the entrepreneurial desire to create change, to delight in ventures. "Several hundred case studies of innovation completed in the late twentieth century and early twenty-first," writes Thomas K. McCraw, Schumpeter's biographer, "confirmed Schumpeter's thesis. Just as forces besides money had motivated Carnegie, Thyssen, and Ford, the same was true of later entrepreneurs such as Akio Morita, Estee Lauder, Andy Grove, Richard Branson, Steve Jobs, and Oprah Winfrey" (McCraw, *Prophet of Innovation: Joseph Schumpeter and Creative Destruction* [Cambridge, MA: Belknap Press of Harvard University Press, 2007], 500).

10. Michelle Singletary, "It's Time to Drop the Consumer Label," *Washington Post*, January 4, 2009.

11. Anthony M. C. Waterman puts it this way: the economic way of thinking "is a way of looking at society that rests on certain assumptions about the human condition. Those assumptions are neither innocent nor uncontroversial. For they stir up baffling moral and theological questions. Is there a higher good than economic welfare?" *Political Economy and Christian Theology Since the Enlightenment* (New York: Palgrave McMillan, 2004), 88.

12. Amartya Sen, *Development as Freedom* (New York: Anchor Books, 2000), 87. On the dangers of the pursuit of economic growth as the chief goal of globalization and of national well-being, see Bob Goudzwaard, Mark Vander Vennen, and David Van Heemst, *Hope in Troubled Times: A New Vision of Confronting Global Crises* (Grand Rapids: Baker Academic, 2007).

13. Sen, *Development as Freedom*, 92. Along this line, see Michael Sandel, *What Money Can't Buy: The Moral Limits of Markets* (New York: Farrar, Straus & Giroux, 2012).

14. Sen, *Development as Freedom*, 86.

15. Robert H. Nelson interprets the rise of the environmental movement as one of the signs of crisis in modern, progressive economics, which has become the religion of our day. See *Economics as Religion: From Samuelson to Chicago and Beyond* (University Park, PA: Penn State University Press, 2001), esp. 303–38.

16. Martin Wolf, "Prepare for a Golden Age of Gas," *Financial Times*, February 21, 2012, www .ft.com/cms/s/0/7d298f50-5c85-11e1-8f1f-00144feabdc0.html. See also the review by Bill McKibben of two books on this subject: "Why Not Frack?," *New York Review of Books*, March 8, 2012, 13–15.

17. Calvin DeWitt, *Caring for Creation: Responsible Stewardship of God's Handiwork* (Grand Rapids: Baker Books, 1998), 43–47. For a more recent and broader ranging argument from a Christian point of view, see Steven Bouma-Prediger, *For the Beauty of the Earth: A Christian Vision for Creation Care* (Grand Rapids: Baker Academic, 2010).

18. For evidence of the liberal structuring of environmental politics and struggles against that structuring, see Matthew Lindstrom, ed., *Encyclopedia of the US Government and the Environment*, 2 vols. (Santa Barbara, CA: ABC-CLIO, 2011); and Magali Deimas and Oran R. Young, eds., *Governance for the Environment* (Cambridge: Cambridge University Press, 2009).

Chapter 13 Politics in One World

1. International affairs commentator David Gardner says of the Middle East, for example, that in the wake of the revolutions in Tunisia, Egypt, Libya, and Syria, the people "will need to develop everything from the rule of law to a pluralist political culture to succeed." The "ultimate test of the Arab awakening will be how sensitively and equitably the emerging order handles minorities, especially in those countries such as Syria that are home to a fragile mosaic of sects and ethnic groups." Gardner, "Middle East: Febrile and Fragmented," *Financial Times*, May 14, 2012, www .ft.com/cms/s/0/99014b20-9b80-11e1-8b36-00144feabdc0.html#axzz2EMrFGqRr.

2. Michael Sandel, "America's Search for a New Public Philosophy," *Atlantic Monthly*, March 1996, 72.

3. Michael Walzer, "International Society: What Is the Best We Can Do?" *Ethical Perspectives* (Journal of the European Ethics Network) 6, nos. 3–4 (December 1999): 201.

4. Sandel, "America's Search," 73–74.

5. Walzer, "International Society," 206–7.

6. Ibid., 208.

7. Richard B. Hays, *The Moral Vision of the New Testament: A Contemporary Introduction to the New Testament* (San Francisco: HarperOne, 1996), chapter 14, 317–46. The discussion of Hays that follows depends in part on an earlier essay of mine written jointly with Keith J. Pavlischek, "Political Responsibility and the Use of Force: A Critique of Richard Hays," *Philosophia Christi* 3, no. 2, Series 2 (2001): 421–45.

8. Hays, *Moral Vision*, 317.

9. Ibid., 337.

10. John Howard Yoder, *The Politics of Jesus* (Grand Rapids: Eerdmans, 1972), 183–214.

11. See James W. Skillen, *With or Against the World? America's Role among the Nations* (Lanham, MD: Rowman & Littlefield, 2005), 95–126, and eight articles from 2002 to 2007 in the *Public Justice Report* (a publication of the Center for Public Justice), available online, beginning with www.cpjustice.org/stories/storyReader%24669 and continuing in sequence, %24806, %24933, %241119, %241153, %241195, %241332, and, finally, www.cpjustice.org/PJR2007Q3/notwar. A thoroughly documented new book on US engagement in Vietnam is also worth noting here. It is devastating in its critique of countless unjust acts and strategies: Nick Turse, *Kill Anything That Moves: The Real American War in Vietnam* (New York: Metropolitan Books, Henry Holt, 2013).

12. See Gideon Rachman, "America's Drone War Is Out of Control," *Financial Times*, December 10, 2012, www.ft.com/intl/cms/s/0/06133786-42c1-11e2-a4e4-00144feabdc0.html#axzz2 Ek719FkY.

13. On this subject see the four-volume work edited by Max Stackhouse, *God and Globalization* (New York: Continuum, 2000, 2001, 2002, 2007).

14. John Kay, "Green Lobby Must Be Treated as a Religion," *Financial Times*, January 9, 2007, www.johnkay.com/2007/01/09/green-lobby-must-be-treated-as-a-religion.

15. Robert H. Nelson, *Economics as Religion: From Samuelson to Chicago and Beyond* (University Park, PA: Penn State University Press, 2001).

16. For background here, see Zhang Weiwei, *The China Wave: Rise of a Civilizational State* (New York: World Century, 2012); and Odd Arne Westad, *Restless Empire: China and the World Since 1750* (New York: Basic Books, 2012).

17. Richard McGregor, "The Pursuit of Harmony," *Financial Times*, April 12, 2007, www.ft.com /intl/cms/s/0/071dbb6c-e893-11db-b2c3-000b5df10621.html#axzz2EMrFGqRr.

18. For additional reflections, see Jason Kindopp and Carol Lee Hamrin, eds., *God and Caesar in China* (Washington, DC: Brookings Institution Press, 2004).

19. Quoted by Vincent Boland, "In Ataturk's Shadow," *Financial Times*, May 3, 2007, www .ft.com/intl/cms/s/2/d11bc366-f8ef-11db-a940-000b5df10621.html#axzz2EMrFGqRr.

20. Ibid.

21. Samuel P. Huntington, *The Clash of Civilizations and the Remaking of World Order* (New York: Simon & Schuster, 1996).

22. See Rex Ahdar and Nicholas Aroney, eds., *Shari'a in the West* (Oxford: Oxford University Press, 2010).

index

kingdom of God, 3–5, 15, 39
  citizenship in, 33–34
  not of this world, 8–11
  and responsibility of public officials, 39–40
Kramer, Richard, 162

Leeuwen, Raymond Van, 23
Locke, John, 109, 128, 138, 170–74, 179, 180
Luther, Martin, xiii
  and the Anabaptists, 86–91
  See also Reformation, the

Machiavelli, Niccolo, 107–8, 129
Mallaby, Sebastian, 173–74
Marsilio of Padua, 84
McGregor, Richard, 191–92. *See also* China
Middle East
  and protests, ix
  Turkey, 192
  wars in Iraq and Afghanistan, 189
Miller, Patrick, 14
mixed sovereignty, 83
monarchies
  biblical definition of kingship, 14
  consolidating territorial power, 84
  God's opposition to, 13
Moral Vision of the New Testament, The (Hays),
  27
Moses, 38

Nicholas of Kues, 85–86. *See also* conciliarists
North Africa, vii
Novak, Michael, 137–39

O'Donovan, Oliver and Joan Lockwood, 48, 49,
  65, 67, 84
Orthodox Church, 102–3, 120

pacifism, 129–31. *See also* Anabaptists
papacy
  papal authority over government, 83–84 (*see
    also* conciliarists)
  Papal Revolution, 67–69, 70, 73, 81
Peace of Augsburg, 87
Pilate, Pontius, 8
Plato, 17–18, 33
pluralism, confessional, 125
polis, 18, 48
Polycarp, 47–48, 49, 58
Porter, Jean, 75
proportional representation. *See* electoral
  systems

Proposition 8, 160
Protestant, x
  St. Bartholomew's Day Massacre, 95
Puritans and Puritanism, xiii, xiv, 112

Radical Reformers. *See* Anabaptists
Reformation, the, 86, 91–92, 101–2, 107
  and Martin Bucer, 92
  and Philip Melanchthon, 92
Renaissance, 106–7
retributive judgment, 25, 118, 119
Roman Catholic Church, xii, xvi, 49, 67, 111
  authority of Jesus Christ, 146
  and canon law, 61–62, 64, 101, 132
  challenges to ecclesiastical authority, 82, 85,
    125
    and conciliarists, 85–86
    and Martin Luther, 86–91
  establishing church hierarchy
  Great Schism, 85
  institutionalization, 68, 81
  and the Orthodox Church, 103
  versus public education, 164–65
  social teaching and solidarity, 114, 136
  St. Bartholomew's Day Massacre, 95
  See also papacy
Russia, 101–4
  and protests, ix

Saleh, Heba, xi
Sandel, Michael, 186. *See also* globalization
secularization, ix, 125–26
Sen, Amartya, 176–77. *See also* economic
  systems
separation of church and state, 10
Shallum (king of Judah), 39
Singletary, Michelle, 176. *See also* economic
  systems
Smith, Adam, 139, 170–74
Stoicism, 66
Stout, Harry, xiv
Sundquist, James L., 147

Tertullian, 48
Thomas Aquinas, 74–79, 81, 85, 87, 101, 107,
  117–19, 121, 139, 187
  versus Augustine, 77, 97
  On Kingship, 74
  Summa Theologica, 74–75
Tocqueville, Alexis de, xiii